BUSINESS IN THE AGE OF REASON

BUSINESS
IN THE
AGE OF REASON

Edited by
R. P. T. Davenport-Hines
and
Jonathan Liebenau

First published 1987 by
FRANK CASS AND COMPANY LIMITED

Published 2013 by Routledge
2 Park Square, Milton Park, Abingdon, Oxfordshire OX14 4RN
711 Third Avenue, New York, NY 10017

First issued in paperback 2014

Routledge is an imprint of the Taylor and Francis Group, an informa business

British Library Cataloguing in Publication Data

Business in the Age of Reason
1. Business—History—18th century
I. Davenport-Hines, R.P.T. II. Liebenau, Jonathan
338.6'09'033 HF5341

Library of Congress Cataloging-in-Publication Data

Business in the Age of Reason.

"This group of studies first appeared in ... Business history, vol. XXVIII, no. 3"—T.p. verso.
1. Great Britain—Commerce—History—18th century.
2. Business enterprises—Great Britain—History—18th century. I. Davenport-Hines, R. P. T. (Richard Peter Treadwell), 1953- . II. Liebenau, Jonathan.
HF3505.6.B94 1986 338.4'7'000941 86-18804

ISBN 13: 978-0-714-63306-0 (hbk)
ISBN 13: 978-0-415-76119-2 (pbk)

This group of studies first appeared in a Special Issue on Business in the Age of Reason of *Business History*, Vol. XXVIII, No.3.

CONTENTS

EDITORS' INTRODUCTION

Although there is a considerable *cadre* of work on eighteenth-century business history, there is also a noticeable divide between business historians interested in the eighteenth century and those concerned with visible hands, managerial revolutions and twentieth-century corporate economies. Distinguished exceptions to this observation immediately spring to mind: but it is to bridge this divide, and to highlight the intrinsic interest and excitement of the Augustan and Georgian eras, that the present set of essays has been collected. Representing a range of eighteenth-century research, these articles clarify or reorientate the historical origins of many of the chief themes of more recent business history.

A. J. G. Cummings's study of the Harburgh Co. depicts company promotion and international speculation at the time of the South Sea Bubble speculative mania. He shows how its lottery proposal reflected the gambling streak in British business life (which, for example, also led insurers to organise tontines), manifest at a time when industry was insufficiently developed to attract the savings of unwary investors. Jacob Price's account of the Sheffeild v. Starke litigation shows the institutional evolution of trade between London and Maryland: it also highlights the large role of debts, and related problems, in eighteenth-century commerce. J.F. Bosher's essay describes the role of private capital in financing the French navy during the Seven Years' War and draws an important distinction between bankers (as those who traded in money and merchandise) and financiers (who dealt in government funds on the basis of tax returns which covered interest and advances). Frank Melton's analysis of the operations of private deposit banks like Drummonds and Hoares is largely confined to London, and develops themes from his new study of the money scrivener, Sir Robert Clayton. Emphasising the irregularity of bankers' cash flows, he shows the continued utility of bankers in mortgage investment and in handling the legal aspects of freehold trusts. Eric Hopkins' reflections on the eighteenth-century growth of trading and services sectors are concerned with the Birmingham economy, and use fire insurance registers to argue that the proportionate size and significance of the town's metal trades has been exaggerated. With steampower not ubiquitous in Birmingham before 1830, he finds little evidence of industrial innovation there in 1750–1800, and believes that new technology was not the chief cause of urban expansion in this case.

Lorna Weatherill traces the complexities of the eighteenth-century pottery trade's distribution network involving wholesalers and shopkeepers in the provinces, factory warehouses, wholesalers and shops in London, itinerants, and sales at the pottery, or direct to consumers.

She also scrutinises the changing consumption patterns and business organisation that were entailed in the genesis of a consumer society. Eric Robinson, writing of sales techniques and fashion, looks at themes related to Weatherill, such as the spread of a taste for innovation by the growth of the periodical and other press. Neither Weatherill nor Robinson consider Boulton or Wedgwood as isolated exponents of new sales techniques, while the latter's description of the button craze of 1775, or of the social gradations which codified the protocol of shoebuckles, brings a vivid touch to the subject. The unique memorandum of office organisation and bookkeeping from the counting house of Herries, dated 1766, the text of which is published as the conclusion to this collection, has several points of interest, apart from its general value as illustrating that the details given in published treatises were mirrored in practice. Points of novelty include the admonition to secrecy; the familiarisation of the clerks with the running of the business; the prescription for the Waste Book; the treatment of Merchandize Charges; the Sundry Creditors Account; and the Check Ledger.

Nevertheless some common themes emerge from this diversity. One of these is the constant institutional evolution that characterised eighteenth-century business life in contrast to some other eras. The imbroglio of the Harburgh Co. in the 1720s demonstrated that European trading monopolies were no longer favoured in British political and commercial circles, where there was also a new willingness to be aroused against the more blatant corruption or the more flagrant efforts to fleece the gullible. The contractual relations of Sheffeild and Starke over Virginian tobacco and Maryland stores were an innovative development halfway between the earlier factor system (where London merchants provided all the capital and took all the risks) and the later eighteenth-century manifestation of independent indigenous merchants on the Chesapeake. Following earlier work by Joslin, Melton too charts developments in the money market and eighteenth-century London banking, while the two studies of consumer goods (albeit by different methods and evidence) demonstrate the complex interplay between economic and social change, and technological, organisational and locational innovation, which created new consumer demand and business modes in the eighteenth century. The growth of Birmingham is depicted as based not simply on workshop manufacture in the metal trades, but as a developing regional capital and transport centre. The final essay recounts not only institutional evolution in French government finance, but other developments, including the steady expansion of French maritime trade after the treaty of Utrecht in 1713.

Debt and bankruptcy dog these essays as a reminder that an eighteenth-century entrepreneur was, as in the classical definition, concerned with taking risks. Many of those concerned with the Harburgh Co. went bankrupt, while the problem of debt collection pervades the story of Sheffeild and Starke, leading Professor Price to argue that debt was an outstanding local problem long before the American revolution of 1776. The risks of bill collection were perpetual and ineluctable to the London bankers, trade debts loom large over the pottery producers and distributors, and debt and bankruptcy problems were the staple work, so Hopkins suggests, of the mushrooming number of attornies in Birmingham. The collapse of Beaujon, Goossens et Cie. in 1759, *pace* Bosher, resulted in 'credit stifled' and 'general consternation' across Bourbon France (p. 127).

The importance of social contacts and social nuances is also repeatedly stressed. It was integral to the high-level operations of those involved in the Harburgh Co., like Case Billingsly the company projector or Lord Barrington the political adventurer. The importance of the social distinctions of their clients to bankers manipulating their deposits, and the specialisation, for example, of Drummonds or Ewers in military clientele, is shown by Melton. Class and social contacts are inherent in several other contributions.

Overall the articles in this collection show a business economy increasing in size, sophistication and integrality. Thus Weatherill writes of the pottery distribution network becoming 'larger, more dense and more sophisticated' and yet remaining 'a composite whole' (p. 71), while Hopkins describes 'each development being both a response and a trigger; industry, commerce and services grew in symbiotic relationship' (p. 92). Other contributors make equivalent comments or suggest comparable conclusions. These essays reveal unexpected congruence in their picture of fluid and experimental business organisation developing towards a more integrated national economy.

Business History Unit
London School of Economics

THE HARBURGH COMPANY AND ITS LOTTERY 1716–23

By A. J. G. CUMMINGS

The years from the middle of the 1690s to the early 1720s were crucial to the development of joint stock companies in Britain. Two distinct waves of company promotion, and their collapse, led to moves to curb the activities of speculators and to restrict the formation of new ventures without the consent of Parliament. The first of these booms occurred in the 1690s and came to an end during the financial crisis of 1696–97 which had been induced by war and its effect on government spending and the restriction of trade. The collapse of many over-ambitious joint-stock enterprises or 'bubbles' led to government measures to curb the activities of stock jobbers who dealt in their stocks. The second boom, based on the plans of the South Sea Company in 1719 and 1720 to assume responsibility for aspects of the national debt by exchanging government securities for South Sea Company stock, was greater in scope and much more severe in its consequences. Speculative mania surrounded the conversion of these stocks and led to the flotation of numerous other schemes, many of which were highly speculative and of doubtful legality. Fear within the South Sea Company that such ventures would drain the flow of capital necessary for its own success led to pressure being exerted on the government to curb the menace of 'bubbles'.[1]

The passing of the Bubble Act in June 1720 had a lasting effect on joint-stock companies in Britain.[2] The act suppressed unauthorised ventures which had sprung up since 24 June 1718 and forbade the flotation of new concerns without the consent of Parliament. Although it did not entirely destroy it, this crisis curbed the speculative mania in company stocks which had been growing steadily during 1720. Thenceforth if a new corporate venture was to be launched, Parliamentary sanction had to be obtained or means found to circumvent the Bubble Act. Moreover, care had to be taken in framing the scheme to make it attractive to an investing public made a little wiser by the South Sea collapse. One such attempt was the launching of the Harburgh Company. As a company originally established abroad, it was felt that it avoided the restrictions of the Bubble Act. To entice the investor it was planned to run a lottery, a device which reflected the element of gambling in many business enterprises of the time and often present in insurance ventures such as tontine schemes. The lottery itself had been used successfully by the government as a means of raising funds in previous years. Uncertainty surrounding its legality and the dubious nature of its plans ensured the failure of the Harburgh Scheme, but a study of the company's affairs reveals some interesting insights into the business methods and ethics of the 'Bubble' era.

I

The town of Harburg, situated on the River Elbe directly opposite the Imperial Free City of Hamburg, came under the control of George I as Elector of Hanover on the death of his father-in-law, Georg Wilhelm, Duke of Celle in 1705.[3] Hanoverian merchants had quickly realised the economic potential of this new acquisition, and in the years 1708 and 1709, attempts were made to encourage trade in the town. In 1716 a further scheme was devised whereby merchants were to be given trade and toll privileges in return for building houses and developing the port. The money for development was to be raised by a lottery and powers were granted to establish a bank with a monopoly.[4]

After the accession of George I to the British throne in 1714, English merchants began to explore the possibility of encouraging trade through Harburg and developing its port facilities. During the seventeenth and early eighteenth centuries there had been a succession of river improvement schemes in England linked to the development of trade and industry in which merchants had played a significant part.[5] Some of those involved in such enterprises were later to be found among the promoters of the Harburgh Company.

At least two men, Thomas Sliford and John Christian Nicolai, were active in promoting schemes to develop Harburg as a centre of British trade. Sliford, writing in 1717, felt that the Dutch were enjoying the trade of the Rivers Elbe and Weser which might conceivably be taken over by British merchants and that Hamburg and Bremen merchants, because of the strength of their position in North Germany, were exploiting British merchants. By opening up trade through Harburg, Sliford thought that greater profits could be made and tolls on the Elbe saved. The cost of the scheme would be high as considerable investment was necessary to make the port facilities at Harburg suitable for handling large ships.[6] Despite this, Sliford was of the opinion, rightly as it turned out, that a joint-stock company was not appropriate from the British point of view as Parliament had been involved, in recent decades, in dissolving monopolies in European trade. Instead he advocated a scheme similar to the British Navigation Acts where Hanoverians would have the greatest privileges but with the British paying less duty on the movement of goods than others, a situation similar to that which had pertained to the Scots in England before 1707. Such a scheme, though, appeared to be contrary to the imperial laws of the Holy Roman Empire of which Hanover was a part and was certain to arouse the anger of the merchants of Bremen and Hamburg.[7]

Interest in trade through Harburg was also demonstrated by John Christian Nicolai. Nicolai travelled several times to Hanover between 1716 and 1722 in order to promote his idea. Nothing came of the plan for several years, perhaps due to uncertainties on both sides of the North Sea. Within Hanover, the Bremen-Verden crisis of 1717 and war in northern Europe meant that the climate was not suitable for such a venture. In Great Britain, the slackening of trade coupled with the threat of war with Spain may also have acted as deterrent factors.[8] After the return of peace in 1720 the scheme was revived. A joint-stock company was decided upon, based on the scheme first proposed in 1716, with John Christian Nicolai as one of the directors.

The Harburgh Company was established on 30 November 1720, when a charter was obtained from George I as Elector of Hanover.[9] The main objective was to foster trade between Britain and the king's German possessions for which concessions were to be given, and an obligation was accepted to deepen the River Elbe and construct a harbour at Harburg. Significantly the company's powers included permission to form a bank in Harburg and to organise a lottery under the king's direction to be drawn in Hanover. Earlier in 1720 George I, again as Elector of Hanover, had granted a charter to a manufacturing concern. This was now to be linked to the Harburgh Company and, in effect, a united company was to be formed. This merger was completed sometime in 1721.[10]

The fact that the company was established abroad so soon after the passing of the Bubble Act, and that it was, in effect, directed from London, suggests that some of its promoters were seeking to circumvent the provisions of the act. This impression is underlined by the fact that meetings of company took place in London rather than in Germany. The attempt to establish a bank possibly indicates that some members were also trying to evade the monopoly of the Bank of England in joint-stock banking. To allay the doubts of some officers and shareholders, a British charter was sought, and some waverers were placated by assurances that this would be forthcoming.[11] Failure to obtain this document meant that the company's proceedings in England were of dubious legality and eventually gave the House of Commons grounds for establishing an investigation into the lottery in 1723, thus making public other aspects of the conduct of the company.[12]

The governor, as with so many other corporate concerns, was a member of the royal family, Prince Frederick, a boy of 15 who took no active part in the company's affairs. Significantly, though, Frederick was resident in Hanover for constitutional reasons and this strengthened the German link. The German trading charter was sought by Alderman Robert Baylis, a city businessman, and Sir John Eyles, among others.[13] Baylis actively came to oppose many of the company's later actions. Eyles, sub-governor of the Harburgh Company under its charter, was a notable business figure of the period. A Whig MP from 1713 to 1734, he sat for Chippenham until 1727 and then for the City of London until 1734. He also served as a director of the Bank of England, the East India Company and the South Sea Company and was the only director of any of these three major joint-stock companies to be directly involved in the Harburgh Company. His connection with the South Sea Company was tinged with hints of malpractice. As sub-governor of that company between 1721 and 1733 he steered that concern through its difficulties following the crisis of 1720, but he and other directors were accused by Edward Vernon MP in the House of Commons in 1732 of carrying on private trade to the detriment of the South Sea Company. This was vigorously denied and it took the Speaker and several others to calm the situation. In the same session Eyles was censured by the House for allowing the secretary of the Forfeited Estates Commission to sign a document for him in his absence which facilitated the fraudulent sale of the Derwentwater estate to another member, Denis Bond. In 1733 Eyles demitted office in the South Sea Company on the grounds of ill-health and in the election of 1734 failed to be returned for Chippenham.[14] It is difficult to determine the exact extent of Eyles' involvement with the Harburgh Company. The House of Commons report on the Harburgh Lottery is singularly reticent about his activities. As Eyles sat on that committee[15] one can point to the possibility of his role being deliberately minimised. On the other hand there was no attempt by others to implicate him when the affairs of the company were under investigation. On balance it seems probable that Eyles took a relatively minor role in the affairs of the company.

The other sub-governor, and one more actively engaged in the company's affairs, was John Barrington, MP for Berwick-on-Tweed, who had been elevated to the Irish peerage as 1st Viscount Barrington in 1719.[16] He appears to have been one of those chiefly responsible for the company's fraudulent activities and it was he who eventually carried most of the blame. However, the man who devised the scheme which was to raise the bulk of the finance by means of a lottery and give rise to a Parliamentary investigation was Case Billingsley. Billingsley, a city merchant and a noted company projector, had been one of those responsible for floating the scheme which ultimately became the Royal Exchange Assurance. He also promoted the acquisition of the York Buildings Company with the idea of using its corporate powers to acquire the estates forfeited after the Jacobite rebellion of 1715. It was the intention of the promoters to make the revenues from the estates the basis of an annuity lottery scheme.[17] Billingsley was, therefore, the ideal man to devise the lottery. Another leading figure was William Squire, a Liverpool merchant and mayor of the town in 1715, who represented an important link with river and port development schemes in England. On 2 December 1719, Squire had been instructed by Liverpool town council to go to London to assist the town's MPs, one of whom, Edward Norris, was his brother-in-law, in petitioning for an act for the improvement of the River Weaver. During the period of the South Sea Bubble, Squire, another brother-in-law, Richard Norris, and Thomas Steers were involved in a dubious scheme to market shares in the Douglas Navigation from Wigan to the River Ribble which saw £5 shares in that concern leaping to £70 before collapsing to £3 3s. (£3.15). Steers was one of the most noted civil engineers of the period. He was involved in river improvements in the Mersey and Irewell completed in 1725 and between 1736 and 1741 surveyed and supervised the construction of the Newry Canal. He was also responsible for dock developments in Rotherhithe and Liverpool.[18] It seems possible, therefore, that Billingsley and Squire provided the bulk of the business acumen surrounding the scheme and that Barrington was merely the front man.

Significantly, several of those nominated as trustees of the Harburgh Lottery were involved contemporaneously in companies with which Billingsley and Squire were concerned, or had other interests in common as illustrated in Table 1.

Parliamentary investigations in 1732 and 1733 were to reveal serious misdeeds within the York Buildings Company and the Charitable Corporation as well as the Harburgh Company.[19] Therefore, the links outlined in Table 1 suggest that there was a distinct group of people involved in manipulating these and possibly other companies for their own individual ends. They were not a coherent body as at times their interests conflicted, and disputes arising from such clashes were fought out in the courts. Speculation and quick capital gains rather than investment for long-term growth and a steady income were the aims of this particular group.

TABLE 1

CORPORATE LINKS AMONG PRINCIPAL HARBURGH COMPANY PROMOTERS

Case Billingsley:	Royal Exchange Assurance; York Buildings Company; English Copper Company
Sir Alexander Cairnes:	Royal Exchange Assurance; York Buildings Company; English Copper Company
Fiennes Harrison:	York Buildings Company; English Copper Company
Peter Hartop:	Charitable Corporation
John London:	Royal Exchange Assurance; York Buildings Company
William Squire:	York Buildings Company; Charitable Corporation; Mines Royal and Mineral and Battery Works

Sources: PRO C11/1816/11, Westmoreland v York Buildings Company; *Daily Courant*, 1 July, 13 August 1720, 29 June 1723; *Daily Journal*, 29 March 1723; *Reports of Committees of the House of Commons* (1803), Vol. 1, p. 439.

This faction met with a fair degree of opposition to their plans from within the company. Baylis, for one, argued against their actions in private and in public. Sir Thomas Webster, a deputy governor, also attempted to bring their conduct into the open. Despite these determined efforts by the more honest group within the company, it took a parliamentary investigation to expose the extent of the activities of this particular group and to terminate them.[20]

II

The exact amount and nature of the capital structure of the enterprise is uncertain. The issue is complicated by the fact that the venture was the result of the amalgamation of two different organisations, one a trading and the other a manufacturing company. The nominal capital of the former was £500,000 and of the latter, £540,800.[21] The difficulty is to ascertain with accuracy how much stock was actually issued. A two per cent call was made which raised £20,000 – £13,000 in cash and £7,000 in notes. The sum taken in suggests stock with a nominal value of £1 million was issued, but all the indications are that only £500,000 was in circulation by the time of the parliamentary report, and that appeared to be the stock of the trading company. The latter was the amount of stock later linked to the £1 million to be issued to holders of blanks in the company's lottery bringing the total nominal value of stock up to £1.5 million. The manufacturing company did lose its separate identity sometime in 1721. Barrington certainly agreed to the giving up of the manufacturing company's charter to accomplish a union between the two ventures.[22] There is no evidence to indicate what became of the stock, or if the £20,000 paid in did include a two per cent payment on the manufacturing company's stock.

The fate of the £20,000 collected on the stock became a cause for concern. The Commons Committee of 1723 was unable to see the books, but believed the sum had been embezzled. The difficulty in eliciting information arose from the fact that the Committee was unwilling to interfere in matters which concerned the king's German territories – and the company had been floated there. However, Billingsley tried to convey the impression that Benjamin Joules, the person charged with carrying out the civil engineering works at Harburg, had taken the money, as in later years he constantly demanded that Joules account for it.[23]

Joules did profit from the flotation of the stock. At one stage £100,000 of trading company stock was disposed of at £15 3s. per cent of which only £2 per cent found its way to the company. Of the other £13 3s. which raised £13,150 – £3,150 went to Joules and the other £10,000 to John Christian Nicolai. Nicolai asserted that the money he received was for services rendered to the enterprise since 1716 and that these had necessitated several journeys to Hanover. Nicolai claimed only to have received £8,800 from Joules and to have laid that out in South Sea subscriptions.[24] The attempt of one director, Nathaniel Brassey, to get an accurate account of these transactions from Lord Barrington, the sub-governor, was unsuccessful. Brassey stressed he was most anxious to see the statement, as he felt Joules could not account for the money he had received. Another enquirer, Moses Raper, met with a similar refusal.[25]

Perhaps the most illuminating account of this particular stock transaction was given to the Commons committee by Andrew Hope, a director, who had purchased £10,000 of stock at £15 3s. per cent. Like the others, he found Lord Barrington unwilling to give him any information and so he turned to Joules. The latter informed Hope that Barrington and Cairnes had authorised him to dispose of £100,000 of stock at this price and that as treasurer he received the money by their order. Hope could find no trace in the records that he had paid for this stock. He also complained that he appeared to have no more privileges than the holders of the remaining £400,000 of stock who had paid only two per cent. Hope therefore appeared to be under the impression that he had paid a call of £15 3s. (£15. 15) rather than a call of £2 and a premium of £13 3s. (£13.15). Also Hope believed one John Lloyd, who had purchased £30,000 of stock at £15 3s. per cent, and sold some at £80 and £60 and more of it from £20 to £30 per cent. He pointed out that for these transactions, no stock transfers were made and no receipts given.[26] What is curious is that the Commons committee did not make any comment on this point in its report, limiting itself only to stamping out the lottery. It could be argued its remit extended only to the lottery, but given the concern of the government and parliament with 'bubbles', one might have expected some comment on the stock transactions.

As the company was chartered in Germany, the stock could not be subscribed for in London. Applications had to be forwarded to Harburg. To facilitate this, Joules was to get a letter of attorney to allow him to act for prospective purchasers. One of the people to whom he offered stock was Case Billingsley, who was sceptical about the enterprise, and he did not agree to subscribe until he had investigated the proposals. Billingsley's caution was underlined by the fact that he did not pay cash for his initial issue, but gave Joules a note which only became valid when endorsed by a quorum of directors of the company. Billingsley also wished to be certain that the stock was transferable.[27] This caution on the part of a known speculator seems a reasonable indication that he was well aware of the dubious nature of the enterprise.

The fact that the company possessed only a German charter meant that its activities in Britain were decidedly limited. Thus many of those involved with the company were anxious to ensure that a British charter was obtained, and Lord Barrington kept assuring people that this was about to happen. The fear of many stockholders was that without this charter, the company would be regarded as fraudulent in Britain. The Bubble Act was no doubt in many people's minds. On 28 May 1722 the company prepared a draft of a British charter similar to that obtained in Germany.[28] Thus the company was trying to obtain powers from the British parliament on the one hand, and George I as Elector of Hanover on the other, which would have given the company a monopoly of trade between Britain and Harburg. The name of Prince Frederick as Governor headed the list of 104 applicants which also included three peers, three baronets, five knights, 29 gentlemen, 42 merchants and 18 others. Barrington was to be Sub-Governor and Sir Thomas Webster, Sir Charles Wager and Robert Baylis, Deputy Governors. The directors included Benjamin Burroughs, Fiennes Harrison, Peter Hartop, John London, John Christian Nicolai and William Squire.[29]

In order to further their case Lord Barrington, Sir Thomas Webster and Sir Charles Wager, all members of parliament as well as governors of the company, had approached Sir Robert Walpole and other members of the government to enlist their aid. The latter had distinct objections to the scheme. In the first place they did not care for the company's German privileges. Second, they were against a joint-stock company. Finally, they felt that the lottery could not be chartered as it was impractical and illegal. Lord Barrington was anxious to keep this decision secret, but Webster ordered George Ridpath, the secretary, to call a directors' meeting to inform them of the decision.[30]

The directors' reaction was swift. On 31 August 1722 a committee was appointed to find ways of overcoming the objections. The committee recommended that its trading privileges be extended to all Britons willing to pay £30 to become freemen of the company. This was in line with general government policy to abandon company monopolies in European trade by opening up such organisations as the Eastland Company and the Russia Company to all those paying a small fee. Those who decided not to avail themselves of this facility would still be free to trade with Harburg but be subject to normal duties and fees. The proposal was adopted by the directors on 4 September 1722 and ratified by a general court later the same day.[31]

Despite the proposed amendments, the charter was rejected. This was hardly surprising since the Hamburg Company, despite powerful lobbying in Parliament had been unable to maintain its rights and privileges to trade just across the river.[32] The decision led to dissension within the company. It was generally felt that it was against the law to proceed with the lottery. For this reason, Lord Barrington was very keen to keep the fact that the charter had been refused a close secret. Men such as Baylis and Sir Thomas Webster refused to have anything more to do with the company.[33] Despite this, the scheme for the lottery appeared in *The Flying Post* for 4–6 December 1722. The editor of this newspaper was none other than George Ridpath, secretary to the Harburgh Company and to the lottery trustees.

III

Even before the scheme was published, the Harburgh Lottery had had a chequered history. The power to conduct a lottery in Harburgh was granted to the company in the original charter of 1720. This was changed in September 1721. In return for an undertaking to carry out the civil engineering projects in Germany, the profits of the lottery were assigned to Benjamin Joules. In October Joules petitioned the king to issue a warrant for a lottery of £1.5 million. On 19 December this was granted subject to the king's approving the method and time of drawing of the lottery. Seven trustees were appointed – Lord Barrington, Fiennes

Harrison, Henry Bendysh, another director, Joules and three Germans. The trustees had powers to co-opt others if the need arose and were authorised to lay a scheme for the lottery before the king. Barrington claimed that in January 1722, three lawyers advised the company that the lottery could be published and tickets issued in England.[34] Sir Thomas Pengelly, Sergeant-at-law and the leading expert on company law in the 1720s was not so certain. He felt that the purchase of tickets might not in itself be illegal under a measure prohibiting certain types of private lottery, but that dealing in tickets could be construed as evidence of the publication of such a scheme which had been made illegal.[35] On 20 January the king approved the scheme for a five-part lottery of £1.5 million.

In July 1722 the company altered its plans for the lottery. It was felt that it was more appropriate that the company carry out the works itself. On a motion by Sir Thomas Webster it was decided to give Joules £10,000 in five instalments of £2,000 to be paid as individual parts of the lottery were drawn, provided that particular part was full. In return Joules promised to re-assign the profits of the lottery to the company. As the lottery had reverted to the company, it was decided to appoint all the British directors as trustees, in addition to those originally named. Most directors agreed to be appointed, and they, together with one Francis Kreinbergh, a proprietor of stock, were appointed on 16 September 1722.[36] It was during this period that the dispute over the British charter arose, and the names of Sir Thomas Webster and Alderman Baylis were significantly absent from the list of trustees. Sir Alexander Cairnes's name was also omitted. He had become bankrupt in October 1720 as a result of the collapse of the stock market.[37]

The scheme of the lottery was devised by Case Billingsley when Joules held the franchise. By a deed of agreement drawn up between the two men on 30 September 1721, Lord Barrington claimed that Billingsley was to receive two per cent of the value of the lottery for his plan if the lottery was filled. If true, this would have netted Billingsley a maximum of £30,000. Billingsley and Joules were in very close collaboration over this, as the latter refused to re-assign the rights of the lottery unless the agreement with Billingsley was upheld. As the large amount payable to Billingsley was only a contingency it was felt that he would sell the rights for £6,000. Despite pressure he refused to renounce any of the concessions made to him by Joules.[38] In a speech to the House of Commons, Lord Barrington claimed that in fact Billingsley's two per cent was to come out of the contingent profits of the lottery and was not on the whole sum of £1.5 million. Therefore, Billingsley would have received nothing like £30,000. Lord Barrington thought it better to offer Billingsley two per cent on the profits rather than an outright payment of £1,000 before the scheme got off the ground.[39]

The whole question of fees and expenses for the lottery was beset with complications and contradictions. In addition to payments to Billingsley and Joules, the wider concept of management costs was later queried.

Nathaniel Brassey, a director, told the Commons committee that at one board meeting he attended, Lord Barrington informed those present that £75,000 was to be provided for the management of the lottery. At the same meeting, Barrington proposed that £75,000 be given to Joules for his rights to the lottery and for work at Harburg, but this was later modified. Brassey objected to the size of the management charge as Alderman William Billers had offered to supervise the scheme for £20,000 provided he, Billers, thought it fair. Barrington turned down the suggestion as royal assent had authorised expenditure of £75,000 on the lottery, and it was necessary to adhere to this sum. On further questioning Barrington as to how the £75,000 was to be spent, Brassey was told this was private and none of his business.[40]

It was further claimed that Billingsley's share was to include the cost of preparing and publishing the lottery as well as printing and issuing the tickets. Billingsley had the tickets printed, and they were issued from York Buildings House, headquarters of the York Buildings Company. The trustees of the lottery received the money for the tickets. Joules, giving evidence to the Commons committee, said he did not know how many tickets were issued. The scheme was first published and the tickets issued on 13 November 1722.[41]

On the surface the lottery seemed very attractive. There were to be 500,000 tickets costing £3 each, payable in five instalments of 12s. (60p.), to be paid before the drawing of the lottery. The prospectus tried to give the impression that the investor had very little to lose.[42] The lottery was to be divided into five equal parts. Prizes were to range from one of £10,000 for the last blank drawn in the entire lottery, to 160,120 prizes of £5 each. Of the £1.5 million collected, £1 million was to be returned as prizes and there was one chance in three of drawing a prize. For the holders of the two-thirds of the tickets drawn blanks, there was to be adequate compensation. Each blank was to qualify for £3 of capital stock of the company, which it was claimed would become more valuable as only five per cent was to be deducted from the scheme for management charges. The prospectus valued the stock at £1 10s. (£1.50) per £3 unit. As an added inducement to prevent any one person running the risk of great loss, there was a special scheme for those purchasing more than 12 tickets. If the purchaser paid 12s. (60p.) extra per ticket, and the total amount of prizes and value per blank of each of these tickets (taking the value of stock on each blank to be £1 10s. (£1.50) cash) fell below an average of £3 per ticket, the promoters would make the value up to £3 by a cash adjustment within two months. In this way, it was claimed the maximum to be lost, if all tickets were drawn blanks, was 10s. (50p.) per ticket.

The prospectus also included a plan whereby the company would lend money on the security of the tickets. On 100 tickets a holder could borrow 9s. (45p.) per ticket, on 50, 7s. (35p.), and on 25 5s. (25p.) per ticket. The sums were to be interest free, and payable in four instalments, together with the instalment on the lottery ticket itself. If any ticket drew a prize in an early part of the lottery, the company was empowered to keep a sufficient sum to pay the outstanding balance due on all holders' tickets. Encouraging investors by means of loans and advances was fairly common at this time. The York Buildings Company had lent money on the tickets of its first lottery.[43] During the speculative mania of 1720 the Bank of England, the South Sea Company and the Royal Africa Company had all lent money to their investors on the security of their own stock.[44]

The stock of the Harburgh Company having mysteriously advanced to a nominal £1.5 million, it was reckoned that the cash injection provided by this scheme would advance the net worth of the company to 29 per cent, or £435,000. In addition the value would be enhanced by privileges such as trading free of customs at Harburg for 40 years, lands given to the company in perpetuity and 25 per cent of sums laid out in building houses. The proprietors of lottery blanks would hold, under the scheme, two-thirds of the stock of the company.[45] Those set to gain most were the proprietors of the original stock who, having paid only two per cent on their investment, now found it could have been manipulated to have an asset value equivalent to 29 per cent. This had all the hallmarks of a 'bubble' and it is scarcely surprising that Parliament was called upon to investigate it.

IV

The House of Commons was quick to react to the Harburgh Lottery. Barrington claimed that without a complaint being received, but at the instigation of John Hungerford, a committee was set up to investigate the Harburgh and other foreign lotteries, but this body concentrated solely on the former project.[46] Hungerford was no stranger to this sort of investigation. He had chaired a committee which, in 1720, had investigated the projected companies which had sprung up in 1719 and 1720. Particularly associated with the South Sea Company, he had been especially critical of Billingsley's role in the promotion of the marine insurance scheme which ultimately became the Royal Exchange Assurance Company.[47] He was, therefore, unlikely to look with favour on Billingsley's latest idea.

Most of those principally involved with the Harburgh Company were examined by the committee, but Billingsley proved too elusive for them. Along with Ridpath, he claimed he was too ill to attend the committee, which ordered that they be interrogated at their own homes.[48] Ridpath was eventually questioned, and a claim was put forward that Billingsley was also, but this was untrue.[49] On 15 January 1723 it was reported that Billingsley had absconded. Accordingly, he was ordered to be taken into the custody of the Sergeant-at-Arms.[50] It was reported that he had fled to Holland but claimed that this could merely have been a rumour, put out by his friends, to cover the fact that he was closer to home.[51] For certain people at least, it was not desirable that Billingsley should appear before the committee.

In the absence of what could have been the star witness, it is hardly surprising that the committee came out firmly against the scheme. When the figures were analysed in detail, it was found to be far from advantageous to the investor as claimed in the prospectus. Table 2 shows how the committee believed the existing proprietors would benefit from the lottery at the expense of those entering by way of the lottery.

Although the holders of blanks were to be given stock of £3 per ticket valued at £1 10s. (£1.50) (or 50 per cent), the real value was nothing like that. In fact their stock would be covered by assets (almost exclusively their own cash) to give a realistic value of 29 per cent.

TABLE 2

DIVISION OF LOTTERY PROCEEDS

500,000 Tickets @ £3 each		£1,500,000
Less Prizes		1,000,000
Value of Blanks to share £1m. stock		500,000
Less Management Changes @ 5% on £1.5m.		75,000
Net Money belonging to holders of blanks		425,000
Add Value of £0.5m. existing stock 2% paid		10,000
Real value of £1.5m. stock representing a price of 29%		435,000
Less One third attributable to existing shareholders		145,000
Value remaining to holders of Blanks		290,000
Real gain to original shareholders	145,000	
Less Original Value of stock	10,000	
Net sum taken from lottery investors	135,000	
Add Management charges	75,000	
Total gain for managers & old stockholders		210,000
Representing 42% of the net sum advanced by lottery investors		
		£500,000

Source: HCJ, Vol. 20, p.124, Report of the Committee on the Harburgh Lottery.

This gives rise to the question as to who stood to benefit from the lottery. First of all, the organisers and managers stood to gain £75,000 less expenses. Second, the original proprietors of the company found the real value of their holding raised to £145,000. If one deducts the £10,000 paid on the two per cent call, this is a real increase of £135,000 or nine per cent of £1.5 million. This meant a total deduction of 14 per cent from the whole scheme as against five per cent stated in the prospectus. Looked at in terms of the £0.5 million the lottery was expected to raise for the company's plans, this meant that 42 per cent was actually going to, or attributed to, managers and old stockholders.[52] No doubt many people appeared in both capacities, but unfortunately data deficiencies preclude detailed analysis. It was hardly surprising that the Commons voted the Harburgh Lottery 'an infamous and fraudulent undertaking', which linked a real subscription of £425,000 with a fraudulent one on which only two per cent was paid. The House resolved to bring a bill to suppress the lottery.[53] It was not, however, the end of plans to develop the River Elbe. George I, who had been actively negotiating such plans with the Prussians in 1721,[54] continued to take an interest in such schemes and even after the collapse of the lottery, Benjamin Joules maintained an interest in Harburgh.[55]

V

The suppression of the Harburgh Lottery not only had repercussions for those directly involved, but brings to light several of the contemporary attitudes to speculative ventures. For Lord Barrington the scheme was particularly disastrous. No doubt, despite his claims to the contrary, he lost the opportunity to make a great deal of money. More important was the fact that he was expelled from the House of Commons for his part in the affair. Barrington felt unjustly treated in being singled out for blame. In particular he was annoyed that Sir Thomas Webster and Sir Charles Wager had escaped censure.[56] The former had in fact given evidence to the Commons committee, in which he claimed to have opposed some of the company's actions. The latter sat on the committee itself.[57] It seems possible, therefore, that Eyles, Wager and Webster had sufficient influence to steer the investigation away from themselves, and that Barrington was made the scapegoat.

Barrington believed that the Harburgh Lottery was being unfairly singled out for opprobrium for claiming 14 per cent for managing the lottery, when the York Buildings Company and other lotteries regularly deducted 19 or 20 per cent.[58] He also felt aggrieved that the House had not spelt out the exact nature of the fraud it claimed existed. He maintained that the lottery would have been more advantageous to the participants than the scheme suggested. On the other hand, Barrington denied any involvement in the printing of the prospectus. Finally, he stated that the Harburgh Company itself had fallen, not due to any misconduct on his part, but to the envy of others, most notably the citizens of Bremen and Hamburg, the Dutch and the court of Vienna, all of whose interests he felt would suffer as a result of the company's success. In his speech to the House of Commons, he stressed the commercial advantages the company would have enjoyed, but most seemed vague and exaggerated. He even went so far as to claim that £150,000 per annum could be made from herring alone. Thus the stockholders coming in via the lottery could have had the £210,000, which was deducted from them, repaid in around 18 months. Such schemes appear wildly improbable, but seem to be indicative of the general conduct of Barrington at this time. During his address to the House of Commons on 14 February 1723, he was interrupted by Walpole, who assured the House that Barrington and his scheme had never had any encouragement from the government.[59] Barrington's speech made little impression on the Commons, who voted to expel him.[60]

Few people had in fact subscribed to the lottery before it was stopped. It was later stated that only £120 had been taken in, and by 4 March 1723 the trustees claimed only £11 8s. (£11.40) was outstanding and invited those entitled to this sum to reclaim their money.[61]

There were several reasons why the Harburgh Lottery failed to catch the public's imagination. The most important was that the events of 1720 had caused a rash of bankruptcies and a crisis of confidence in the business community. This has best been summed up by Ashton:[62] 'It was only slowly that confidence was restored and that money trickled out of the iron chests of merchants and the stockings of smaller tradesmen'. Investment from these sources was essential for the success of the Harburgh scheme, and it was not forthcoming. Second, the general trend in the stock market in 1722 was for the prices of leading stocks to fall. Between 15 January and 1 November 1722, South Sea Company, Bank of England, East India Company, Royal Africa Company and Royal Exchange Assurance stocks all fell. A slight recovery was noted in the latter half of October 1722 in respect of the first of these stocks, but this could not be sustained.[63] Finally, lotteries, with their added risks, were not a suitable type of investment for the financial climate of the period following the collapse of the bubbles of 1720. This was confirmed by the fact that the York Buildings Company lotteries of the same period also failed.

The evidence clearly points to the fact that the Harburgh Company's lottery was designed to defraud the public. There is no doubt that the lottery would have increased the value of the existing stock, and transferred title to assets to established shareholders from the participants in the lottery. One must also doubt the intention of some of the participants to complete the works at Harburg, as Billingsley did. Undoubtedly, George I and others such as Joules took such plans seriously and the former had even gone so far as to lend his surveyors to assist in the work of constructing a network of canals to open up trade in northern Germany. The King was thus distinctly embarrassed when the fraud came to light.[64] Even if the intentions of the company were serious in this respect, one feels that in common with the ideas behind the South Sea Company, trading schemes were subordinate to financial ones. Parallels with the York Buildings Company lotteries were also strong as Case Billingsley was the promoter for both companies. One contemporary commentator complaining of the York Buildings Company's conduct in 1724 went as far as to suggest there was a strong link between the two organisations and stated that Parliament should investigate the York Buildings Company.[65] This demand was not implemented at that time.

The complexities of the Harburgh Lottery scheme, including facilities for loans upon partially paid tickets left tremendous scope for malpractice. The House of Commons was undoubtedly correct in quashing the lottery, but unfortunately did not look closely at the company's stock transactions. However, the committee was not wholly a disinterested body safeguarding the public interest. It contained two of the principal figures involved in the company in Eyles and Wager. Therefore, it is possible that certain crucial areas were avoided during the enquiry especially if royal interests were also involved. On the trading side, despite Barrington's optimistic forecasts, one feels that the ports of Bremen and Hamburg and, of course, the Dutch, would have ensured the crushing of this upstart rival.

The whole plan behind the Harburgh Company was built on an entirely insecure foundation, both on the capital side and as a trading venture. Had the lottery been allowed to proceed, there seems little doubt that anyone who had invested in it would have found themselves possessors of stock in a worthless foreign company. By this time, the projectors would have attempted to unload their own holdings on to the market, as happened in the case of the York Buildings Company and the English Copper Company, in which Case Billingsley had also been involved.[66] What would have happened to the lottery investors' cash is a matter of pure speculation.

The case of the Harburgh Company also calls into question the effectiveness of the Bubble Act. As the company was technically a foreign operation, simple legal proceedings could not be taken under its provisions, and a full-scale parliamentary enquiry was necessary. Given the poor response of the public to the lottery, it appears to be a case of over-reaction, unless there were political motives for such a move which are not readily apparent. On the other hand, the refusal of Walpole and his colleagues to approve the requests for a British Charter and the speed of the House of Commons in setting up an investigation into the affair can be seen as an attempt to enforce the spirit as well as the letter of the law. In the aftermath of the crisis of 1720, this commanded a great deal of public support.[67]

The case of the Harburgh Company, therefore, brings to light some interesting aspects of business life in the 1720s. In the first place, despite the crisis of 1720 there would appear to have been sufficient funds around, either from agriculture or trade surpluses, to tempt speculators to float speculative projects in order to make a quick profit. This was done by holding out the prospect of sizeable capital gains and were designed to tempt the unwary. The speculative money market was fairly young at this time and many people were still comparatively oblivious to its dangers despite the recent crisis. Also industry had not yet developed to a sufficient extent to provide an outlet for such funds. Thus the way was open for groups of businessmen such as Case Billingsley and his associates to design schemes with the intention of fleecing a gullible public. The fact that Parliament was willing to investigate such enterprises, in the case of the Harburgh Company even before its plans came to fruition, indicates that despite ideas of indolence and corruption it could act when it had a mind to. The more honest sections of the business community also appeared willing to see such activities brought to light and stopped. Ventures such as the Harburgh Company also demonstrated the new attitude to joint-stock enterprises. Government thinking, reflecting the wishes of many in the business community, no longer favoured trading monopolies, at least in Europe, and thus the trading company never stood a chance of receiving approval from Parliament. The more fraudulent aspects of the Harburgh Company and other such ventures ensured that aspects of joint-stock company development, other than those concerned with large-scale public utilities, would be looked upon with a jaundiced eye until the middle of the nineteenth century.

University of Strathclyde

NOTES

1. For the early development of joint-stock companies, the classic work is still W. R. Scott, *The Constitution and Finance of English, Scottish and Irish Joint-Stock Companies to 1720* (3 vols., Cambridge, 1912). I am grateful to Professor John Butt and Dr Gordon Jackson, Strathclyde University, for their comments on early drafts of this article.
2. 6 George 1, c.18. For detailed treatment of the South Sea Bubble, see J. Carswell, *The South Sea Bubble* (London, 1960) and P. G. M. Dickson, *The Financial Revolution in England, A Study in the Development of Public Credit* (London, 1966), especially Chs. 5–6.
3. Ragnhild Hatton, *George I Elector and King* (London, 1978), p. 79.
4. Thomas Sliford, *A Brief Account of what hath been done towards making a settlement of Trade at Harburg* ... (1717), pp. 5–6.
5. T. S. Willan, *River Navigation in England 1600–1750* (London, 1964 ed.), p. 62.
6. Sliford, *Account*, p. 12; *Journal of the House of Commons* (henceforth *HCJ*), Vol. 20, p. 115.
7. Sliford, *Account*, pp. 4, 7–10.
8. *HCJ*, Vol. 20, p. 120. For the general situation as it affected Britain's relations with Europe and with Hanover see Hatton, George I, Chs. VII–VIII, *passim*. and W. A. Speck, *Stability & Strife, England 1714–1760* (London, 1977), Chs. 7–8, *passim*.
9. *Lord Viscount Barrington's Case in Relation to the Harburgh Company and the Harburgh Lottery* (1723), p. 3.
10. PRO E112/1172/556/1 Billingsley v Joules, Complaints of Billingsley; *HCJ*, Vol. 20, pp. 116–18; *Barrington's Case*, p. 3.
11. Ibid., p. 6; *HCJ*, Vol. 20, p. 118; Hatton, *George I*, p. 128.
12. *HCJ*, Vol. 20, pp. 115–25, Report on the Harburgh Lottery.
13. *Barrington's Case*, p. 3.
14. R. Sedgwick (ed.), *The History of Parliament: The House of Commons, 1715–1754* (London, 1970), Vol. 2, p. 21; Dickson, *Financial Revolution*, p. 117.
15. *HCJ*, Vol. 20, p. 75.
16. Sedgwick, *Commons*, Vol. 1, p. 438.
17. A. J. G. Cummings, 'The York Buildings Company, A Case Study in Eighteenth Century Corporate Mismanagement' (University of Strathclyde, unpublished Ph.D. thesis, 1981), pp. 32–3.
18. Sir James A. Picton (ed.), *City of Liverpool. Municipal Archives and Records from A.D. 1700 to the Passing of the Municipal Reform Act, 1835* (Liverpool, 1886), p. 51; Willan, *River Navigation*, p. 70; L. T. C. Rolt, *Navigable Waterways* (London, Arrow ed., 1973), p. 22; D. Swann, 'The Engineers of English Port Improvements 1660–1830. Part I', *Transport History*, Vol. 1, (1968), p. 158.
19. See *Reports of Committees of the House of Commons* (1803), Vol. 1.
20. *HCJ*, Vol. 20, pp. 119–20.
21. Ibid., pp. 117–18.
22. *Barrington's Case*, pp. 19–21.

23. PRO E112/1172/56, Billingsley v. Joules· *HCJ*, Vol. 20, p. 115.
24. Ibid., p. 120.
25. Ibid., pp. 117, 119. Raper was a director of the Bank of England, *Weekly Journal or British Gazetteer*, 8 April 1721.
26. *HCJ*, Vol. 20, p. 120.
27. PRO E112/1172/556/1, Billingsley v. Joules, Complaint of Billingsley. The subscription was for £18,000 of stock at £2 per cent or £360. Later Billingsley gave another note for £120.
28. *HCJ*, Vol. 20, pp. 118–19.
29. BL Add. MS. 6406, Charter of the Harburgh Company, 28 May 1722.
30. *HCJ*, Vol. 20, p. 119.
31. Ibid., p. 123. P. Griffiths, *A Licence To Trade* (London, 1964), pp. 39–40; R. Roberts, *Chartered Companies* (London, 1969), p. 55.
32. D.C. Coleman, *The Economy of England, 1350–1750* (Oxford, 1977), p. 149.
33. Ibid., p. 119.
34. *Barrington's Case*, pp. 4–5.
35. BL Add. MS. 22675, f63r. Opinion Book of T. Pengelly, 25 Jan. 1721/22; 8 George 1 c.2.
36. *Barrington's Case*, pp. 4–5.
37. David Murray, *The York Buildings Company: A Chapter in Scotch History* (Glasgow, 1883), p. 28.
38. *HCJ*, Vol. 20, p. 116; *Barrington's Case*, p. 15.
39. *A Speech on the Question That the Project called the Harburgh Lottery is an Infamous and Fraudulent Undertaking* (1723), p. 8. The speaker is not identified but internal evidence points to Barrington.
40. *HCJ*, Vol. 20, p. 118.
41. Ibid., p. 116; *Barrington's Case*, p. 8; *Speech on the Question*, pp. 8–9.
42. *HCJ*, Vol. 20, pp. 121–2.
43. Cummings, 'York Buildings Company', p. 116.
44. Dickson, *Financial Revolution*, pp. 143–5.
45. *HCJ*, Vol. 20, pp. 122–3.
46. *Barrington's Case*, p. 8.
47. *Special Report from the Committee appointed to enquire into and examine the several subscriptions for fisheries, insurances annuities for lives* ... (1720), p. 5. A copy of the report is to be found in the British Library at 357.b.3(30); *HCJ*, Vol. 19, p. 341; Sedgwick, *Commons*, Vol. 2, p. 161.
48. *British Journal*, 29 Dec. 1722.
49. *HCJ*, Vol. 20, pp. 116–17; *British Journal*, 5 Jan. 1723.
50. *Daily Journal*, 15 and 19 Jan. 1723.
51. *London Journal*, 23 Feb. 1723; *Mist's Weekly Journal*, 9 March 1723.
52. *HCJ*, Vol. 20, p. 124.
53. Ibid., p. 125.
54. BL Add. MS. 37387, Whitworth papers f4 Letter to Mr Tilson, 21 Nov./2 Dec. 1721.
55. PRO SP43/5, Letter, Tilson to Delafaye, 26 Oct./6 Nov. 1723.
56. *Barrington's Case*, p. 12.
57. *HCJ*, Vol. 20, p. 75.
58. *Barrington's Case*, p. 13.
59. Sedgwick, *Commons*, Vol. 1, p. 438.
60. *HCJ*, Vol. 20, p. 141.
61. *Daily Courant*, 4 March 1723; *The Case of the Trustees of the Harburgh Lottery* (1723).
62. T.S. Ashton, *Economic Fluctuations in England, 1700–1800* (Oxford, 1959), p. 121.
63. *Daily Courant*, 1 Jan., 15 Oct., 1 Nov., 1 Dec., 15 Dec., 1722.
64. Hatton, *George I*, pp. 292–3.
65. *A Letter from a Citizen to J— B— Esq., Member of Parliament, Relating to the York Buildings Company's Affairs* (1724).
66. Cummings, 'York Buildings Company', Ch. 3, *passim*.
67. A.B. DuBois, *The English Business Company after the Bubble Act, 1720–1800* (New

York, reprinted 1971), p.24. For details of another dubious scheme and its consequences, see J.M. Treadwell, 'William Wood and the Company of Ironmasters of Great Britain', *Business History*, Vol. 16 (1974), pp.97–112.

SHEFFEILD V. STARKE: INSTITUTIONAL EXPERIMENTATION IN THE LONDON–MARYLAND TRADE *c.* 1696–1706

By JACOB M. PRICE

Relatively few records survive of firms engaged in British–American trade in the century and a half preceding the American Revolution. For the Chesapeake tobacco trade – the largest component of British trade with North America, both in value and in shipping tonnage employed – papers survive of some larger planters and some small American merchants, but hardly anything on the British side. The three major collections of British firm records that do survive were preserved because they were presented as evidence in lawsuits and not reclaimed by the litigants.[1] These three, however, all date from the years immediately preceding the revolution. It may therefore be considered particularly noteworthy that there has recently come to light in the *fonds* of the Court of the Exchequer in the Public Record Office in London some papers of a London firm trading to Maryland in the 1690s. These records (accounts and correspondence) were brought into court in connection with a suit – Sheffeild v. Starke – between the executors of a London merchant, Thomas Starke, and his former apprentice, John Sheffeild. No other Chesapeake trade records of this character and antiquity are known to survive. In the first half of the article, the nature and progress of the lawsuit will be sketched; in the second part, the documentary sediment left behind by the lawsuit and other evidence will be sifted and analysed for a fuller picture of the firm's activities and of commercial practice in this significant branch of Anglo-American trade in the war years after 1689.

(i) Sheffeild v. Starke

Thomas Starke, 'of the parish of St. Dunstans in the East, citizen and haberdasher of London', was born in Norfolk ca. 1649. He apparently did not serve an apprenticeship in London but may have acquired his merchant's skills as a supercargo or factor representing some English merchant in Virginia or Maryland in the late 1660s or early 1670s. Although he later alleged in 1692 that he had been trading to Virginia for more than 20 years,[2] he does not appear as an importer of tobacco in the London port books of 1672[3] or 1676[4] – but does so in 1677 when he imported 24,252 lb. of tobacco.[5] It is possible that he was associated then – as later – with George Richards, at the time the second largest importer in London. (Richards, originally from Southampton, imported 358,374 lb.

of tobacco in 1672; 529,186lb. in 1676 and 435,541lb. in 1677.)[6] By 1679 Starke was sufficiently prosperous to be admitted a freeman of the Haberdashers' Company by redemption.[7]

By 1686, the rising Starke had become the third largest importer of tobacco in London, entering 833,175lb., while Richards was now in fourth place with 670,964lb.[8] We do not know the precise connection between them, but in a hearing on a later lawsuit, a customs officer deposed that between 24 June 1685 and 1 May 1696 'Mr Starke or George Richards or others for him Imported into the Port of London and other ports' 5,014,715lb. of tobacco.[9] There is nothing to suggest that Starke and Richards were general partners; more likely they were co-participants in one or more 'adventures' to the tobacco colonies. At the start of the war in 1689, both appear as part-owners of two very large armed merchantmen which received letters of marque and reprisal.[10] Whatever the connection had been earlier, it was not close then for, when George Richards died in 1695, he did not mention Thomas Starke in his will.[11]

The war years were very difficult for the Chesapeake tobacco trade as for many other branches of English commerce. Insurance was expensive and not routinely used, as we shall see. Merchants had to depend more on dividing their ventures among many, preferably armed, vessels, and hope for the best. Some prospered in these dangerous times – but not Thomas Starke. One of the last surviving port books for London is the export or outward book for 1695. Since exporters of tobacco were entitled to a refund or drawback of most of the duties paid at importation, each entry outward of tobacco is accompanied with a notation of when and by whom the leaf was imported. These show that of the nine million lb. exported, Starke accounted for the importation of only 30,090lb. and thus ranked 40th in the trade in London instead of third or fourth in 1686.[12] However, the year may be atypical for a 1702 list of bonds outstanding for tobacco duties shows Starke owing £5,900 and in seventh place at London.[13]

Thomas Starke died in February 1705/6 leaving a widow and six children. By his will, he left bequests to his widow Sarah, his only son John, his married daughter Mary Sherman and his four unmarried daughters, all apparently minors: Sarah, Martha, Frances and Elizabeth. He left all his real estate in Virginia, including five plantations, to his son John. Some real estate in Suffolk was encumbered to meet the £2,000 to which his widow was entitled – but was to go eventually to his son also. The unmarried daughters were at marriage each to get one-fifth of his personal estate up to a maximum of £1,000 or £1,500, with the balance of the personal estate going to his son John.[14] A more sombre picture, however, is suggested by the inventory of Starke's estate submitted to the London Orphans Court. Starke had some £20,000 owing him in Virginia at the time of his death, the collection of which was entrusted to James Joyeux, his current chief factor there. This £20,000 included £6,000 considered 'desperate', owed by about 30 named individuals (including some with well-known Virginia names like Bushrod, Wormeley, Cole,

Tandy and Warner) plus £14,000 owed by his former chief factor in Virginia, Henry Fox. The £6,000 probably included credits Starke had extended to planters and others in the Chesapeake who consigned him tobacco; the £14,000 on the other hand would appear to represent resources invested or sunk in his direct trade with the colony, that is, the value of goods (including slaves) sent to Fox for sale – on Starke's account – to planters and others, and which had not yet been accounted for. In addition, there was a large debt owed by one William Leigh in Virginia, the value of which was not yet established. Starke was actively trading at the time of his death, his estate including £1,732 worth of leaf tobacco. He had recently sent an £800 venture on the *Anthony Galley* to the Guinea Coast and a £1,637 venture to Joyeux in Virginia. In addition he had shares in two vessels (the *Jeffreys* and the *Merchants Adventure*) chartered to the government as well as in two others that had recently met unhappy fates: the *Concord* seized in Saõ Thomé and the famous *Worcester* seized in Scotland.[15]

It is not clear whether Starke was solvent at the time of his death. In 1716 the crown still claimed against the estate £2,740 for unpaid tobacco bonds and included the estate on a list of debtors believed to be insolvent. However, since the payment of many of those bonds had been under litigation for many years, it is not clear exactly what the crown's claim represented.[16]

Over the years Thomas Starke had had a number of apprentices. The records of the Haberdashers Company show that on 29 July 1692 he took as apprentice 'John Sheffield [*sic*] sonne of John Sheffeild [*sic*] of the Inner Temple London Gent'.[17] Young Sheffeild, born in Winchester, was then about 17. His father was not a member of the Inner Temple but could have had a residence or office there.[18] In late 1696, Starke resolved to send his apprentice Sheffeild to Maryland. Although Starke's main trading interests were with Virginia he had some interests in Maryland which were not cultivated after he broke with his former factor there, a merchant-planter-politician named Philip Lynes. To renew his Maryland activity, he resolved to send out Sheffeild not as an employee or even as a factor working on commission but as a partner in a joint venture. Sheffeild was then 21 and legally competent to conduct most business even though his apprenticeship still had three more years to run. The articles of agreement of 8 February 1696/7 specified that the arrangements were made 'for the Advantage of the said John Sheffeild and to the end he may get more Experience in Commerce . . . [and] att the Request of the said John Sheffeild'. Sheffeild was to sell all the goods consigned him for the account of the partnership to which he was also to charge most of his travel and living expenses. In addition, as Starke's apprentice, he was to endeavour to collect debts owing to Starke in Maryland for which service he was to charge no commission until the end of his apprenticeship, though he could charge Starke for his travel expenses when on the latter's business. Starke, however, was authorised to charge the usual commission on all buying and selling for the partnership.[19] The terms were not overly generous to Sheffeild but he very likely attached more value to the experience he would gain in Maryland. Starke undoubtedly saw prospects of profit if tobacco prices remained high, and, whatever happened to prices, there was the added almost cost-free chance of collecting some of his debts in Maryland.

The young and inexperienced Sheffeild arrived in Patuxent River, Maryland, in July 1697 and set up his 'store' in Calvert County. He very soon got into trouble with the litigious and difficult Philip Lynes.[20] When Lynes realised that Sheffeild would try to collect from him debts allegedly owed to Starke, he decided to strike first. Claiming that Starke owed him over £10,000, Lynes initiated two successive suits in Calvert or Charles County against Sheffeild and attempted to attach all the merchandise in the latter's possession on the grounds that, as Sheffeild was Starke's apprentice, such goods really belonged to Starke. The cases were long, drawn-out and complicated, involving ultimately the governor and chancellor of the colony. At one stage Sheffeild was imprisoned until he could give bond. Lynes was at various times a rather important resident of Charles and St. Mary's Counties with many influential friends; Sheffeild to defend himself had to cultivate influential acquaintances of his own. He repulsed the attacks of Lynes, but only at a great cost. There were not only the heavy expenses of transporting himself, witnesses and bondsmen to the seat of the provincial court, the chancellor and the governor; there were also losses of business and merchandise. At one stage, Sheffeild tried to keep some goods out of Lynes's clutches by sending them by water to another county 'up the bay'. The sloop capsized in a winter storm near the mouth of the Patuxent and many of the goods on it were lost, damaged or stolen.[21]

For all its disappointments, the 'voyage to Maryland' could not have been an unmitigated disaster for Sheffeild who was determined to persevere in the trade. His apprenticeship had ended in July 1699 and in the fall of 1700 he returned to London to put his relations with Starke on a new footing. Now that he was no longer an apprentice, the terms between the partners needed to be made more equal, particularly with regard to commissions. Sheffeild also wanted to persuade Starke to send out a further 'cargo' of goods for him to sell on the account of the partnership.

During his brief visit to London (*c.* October 1700–January 1700/1) Sheffeild discussed with Starke both his hopes for the future and the current state of their accounts. Sheffeild later alleged that Starke at first claimed that he was unable to give him a definitive state of their balance since he had yet to receive accounts of sale of some tobacco sent abroad. However, Starke agreed to send him back to Maryland with a cargo worth at least £400 provided that Sheffeild paid him £300 on account. In effect, £200 of this would be Sheffeild's half of the £400 cargo while the remainder would reduce the balance owed by him to Starke. Sheffeild agreed and his father paid Starke £200 towards his son's obligation. Sheffeild had had opportunity to glance at his account in Starke's books if not to scrutinise it carefully. He may have thought that there was no point in his making such an audit until Starke gave him a copy of his version of their accounts. Such was the situation when on 23 January 1700/1, on the eve of his embarkation for Maryland, Sheffeild visited Starke to say good-bye. Starke surprised him by pulling out a statement of accounts between them and asking him to sign a bond for £868. 16. 4 allegedly owed him. Even without a close examination of Starke's books, Sheffeild quickly detected what he considered errors in the statement and refused to sign the bond. Starke replied that, if Sheffeild would sign the bond, he, Starke,would give him a *letter of defeasance* which would remove from the scope of the bond any errors which might subsequently be found in the accounts. With his embarkation imminent, Sheffeild felt constrained to agree to Starke's compromise proposal. A solicitor was summoned who hastily prepared the letter of defeasance which was signed by Starke as Sheffeild signed the bond. The same persons witnessed both.

On his second voyage, Sheffeild remained in Maryland only two years. This second trip was apparently more successful than the first, and Sheffeild was able to remit a considerable quantity of tobacco and bills of exchange: he later alleged that he had sent Starke 700–800 hogsheads of tobacco and £700–800 in good bills of exchange for account of the partnership plus £600–700 in bills of exchange on his own private account. On his return to London during the winter of 1702–3, Sheffeild once again entered into discussions with Starke about settling their accounts. The shoe was likely now on the other foot. In 1700 Sheffeild obviously owed something to Starke, though probably not the full £868 claimed. By 1703 it seems more likely that Starke owed something substantial to Sheffeild. Starke, obviously short of ready cash, allegedly used one excuse after another to delay reaching a final settlement. Although Sheffeild spoke of legal action, he did not break totally with Starke and was still signing some of Starke's tobacco duty bonds as surety during the winter of 1705–6. Everything was still very much up in the air when Starke died on or about 9 February 1705/6.

Starke's executors were his widow Sarah and his only son, John, who was just 20 when his father died. They must have been shocked to find the estate of the defunct in so illiquid a condition, even though it might be considered technically solvent if much credit were given to the sums owed them in America. John Starke was later to go out to Virginia to try to collect some of his father's debts there, leaving his mother as sole acting executrix. Much responsibility for the litigation that followed belongs to Mrs Sarah Starke. Experienced merchants avoided the law courts wherever they could and settled their disputes by compromise or arbitration. The Starke–Sheffeild dispute was simply a question of settling accounts, an everyday commercial problem. It was primarily Mrs Starke's intransigence and perhaps inexperience that converted it into a subject for years of litigation.

Following Starke's death Sheffeild submitted to the executors an account by which the estate owed him £1,430. 13. 2. The executors replied not with detailed counter-accounts but only with summary statements, one claiming that Sheffeild owed the estate £2,000, the other £576. 6. 5. (Later the Starkes claimed that Sheffeild owed them £813. 16.10½ on the 1701 bond plus £312. 9. 8½ on later transactions for a total of £1,126. 6. 7.) To avoid litigation, Sheffeild proposed arbitration, a procedure now formally encouraged by the act of 1698 which gave agreements to arbitrate the force of court rules or orders.[22] The Starkes seemed to agree, signed the appropriate arbitration bonds and named Francis Lee, a Virginia merchant of London, as one arbitrator; Sheffeild named Heneage Robinson, another local Virginia merchant, as the other arbitrator. Francis Lee (son of Colonel Richard Lee of Virginia) was a trustee under the will of Thomas Starke and very familiar with that family's financial problems. It soon became evident that the arbitrators could not agree on the accounts or on naming a third merchant as umpire. To break the log-jam, Lee apparently on his own initiative proposed a compromise to Sheffeild by which, in return for a general quitclaim of all his demands against the estate, the Starkes would allow him all the debts owed the partnership in Maryland plus £500–700 (£700 cash, according to Sheffeild, but, according to the Starkes, only the remission of £576 he owed them). Sheffeild rejected Lee's proposal which the Starkes later insisted they had never approved.

With the failure of arbitration, the executors of Thomas Starke in the Michaelmas term of 1706 put the 1701 bond for £868 in suit in the Court of Common Pleas and forced Sheffeild to give security. Sheffeild replied by commencing suit in the equity side of the Court of Exchequer in the Hilary term 1706/7. Tactically this action was necessary both to stop the Starkes' effort to enforce the bond and to gain access to the books of the Starke firm and establish just how they came at the figures that they tossed around. In his bills, Sheffeild ascribed some of the differences in the accounts to the fact that the Starkes were not prepared to allow him all his expenses in America or his personal losses there caused by the Lynes suit. He also alleged that they, particularly young John, were inclined to 'cook the books' and among other things not allow him the full prices actually received for tobacco remitted by him for the account of the joint venture, 'it being noe new thing for ... Tho: Starke to wrong yor Orator [petitioner] & other his correspondents for a penny or two pence a pound in the sale of a parcell of Toba[cco]s'.[23]

As the suit evolved, the fundamental tactical issue became access by Sheffeild's side to the books and papers of the Starke firm. On a motion by his counsel, the court on 31 January 1706/7 ordered that Sheffeild and his solicitor, on giving due notice, be permitted to examine the books and bills of exchange of the Starke firm and to take notes thereof.[24] When the Starkes failed to co-operate, the court on 25 February ordered that John Starke prepare copies of all bills of exchange and entries in his books relating to the 'Joynt Account' and deliver the same within one month to Sheffeild who would have liberty to compare copies with originals.[25] At the next term, however, Sheffeild's counsel were back in court with a complaint that Starke had given them accounts of sale of only 95 hogsheads of tobacco instead of the 682 previously referred to. On 10 May 1707 the court ordered that Starke speedily produce copies of the accounts of sale of all 682 hogsheads which Sheffeild could compare against the originals.[26] Sheffeild continued to complain of the quality of the 'copies' received, and on 27 June 1707 the court ordered the Starkes to deliver the books, etc. in question into the temporary custody of the deputy king's remembrancer, R. Barker, for investigation. After examination Barker reported on 15 July that he had found numerous omissions in the copies supplied by the Starkes, and – more sinister – had found two pages of Thomas Starke's factory book stuck together with wax wafers thus concealing the accounts of sales of 123 and 132 hogsheads of tobacco on the joint account which were also omitted in the copies.[27] After still further complaints, the court on 23 October 1707 ordered that the books, etc. of the late Thomas Starke be left in the custody of his executors' solicitor, Steele, where Sheffeild and his solicitor could examine them.[28]

Learning that John Starke was planning to go to Virginia, Sheffeild had him arrested in 1707 and released only after giving bond. Some half-serious discussion ensued about submitting the case once more to arbitrators, but again Mrs Starke decided against this course; instead, in the spring of 1708, she commenced a counter-suit against Sheffeild in the Court of the Exchequer. This was ostensibly an action to collect the debt covered by the 1701 bond but tactically was a necessary move to force Sheffeild in turn to divulge details of his own accounts and transactions.[29] The Starkes' lawyers kept up pressure in court for several months to force Sheffeild to divulge further information, and to prevent any progress on the original suit.[30] They also arranged for depositions in the spring of 1708 to show, inter alia, that Starke's commission charges were normal;[31] and questioned in court whether the 1701 letter of defeasance was still in its original state or had been altered by erasures or additions. This led to a postponement of the case from November 1708 until the next term so that in the interval the witnesses to the 1701 document could be interrogated.[32]

The case finally came before the barons of the exchequer for decision on 26 February 1708/9. The barons recognised it for what it was: a simple case of settling accounts. They admitted the validity of the 1701 bond but ruled that the amount covered could be altered if errors were found in the underlying accounts – in effect recognising the letter of defeasance without mentioning it. They referred the final establishment of the account to Henry Stevens, deputy king's remembrancer, who had authority to call for all relevant books and papers and examine both sides and others 'upon interrogatories' (under oath). Stevens was to make his report 'with all Convenient speed'.[33]

In fact, there is no indication in the surviving court records that Stevens ever made a report. Instead the two sides a year later once more endeavoured to settle the matter by arbitration: in May 1710 they recorded in court their agreement to refer the matter for arbitration to

Richard Lee (nephew of the deceased Francis), Thomas Wharton and Isaac Millner, Chesapeake merchants of London.[34] But nothing came of this arbitration effort either. In November 1711, Sheffeild's lawyers sought to have the matter referred once more to a deputy king's remembrancer.[35] Finally in November 1712, the parties agreed to refer the matter to a fourth set of arbitrators: Benjamin Brayne, Captain Francis Willis and Thomas Sandford, three more Chesapeake merchants of London. This agreement was recorded and made a rule of the court on 1 May 1713.[36] No further references to the case have been found in the records of the Court of Exchequer and one must assume that this final arbitration effort was successful.

That same year – 1713 – John Starke, having returned from the Chesapeake, left for the 'East Indies'[37] and intrudes no more upon the record. Sheffeild also disappeared shortly thereafter.

(ii) Commercial Practice and Experimentation

On the surface, this is simply a case about settling accounts. It does suggest, however, the extraordinary importance of mutual trust in the 'correspondence' system which linked a merchant in one place to a correspondent in another, with each buying and selling and handling bills for the other. Buttressing this trust was the confidence that, should any difficulties arise in settling their accounts, both sides would readily submit the matter to arbitration and thus avoid legal trouble and expense. Mrs Starke perhaps did not appreciate this and at the very least must have incurred very heavy legal expenses. (Three counsel appeared for each side at the major hearings before the barons of the exchequer.)

But, from our standpoint, the case has another interest. Both sides, as we have seen, brought into court a considerable body of business records for scrutiny by a deputy king's remembrancer (the Exchequer's equivalent of a master in chancery). The Starkes appear to have retrieved all their records, but Sheffeild did not. Documents he left have survived among the 'clerks' papers' in the records of the court.[38] They include some of his original Maryland accounts as well as some of the copies of the Starkes' records delivered to him by court order. The survival of these records enables us to dig below the level of formal court records and to seek to learn more about the character of this firm and the London–Maryland trade *c.* 1700.

Let us start by looking at the previously noted contract of 1697 between Thomas Starke and John Sheffeild, his 21–year-old apprentice. It reminds us once again that apprentices were not mere 'teenagers' but could be more mature young men capable of assuming considerable responsibility. Nor should one assume that the equal shares (50–50) joint venture between the two was an isolated phenomenon. Other merchants at the time experimented with similar arrangements including John Hyde, the leading Maryland merchant of the first third of the eighteenth century.[39] This mode of organisation, in which each side provided roughly half the capital and took half the risks, can be seen as a half-way house between the earlier factor system in which the London merchant provided all the capital and took all the risks (his American agent working only on commission) and the later mid-eighteenth century arrangement in which we find independent indigenous merchants in the Chesapeake operating on their own capital and employing English merchants as their 'factors' or commission agents. The evolution measures the emergence over time in the Chesapeake of a class of merchants with enough capital to act by themselves.

Next, we may wonder, why was Starke so anxious to send Sheffeild out to Maryland in 1697 and 1701? Sheffeild, of course, could help collect the debts owed him there. But what was the origin of these debts? Were they all for merchandise sales? In the Exchequer Court bills and answers and in some of the miscellaneous firm records left in that court we find interesting references to Sheffeild's selling slaves for Starke. Thomas Starke, in fact, appears to have been one of the pioneers in the importation of slaves into the Chesapeake directly from Africa, rather than from the West Indies. As an owner of plantations in Virginia,[40] he must have been more than familiar with labour problems there. In 1692 he headed a group which petitioned the Privy Council for permission to send his ship (the *Concord*) to the Guinea Coast for slaves to be carried from thence to Virginia. The petitioners pointed out that no slaves had been imported into Virginia since the start of the war with France in 1689 and that, with the expiry of prewar indentures, the number of white servants was also declining, creating a serious labour shortage in the bay. The council granted permission for the *Concord* (150 tons, 20 men) but ordered customs to delete the number of sailors it carried from the quotas allotted that year to Virginia generally and to its owners specifically.[41] As Starke sent several vessels to Africa during the war, his shipping quota for his ordinary tobacco trade must have been significantly reduced, perhaps helping to explain the marked decline in his tobacco import business after 1689.

Starke and associates were more persistent than fortunate in their slaving ventures. Returning from Virginia after her first slaving voyage of 1693–94, the *Concord* was captured by a French privateer but recaptured by a Guernsey privateer whose crew rifled her.[42] Starke's slaving activity in the next few years is unclear but he evidently sent out some vessel in 1697–98, for Sheffeild was selling slaves for him by 1698.[43] With the return of peace in 1697 and the regularisation of the interloping trade by parliament in 1698,[44] there was an increase of activity by private slave traders. Starke sent out two vessels in 1698–99. One of these, the *Africa Galley*, under Captain Henry Bradshaw, arrived in Annapolis in August 1699 with only 77–102 saleable slaves; it lost close to 400 others to disease either at sea or immediately after arrival in the colony.[45] The other ship, the *Concord*, was equally unlucky. Her captain and both mates died on the African coast and only with some difficulty was the ship's doctor, with help from a Dutch captain, able to get her to the Portuguese island of Saõ

Thomé where the vessel and her cargo were seized by the governor. A year later Starke was still trying to find out why.[46] In 1700–1 Starke sent out two vessels again. He expected that the *Africa Galley*, now commanded by James Westmore, would be able to purchase 300–450 slaves, but, in the event, Captain Westmore arrived in Virginia with only 57 live slaves. The other, the *Two Brothers*, under Captain Roger Gray, was somewhat more fortunate: it purchased 75 slaves and delivered 60.[47] With the resumption of war in 1702, Starke temporarily suspended further African activity until 1705 when he sent out one last vessel just before his death.[48]

Starke's first slave ventures were evidently consigned for sale to Henry Fox at Mattaponi in King and Queen County, Virginia. Fox's selling slaves on generous credit terms may well have accounted for part of the very large balance he owed Starke's estate in 1706.[49] As soon as Starke made arrangements to send Sheffeild to Maryland in 1697, he also made arrangements to send part of his slave shipment of 1697–98 (about 50 slaves) to him there for sale. Sheffeild managed to sell them almost entirely for bills of exchange avoiding the pitfalls of too easy credit sales to planters.[50] Starke must have been satisfied with his apprentice's slave sales in 1698 for he decided to entrust Sheffeild with the much larger slave shipments planned for 1699. And the prospect of earning commissions on such sales (since his apprenticeship expired in July 1699) may well have persuaded Sheffeild to postpone his return home from 1699 to 1700. On Sheffeild's return to London in the fall of 1700, the most pressing reason for Starke's eagerness to send him back to America so quickly was almost certainly the fact that he then had the two vessels just mentioned on their way to the Slave Coast and the Chesapeake.[51] The surviving orders to Westmore, the master of one of those vessels, instruct him on arrival off York River to report to Henry Fox, who was to notify Sheffeild to whom the slaves were consigned. Sheffeild was then to travel from Maryland to York River to supervise the sale.[52] Lists surviving among Sheffeild's papers of bills of exchange received for slaves[53] suggest that he continued to be able to sell most of those received without granting much credit. This efficiency plus the value of the African cargoes consigned him suggest that Sheffeild's performance in selling slaves was probably more important to Starke than his services in disposing of the small trading 'cargoes' which the young man received between 1697 and 1701.

But to Sheffeild, the little 'cargoes' were probably quite important for his meagre capital was tied up in them and he shared in the profits earned on them while he was not entitled to even a commission for the sale of slaves or collection of Starke's debts until his apprenticeship expired in 1699. From the surviving invoices we can identify the following English 'cargoes' sent out to Maryland on the joint account of Starke and Sheffeild (see table on opposite page).

Cargoes thus were sent out nearly every year from 1696/7 to 1700/1. In 1696 and 1698 it will be noted that a large and a small cargo were sent out together. In 1698 the smaller cargo is clearly labelled the 'Indian Cargo',

Date		*Ship/Master*	*Value*	
29 Dec.	1696	*Jeffreys* (Wm. Cooper)	£524. 18. 4	
29 Dec.	1696	*Jeffreys* (Wm. Cooper)	103. 4. 1	(£182)
8 Oct.	1697	*John* (John Tanner)	710. 13. 5	
11 Oct.	1698	*Jeffreys* (Wm. Cooper)	994. 8. 1	
11 Oct.	1698	*Jeffreys* ('Indian Cargo')	129. 3. 1	
14 Nov.	1700	*Providence* (Thos. Martin)	417. 12. 7	
14 Nov.	1700	*Providence* (Thos. Martin)	428. 0. 3	

that is, the goods (including tomahawks) designed for the Indian trade. In 1696 two versions of the smaller invoice survive, one totalling £103 (marked 'prime costs') and one with rather higher prices for the same goods, totalling £182. Presumably when Sheffield haggled with the Indian traders he could have shown them the second or dearer invoice in order to justify his asking prices. The 'prime costs' invoice was apparently sent only for his own counsel. Aside from the tomahawks and a few other such items, the goods sent in the general and Indian cargoes were similar, with large components of woollen and linen cloth, ready-made clothes (hose, shirts) hardware (including brass kettles), flints and gunpowder. A single cargo worth £500 could come from about 30 separate suppliers. In addition, Starke arranged for a correspondent in Barbados to ship Sheffeild annual cargoes of rum, sugar and molasses worth from £100 to £200 each.[54] The rum supply was considered particularly important to attract customers.

It was to prove much easier to put together 'cargoes' for Maryland than it was to devise effective ways to sell them. The biggest problem facing the young and inexperienced Sheffeild when he arrived in Maryland in 1697 was that he was landing in a country with a population quite thin on the ground. In fact, the total population of Maryland in 1690 is estimated at only about 24,000, not one-tenth of what it was to be 90 years later in 1780 (245,000).[55] This meagre population moreover was scattered over both shores of the Chesapeake Bay and for considerable distances up many rivers, particularly the Potomac and Patuxent on the Western Shore. No matter where Sheffeild 'opened his store' he would find customers rather sparse and have to exert himself to reach them. But what exactly was this 'store' he 'opened' in 1697? The very word 'store' is a problem for modern readers and researchers. A glance at the *Oxford English Dictionary* will remind one that 'store' in the seventeenth century did not normally mean a shop or salesroom but most commonly implied either a supply or a place (a storeroom or storehouse) where supplies were kept. The more modern meaning of 'store' as a place where things are sold is described by the *O.E.D.* as an Americanism first noticed about the 1740s. The prevalence of the earlier meaning of 'store' even in America is confirmed by Gloria Main's exhaustive study of Maryland probate records. She has found that 34 per cent of the colony's surviving inventories for 1660–1719 list a room or structure called a 'store' and used for the storage of new supplies, textiles, hardware, soap, etc. Such a facility was more common in larger plantations than in smaller and in the largest was more likely to be a separate building rather than a room attached to the residence.[56] No one should confuse such domestic 'stores', appearing in so large a proportion of inventories, with the later commercial facilities designed for the display and sale of goods.

Sheffeild's use of the term 'store' is ambiguous. When we read that he 'began to open his store'[57] or 'my store in Patuxent',[58] we assume the modern connotation even though the sentences could be interpreted in more than one way. However, when he wrote that he 'divided his store', it is clear that he was not referring to a space at all but only to a supply.[59] In fact, both Sheffeild's practice and language represent a half-way stage in the evolution of the meaning of the word 'store' towards the commercial sales place of the 1740s.

On his arrival, Sheffeild 'opened his store' on the Patuxent River in Calvert County. Later he moved his base of operations to Benedict Town in Charles County on the other side of the Patuxent River. In neither place could he wait passively behind the counter for customers to appear. In fact it is likely that in both places he only kept his 'store' open a few hours a week and spent the rest of his time riding about, meeting merchants and planters and negotiating with them for the sale of imported goods and the purchase of tobacco. Some of his biggest customers were merchants on both the Eastern and Western Shores of Maryland.[60] But much of the Sheffeild's business involved dealing with planters who required more laborious cultivation. Even riding about and visiting was not enough; the goods also had to be moved. We have already referred to the misadventure (mentioned in the law suit) when a chartered sloop carrying some of his imported goods to the upper part of the bay went aground in a winter storm near the mouth of the Patuxent River and lost most of its cargo. We find traces of similar operations in his surviving papers.

In May 1698 Sheffeild reached an agreement with Benjamin Scrivener, master of a sloop (usually in the West India trade), to take a cargo of 'wet' and 'dry' goods worth £466. 0. 4 (by his invoice) and set up a temporary store on or near Gunpowder River in Baltimore County in northern Maryland. The goods had been priced by Sheffeild at what he thought the market would bear but he gave Scrivener authority to reduce prices by up to 10 or 15 per cent if necessary. However, in buying tobacco with goods, he was not to pay for 100 lb. of tobacco more than 8s. 6d. sterling prime cost of goods. He was instructed to try to keep his cargo assorted and not sell out any one article too early just because it was in demand. If necessary, he could conceal the most wanted goods and save them for the best customers. Sheffeild hoped that Scrivener would be able to barter the goods for tobacco and thus avoid credit sales. However, he authorised credit to persons whose 'substance' Scrivener was sure of.[61] Scrivener must have been able to sell a good bit without credit. A later list of the debts to the firm in Baltimore County originated by Scrivener comes to only 9,697 pounds of tobacco, equal to an original cost of goods of only £41 sterling at 8s. 6d. per hundred pounds.[62]

Scrivener's sales must have been promising enough to persuade Sheffeild that the firm could benefit from a continuing presence in the northern part of the Western Shore of the colony. He visited the area in November 1698 and reached an agreement with one Mark(e) Swift, 'of Baltimore County gentleman': Swift was to represent the firm in the Bush River and Gunpowder River areas as a factor on commission. For selling goods for tobacco he was to receive a commission of ten per cent (in effect five per cent for selling the goods and five per cent for buying tobacco) payable in store goods 'as usuall sould to ye seuerall traders there', that is, at wholesale. He was also to receive a five per cent commission for collecting any old debts left by Scrivener. The firm was 'to bear the expence of liquours [entertainment] ... as usuall in such stores also to alloe him for storage [i.e. store rent and expenses] two hundred and fifty pounds of tobacco per month'. In return Swift was to provide his own horses and meet all other incidental expenses. The arrangement was to last for six months and was probably extended at least once, even though Sheffeild was initially disturbed to 'hear you keep store at Mad:^{m} Wellses w:^{ch} I believe will be amiss by reason her Neighbours do not estemme her'.[63]

Even with an outlet in Baltimore County, Sheffeild found it difficult to sell all the goods he received. With the end of the war in late 1697, ships flooded into the Chesapeake in 1698 and 1699 only to find the Maryland crop of 1698 disappointingly low. Competition forced up the price of tobacco to 20s. and higher per 100 lb. (equivalent to *c.* 15s. sterling). Sheffeild reported to Starke that he had still been able to sell slaves and indentured servants easily (slaves for bills of exchange and servants for tobacco) – but even the price of indentured servants went down from *c.* 2,000 lb. of tobacco in 1698 to 1,200 lb. in 1699. Rum generally continued to sell easily and sales sometimes had to be restricted to cash customers and those who supplied superior tobacco. But European goods, so scarce during the war, were now too plentiful. In 1699, in order to have more time for business travel, Sheffeild put his store at Benedict Town in the care of an English factor, John Bird, on the same terms as those agreed with Swift. In early 1699 Sheffeild had visited Virginia to look after Starke's slave sales and had to report that Starke's reputation there was being undermined by tales circulated by his erstwhile 'friend' the councillor and merchant Colonel Edward Hill. Sheffeild also visited the northern part of the bay to see what luck Swift and his assistant Clerke Skinner had been having. There were now substantial sums owed the firm in Baltimore County. Sheffeild wrote Starke that he planned 'to divide my store ... into four parts and to sloop it up and down ... to gett Toba' – that is, divide his stock of trading good into four parcels and send them on sloops for bartering expeditions. One such venture he took himself in the winter of 1699–1700 to the lower Eastern Shore where he established a store left afterwards in the care of Joseph Kennerly of Fishing Creek, Little Choptank River, Dorchester County. Operations there also resulted in the accumulation of debts not too easy to collect.[64] The next year (1700), shortly before his return to England, Sheffeild established another small 'store' on 'Meggatty' (Magothy) River in Anne Arundel County north of Annapolis; it was entrusted to Charles Brebaud presumably on the usual factor's (commission) basis.[65]

Although compulsory public warehouses for export tobacco were not established until 1730 (Virginia) and 1747 (Maryland), there already were in the 1690s private warehouses in the colonies (usually called 'rolling houses') where planters and merchants could store tobacco pending shipment. When a vessel arrived on which Sheffeild planned to ship tobacco (usually one on which Starke had chartered freight space for a certain number of hogsheads), he would give the master lists of tobacco to be picked up at different locations, along with 'notes' or warehouse receipts for the hogsheads so stored. A surviving charter party for 50–100 hogsheads contracted by Starke provided that Sheffeild must deliver the notes to the master within 26 days of the delivery of the outbound European goods in Patuxent River and that the tobacco must be stored at a 'Usuall Shipping Place in the said River . . . where the Boat or Shallop of the said Vessell may safely come, not exceeding a Mile from the Waterside'. Sheffeild put as much tobacco as he could on board the ships chartered (and perhaps partly owned) by Starke though he was sometimes tempted to do otherwise when freight rates in the colony fell very low in 1699. He feared with some justice that Starke may have chartered space at rates higher than those then prevailing in the bay and would charge the higher rates for the tobacco returned on their joint account.[66]

Sometime after 13 July 1700, John Sheffeild began his return to England,[67] and had reached London by October. He left with John Bird at Benedict Town the major part of his unsold goods plus warehouse notes for over 76,000 lb. of tobacco and lists of as yet uncollected debts in money and tobacco. He also left Bird a power of attorney making him superior to the firm's other factors in the colony: Charles Brebaud in Anne Arundel County, Mark Swift in Baltimore County and Joseph Kennerly in Dorchester County (Eastern Shore).[68] Before Sheffeild departed the colony, he had ordered a cargo of rum and sugar from Barbados to be delivered to Bird to keep their stores suitably 'assorted'. While in London, Sheffeild sent Bird detailed familiar instructions concerning the importance of rum for retaining the best customers, the necessity of cultivating planters who produced superior tobacco and the futility of doing any favours for 'freighters', that is, planters who consigned their tobacco to commission merchants in England. These letters suggest that Sheffeild had every intention of returning soon to Maryland. He realised that Bird would be hard pressed in the interim to manage the store and still visit planters, and promised to send him an indentured servant who could be left in the store while he travelled about. Other servants he now found it impossible to procure except at 'prodigious' prices.[69]

After Sheffeild's return to the Chesapeake in the spring of 1701, we have few additional documents relating to the Maryland side of the business except for two letters from Starke to Bird (or Burd) and Brebaud. Sheffeild knew what kinds of Maryland tobacco were most in demand for the Dutch market and had tried to get as much of these as possible. Bird and Brebaud seem to have been less experienced and more easily imposed upon. Starke was convinced that crafty planters shipped their best tobacco on consignment to commission merchants in England and used the inferior residue to pay their taxes and tobacco debts in Maryland. Buyers in London therefore preferred consigned tobacco over 'received tobacco'. Starke warned them that it had become very difficult to sell the poorer grades of tobacco in London now that the Spanish market was closed (by the Bourbon accession). Bird and Brebaud would therefore have to try harder to procure better grades.[70]

The returns from the Chesapeake received by Thomas Starke in London were either in bills of exchange or tobacco. Almost all bills were either payments for slaves sold on Starke's private account or remittances on account of the joint concern. Payment for slaves was usually made in bills drawn by Virginia planters on a house in London and made payable to Thomas Starke. The bills received for the account of the joint concern were usually drawn by merchants or planters in Maryland on houses in London payable to John Sheffeild and endorsed by him to Starke. The slave trade bills were heavily weighted towards firms in London specialising in the Virginia trade while the bills acquired by Sheffeild for goods sold in Maryland were necessarily drawn on firms trading thither. All told the bills remitted were drawn on 38 different English houses (35 in London): of these, 20 firms were drawn on only for bills covering slave purchases; eight other houses were drawn on only for sums owed the joint concern, while ten further houses were drawn on for transactions arising in *both* trades. All told this bill network involved a larger number of London firms than some recent scholarship has led us to expect.[71]

In the litigation between Sheffeild and Starke's executors reference was made to 682 hogsheads remitted from Maryland on the account of the Sheffeild–Starke joint venture. The firm's surviving papers contain manifests or lists covering only part of these. The fragments, however, enable us to reconstruct the dramatic shifts in freight rates midst the alternation of war and peace. From a 1690s wartime high of *c.*£14–15 per ton of four hogsheads, freight rates for tobacco from Maryland to London dropped to £8 in 1698, £7 in early 1699 and £6 by the latter part of that year (with even £5 reported by Sheffeild). By 1701 rates had recovered to only £7 and £8 but shot up to £10 by March 1701/2 as rumours of war became more pressing. The reality of war raised rates to £14 by the following November.[72] Insurance should have been subject to the same gyrations except that insurance was not then always available and Starke seems to have deliberately avoided buying it. When Starke's heirs included a charge for insurance in one of their accounts, Sheffeild, knowing the defunct's normal practices, immediately challenged it.[73]

One of Sheffeild's primary objectives in the suit he initiated was to get Starke's heirs to give him full and detailed accounts of Starke's sales of the

682 hogsheads remitted on the account of their joint venture. After the start of the war in 1702, Starke exceptionally shipped a few hogsheads to Holland on the account of the firm.[74] Normally, almost all the partners' tobacco was sold in London even though much of it, like most Maryland tobacco, was destined for export to the Low Countries and northern Europe.[75] The surviving accounts of sale of the joint venture show some of its tobacco sold at a 'home' or 'inland' price which included the duty, while other hogsheads were sold at the much lower export or 'on board' price that excluded the duty drawn back at exportation and retained by the seller. Both sorts of sales are subject to possible misunderstanding by the modern researcher. In the former case, the fact that the tobacco was sold at the inland price including the duty does not always mean that it was destined for the home market; the buyer might subsequently export it and draw back the duty himself.[76] In the latter case, the firm's records clearly indicate that the importer sold the tobacco for export by the buyer but the customs port books would show the importer-seller (Starke) as the exporter because he drew back the duty, swore to the exportation, and paid the fees at the customs house.[77] In fact, of course, the buyer (not the importer-seller) exported the tobacco and the port books (but not the firm's records) are misleading.

Among the 'accounts of sale' in the papers of the Sheffeild–Starke suit are numerous citations of tobacco prices: it is difficult to interpret them because we know nothing of the origin or quality of the tobacco sold and because the dates of sale are usually omitted. Even so, they suggest substantial fluctuations in yield even in peacetime. The poor harvest in Maryland in 1698 led to relatively high prices in 1699 and early 1700 followed by a decline through 1701. Thus the net yield (after deducting all expenses) on Sheffeild's consignments on the joint account could decline from £3. 17. 9 sterling per hogshead in early 1700 to £2. 7. 0 in late 1701. Other parcels later produced as little as £1 per hogshead or even lost money. Sheffeild subsequently alleged that the Starkes cheated on the prices quoted in the accounts of sale. However, most of Sheffeild's shipments were 'received tobacco' and could not, according to Starke, expect prices as high as those received by the more select consigned tobacco.[78]

In summary, the papers of the Sheffeild–Starke suit are of value primarily because of their rarity and early date. They are not the complete records of a firm. We have no ledgers or balance sheets or letter books. But the fragments which we do have are the earliest known records of a British firm trading to the Chesapeake. They represent a stage of institutional evolution in which business organisation was still quite fluid and experimental. Thomas Starke was a direct trader to the Chesapeake dealing through factors (working on commission) in Maryland and Virginia. He also received consignments from planters (and probably from independent merchants) there who trusted him. When the labour shortage caused by the war of the 1690s created an exceptional demand for slaves, he was capable of letting a good part of his pre-war trade languish and of re-allocating resources to the slave trade. This proved less profitable than it might have been, both because of high mortality on some of his ships and because his factors in the Chesapeake apparently sold too many of his slaves on credit. In this juncture he was prepared to gamble by sending out his apprentice Sheffeild both to collect debts and to try to sell slaves primarily for bills of exchange. Sheffeild's apparent success in such sales encouraged Starke to venture even further into the slave trade. He could not, however, entrust slave sales and debt collections to an apprentice entitled to no compensation for such services without adding some *douceurs* to excite the young man's zeal. Hence his initial decision to enter into a small 'partnership' with Sheffeild involving the export of *c.* £500–600 worth of goods per annum to Maryland. In practice, it proved impossible for Sheffeild to perform all these varied tasks and travel too. Lesser stores under subordinate factors were needed in different parts of Maryland. Improvisation followed improvisation until the whole experiment ended with Sheffeild's return to England in 1703 and Starke's death in 1706.

Starke was not the only merchant in London then who attempted to sell goods in Maryland through partners rather than factors. He may, however, have been the only one who converted a current apprentice into a 'partner'. Because the experiment was not entirely successful, a lawsuit ensued which left behind in the court records paper relics of this novel venture.

Historians have long been aware of the importance of debt in the rural economy of the American south, particularly in the generation immediately preceding the Revolution. For that generation, we have the ample evidence of the post-war debt claims and the post-war debates on the debt questions in the American states. Historians have, however, been less sure how far back in time this debt problem went. A particular interest of the Sheffeild–Starke papers is their revelation of the importance of debt in the Chesapeake *c.* 1696–1706. With determination slaves could be sold primarily for bills of exchange and indentured servants for tobacco. However, European goods when plentiful could be 'moved' only if considerable credit was allowed. This helps to explain the many lists of uncollected balances we find among Sheffeild's papers and the large total of Virginia debts outstanding in the inventory of Starke's estate. The debt problem had begun its gestation in the Chesapeake of the 1690s.

University of Michigan

NOTES

The author is particularly indebted to Professor L. S. Pressnell who directed his attention to Public Record Office (hereafter PRO) E 219/446, the most important body of records used in this article.

1. The most numerous body of surviving colonial merchants papers are those of Philadelphia explored in the forthcoming book on that city by Thomas Doerflinger (University of North Carolina Press). Some of the principal surviving Chesapeake mercantile records are listed in Jacob M. Price, *Capital and Credit in British Overseas Trade* (Cambridge, MA, 1980), pp. 210–12. The three major bodies of records of British firms trading to the colonial Chesapeake surviving as court evidence are the papers of Joshua Johnson (Hall of Records, Annapolis); Lawson & Semple; and Buchanan & Simson (the last two in the Scottish Record Office, Edinburgh). On the first see the introduction to *Joshua Johnson's Letterbook 1771–1774: Letters from a Merchant in London to His Partners in Maryland*, ed. Jacob M. Price (London Record Society, XV) (London, 1979). On the last see J.M. Price, 'Buchanan & Simson, 1759–1763: A Different Kind of Glasgow Firm Trading to the Chesapeake', *William and Mary Quarterly*, 3rd series, Vol. XL (1983), pp. 3–41.
2. PRO HCA 13/80 Deposition of Thomas Starke, 25 April 1692.
3. PRO E190/56/1 and E190/58/1. I am indebted to Professor Paul Clemens for this information.
4. PRO E190/64/1.
5. PRO E190/68/1. I am also indebted to Professor Paul Clemens for this information.
6. As in notes 3–5.
7. Guildhall Library, MS. 15,857 Vol. 2, p. 189 (Haberdashers' Company Freedoms, 1642–1772); MS. 15,858 Vol. 1, s.v. 'Starke'.
8. PRO E190/143. If the activity of London merchants at Cowes is included, William Paggen moves up to third place, while Starke drops to fourth and Richards to fifth place.
9. PRO E134 3 Anne Easter no. 20 (London): Depositions by commission: examination of Ebenezer Crocker (12 Oct. 1703). Crocker did not mention Richards in his later examination of 12 April 1704, nor did another customs officer, Richard Pooley, at that time.
10. PRO HCA 26/1. The ships were the *Jeffreys* (450 tons, 26 guns, 60 men) and the *Loyal Effingham* (400 tons, 50 men, 24 guns). Others who appeared as part owners of both were the London tobacco merchants Jeffrey Jeffreys, Robert Bristow, Gawen Corbin and James Carey.
11. PRO Prob. 11/421 (PCC 421 Box).
12. PRO E190/152.
13. PRO T38/362.
14. PRO Prob. 11/487 (PCC 72 Eedes) dated 30 January 1705/6 and proved 4 March 1705/6, with summary in *Virginia Magazine of History and Biography*, Vol. XIV (1907), pp. 303–4. He was buried on 3 March: R.H. D'Elboux and W. Ward (eds.), *The Register of St. Dunstans in the East London, Part III* (Harleian Society, LXXXVI–VII) (London, 1958) p. 121. According to Sheffeild, Starke died 9 February. For Starke's land in King William and King and Queen Counties, see *Virginia Magazine of History and Biography*, Vol. XIV (1907) p. 304; Vol. XXXI (1924), pp. 73, 155.
15. London Corporation Record Office, Orphans Court inventory 2754 (18 April 1706); Common Serjeants Book V, fo. 162B. For the *Worcester*, see George Macaulay Trevelyan, *England Under Queen Anne, II: Ramillies and the Union with Scotland* (London, 1932), pp. 249–56. For Starke's consignment business, cf. *Virginia Magazine of History and Biography*, Vol. XIX (1911), p. 186.
16. PRO E122/231/18. The records of the Court of the Exchequer contain much documentation on the law suit, Starke v. Attorney-General, concerning these bonds. For example, cf. PRO E112/838/900; E133/117/45, 47; E134 3 Anne Easter no. 20; Trinity nos. 5, 13; 6 Anne Michaelmas no. 36; 11 William III Michaelmas no. 25.
17. Guildhall Library MS. 15,860 (Haberdashers' Company, Register of Apprenticeship

bondings), Vol. 7, p. 320.
18. Deposition by Sheffeild in PRO HCA 13/81 ff. 210, 364v.
19. PRO E219/446.
20. For example, Carroll T. Bond and Richard B. Morris (eds.), *Proceedings of the Maryland Court of Appeals 1695–1729* (Washington, DC, 1933) pp. xlv, xlviii, 1, 6, 12–22, 24, 88, 96, 108, 114–15, 121–6, 138–9, 153, 164, 171–7, 196.
21. The account of Sheffeild's activities in Maryland and relations with Starke, *c.* 1697–1706, in this and the following paragraphs, is based on the bills and answers in PRO E112/838/915 and E112/842/1124 and in the summary contained in the decree of 26 Feb. 1708/9 and PRO E126/19 ff. 109–10. For the theft of his goods, see W. Hand Browne (ed.), *Proceedings of the Council of Maryland 1696/7–1698* (*Archives of Maryland*, XXIII) (Baltimore, MD, 1903), pp. 387–8. Lynes brought his suit against Sheffeild in the Charles County Court and was successful. Sheffeild, however, was able to get from the chancellor a writ of *audita querela* on grounds that no resident of Calvert County (where Sheffeild lived) was on the jury that found for Lynes. The case was reheard in the Provincial Court which found for Sheffeild in May 1699. See C. Ashley Ellefson, 'The Writ of *Audita Querela* in Eighteenth-Century Maryland', *Maryland Historical Magazine*, Vol. LIX (1964), pp. 370–73.
22. 9 & 10 William III c. 15 (*Statutes at Large*, ed. Danby Pickering, Vol. X, pp. 139–140). The chronology at this point is that in the decree of 26 Feb. 1708/9 in PRO E126/19 ff. 109–10.
23. PRO E112/838/915 contains Sheffeild's original 'English bill' with supporting accounts, the 'answer' of Sarah and John Starke with accounts, Sheffeild's 'replication' and 'exception' to the Starkes' answer, and the Starkes' 'further answer'.
24. PRO E127/27 fo. 17 (Hilary Term 1706/7 no. 45).
25. Ibid., ff. 75–75v (no. 215).
26. Ibid., ff. 104v–105 (Easter Term 1707, no. 57).
27. Ibid., ff. 194v–195 (Trinity Term 1707, no. 73); E194/6 Reports and Certificates, 1707, no. 15.
28. PRO E127/26 fo. 180 (Trinity Term 1708, no. 125).
29. PRO E112/842/1124 contains the Starkes' bill (Hilary Term 1707/8), Sheffeild's answer (17 April 1708) and two Further Answers, and the Starkes' Exceptions to his answer.
30. For example, PRO E127/26 ff. 162v, 192v, 199.
31. E133/111/17.
32. PRO E126/19 fo. 75v; E133/111/18.
33. PRO E126/19 ff. 109–10.
34. PRO E127/28 ff. 168–168v (Easter Term 1710, fo. 181).
35. PRO E131/16 (Michaelmas Term 1711, no. 89). The order book for 1711–13 is missing, but the original orders survive.
36. Ibid. (Easter Term, 1713), no. 172).
37. *Virginia Magazine of History and Biography*, Vo. XIV (1907), p. 304; *William and Mary Quarterly*, 1st series, Vol. V (1896–1897), pp. 256–7. *C.* 1713–16 Sheffeild was active as a tobacco merchant of London but had disappeared from the trade by 1719. Cf. PRO C11/6/43.
38. Unless otherwise indicated, all the documents cited in the remainder of this paper are in PRO E219/446. Documents in this box are not numbered or foliated.
39. Cf. Carroll T. Bond (ed.), *Proceedings of the Maryland Court of Appeals 1695–1729* (American Legal Records, I) (Washington, DC, 1933), pp. 207–18; and 'Extracts from account and letter books of Dr Charles Carroll of Annapolis', *Maryland Historical Magazine*, Vol. XVIII (1923), p. 218.
40. Starke's will refers to five plantations in Virginia. PRO Prob. 11/487 (PCC 72 Eedes).
41. Elizabeth Donnan (ed.), *Documents Illustrative of the History of the Slave Trade to America* (Carnegie Institution of Washington, publication no. 409), 4 vols. (Washington, DC, 1930–34), Vol. IV, p. 65; *Calendar of Treasury Books*, Vol. IX, pp. 1926–7. For Starke's purchase of the *Concord* for £885 in 1692 and her safe arrival in Barbados and Virginia, see PRO HCA 13/81 Examination of John Hyde, 30 March 1696.
42. PRO HCA 13/81 fo. 364v Examination of John Sheffeild and John Jones, 6 April, 4 May 1696.

43. PRO E112/838/915 (Sheffeild's bill and Starke's answer).
44. Cf. K.G. Davies, *The Royal African Company* (London, 1957), Ch. 3.
45. PRO E219/446 Sheffeild to [Starke], 2 Aug. 1699. An account in ibid. dated 13 July 1700 indicates that, in addition to 76 on the Western Shore, 26 slaves were also landed on the Eastern Shore.
46. Donnan, *Documents*, Vol. IV, pp.76–7.
47. Ibid., pp.71–5, 82–3; PRO E219/446 Sheffeild to [Starke], 23 Aug. 1701.
48. PRO T70/1199 (kindly supplied by Professor K.G. Davies).
49. See n. 15.
50. see n. 43 and *Archives of Maryland*, Vol. XXII, pp.160, 165, 222.
51. See n. 47.
52. Donnan, *Documents*, Vol. IV, p.75.
53. PRO E219/446.
54. Ibid., invoices.
55. United States Bureau of the Census, *Historical Statistics of the United States*, 2 vols. (Washington, DC, 1975), Vol. II, p.1168.
56. Gloria L. Main, *Tobacco Coast: Life in Early Maryland 1650–1720* (Princeton, NJ, 1983), p.294.
57. PRO E112/838/915 Sheffeild's bill.
58. PRO E219/446 Sheffeild to Marke Swift, 9 Dec. 1698.
59. Ibid., Sheffeild to Starke, 9 May 1699.
60. Ibid., bond for £237. 17s. to Sheffeild from Dennis Herbert, merchant of St. Mary's County, 2 Nov. 1699. On the Eastern Shore Sheffeild sold to merchants Richard Bennett and Robert Goldsborough.
61. Ibid., Sheffeild to Scrivener, Benedict Leonard Town, 13 May 1698; landing permit from E. Jennings, 16 May 1698.
62. Ibid., 'Lists of Debts in Baltimore County contracted by Benjamin Scrivener'.
63. Ibid., 'Article of agreement' with M. Swift, 11 Nov. 1698; Sheffeild to Swift, 9 Dec. 1698, 29 July 1699.
64. Ibid., Sheffeild to Clerke Skinner, 28 Nov. 1699; same to Thomas Starke, 9 May, 2 Aug. 1699. In a contract to purchase rum, dated 3 Feb. 1699/1700 John Sheffeild is described as 'of Dorchester County'. There is a list of debts owing from Eastern Shore residents, including Robert Goldsborough and Richard Bennett. Bird's terms are specified in his account current.
65. Ibid., Sheffeild to C. Brebaud, 24 June 1700, and invoice of goods (£191. 12. 9) left with him. In ibid. are ledgers kept by Brebaud in Anne Arundel County and by Kennerly in Dorchester County.
66. Ibid., Sheffeild to Starke, 9 May 1699; to Bird, 17 June 1700 and lists of tobacco to be collected. In ibid. is a 1698 bill of lading at £8 per ton and a 1699 one at £6 per ton to London or £7 to Holland. There is also a charter party of 6 Dec. 1697 for 50–100 hogsheads on the *John* (John Tanner, master) at £8 per ton to London or £9 to Holland. They both presumably refer to a transit option under which the vessel unloaded at a channel port and immediately reloaded for Holland. Nothing in the surviving papers indicates that such an option was exercised although Starke did send some tobacco from London to Holland on the account of the joint venture. See n. 74.
67. Ibid., Sheffeild to Brebaud, 24 June ; to G. Plater, 13 July 1700.
68. Ibid., Power of attorney and lists of tobacco notes and debts left with John Bird, July 1700.
69. Ibid., Sheffeild to Bird, 14 Oct., 12 Nov., 10 Dec. 1700. Sheffeild had also hoped to recruit some skilled building workers, but found this impossible.
70. Ibid., Starke to J. Burd and C. Brebaud, 4 Nov. 1701.
71. Ibid., various lists of bills of exchange and original bills.
72. Ibid., notebook of shipping accounts.
73. PRO E112/838/915 membranes 5 and 6.
74. PRO E219/446. Invoices and accounts of sale indicate that Starke shipped 50 hogsheads in 1703 and 44 hogsheads in 1705 to Sebastian Molewater in Rotterdam and 38 hogsheads in 1703 to Isaac Simkinson in Amsterdam.

75. Ibid., Destinations specified in 'petty cash book' include Rotterdam, Amsterdam, Hamburg, Bremen, Russia, Dunkirk and the Guinea Coast of Africa.
76. Buyers at the inland price included Sir Richard Levett, a great manufacturer, as well as Josiah Bacon, one of the largest exporters of the time.
77. While the 'accounts of sale' show that Starke sold tobacco to the following at the export price 'on board', the 'petty cash' accounts show that he swore to the exportation (including destination) at the customs house and paid the outward fees: Charles Bollinger, Edward Carleton, Cornelius Denn, John Mollar and Charles Chaney. PRO E219/446.
78. PRO E219/446 'Accounts of sale'.

DEPOSIT BANKING IN LONDON, 1700–90

By FRANK T. MELTON

Since the late Professor D. M. Joslin's two articles appeared in 1954 and 1960 describing the structure of private banking in London from 1700 to about 1785, no overview of the same period has rivalled his grasp of the sources and his deep understanding of the interplay (and contradiction) of the various forces at work in banking practice. Today students of the period must acknowledge the pioneering work he made in the archives of London banks. Joslin was the first historian to scrutinise critically and comprehensively the accounting records of London banks, recognising the omissions and other serious limitations in interpreting these records. His own caveat that any conclusions must be tentative concerning the subject of eighteenth-century banking has inspired this article, which is intended to be a supplement to Joslin's work. The seventeenth-century background to the succeeding century is examined here, briefly, as well as the few sources Joslin did not cover; at the same time, and in contrast, Hoare's and Gosling's records are re-examined in light of these conclusions.

According to Joslin's study, the money markets of eighteenth-century London spurred the extent and variety of banking functions, which were necessarily more developed than those of the seventeenth century. Private banking developed continually during the Stuart period, which saw the critical appearance of cheques and notes during the 1650s. However, the context of banking changed remarkably after 1688, so Joslin thought. The revolution in governmental finance brought the practice of deficit finance during the war years, and following the peace, the solvency of the government's debt which made it less dependent upon borrowed capital to answer its needs. 'The eighteenth century money market was therefore radically different from earlier times, as the various issues of government paper provided a wide variety of liquid securities both for investment or for use as collateral security for loans.' Both Exchequer bills and the government's long annuities were attractive investments which bankers bought for their clients. London bankers during the war years often collected the high land taxes, which increased their money on deposit. And the process whereby private companies, such as the South Sea Company and East India Company, funded their investments provided other liquid interest-bearing securities bankers sold.

By the terms of the Bank Act of 1708 the Bank of England enjoyed a monopoly of joint-stock banking, and this privilege lasted until the early decades of the nineteenth century. The bank's notes came to be accepted everywhere. While private banks issued notes also, the ratio of notes to cash in the private sector was never impressively large. On the other hand, private banks dealt extensively in mortgage securities, to which the Bank of England was never heavily attracted. Discounts of private banks were more active than those of the Bank. Thus there were roughly two spheres of activity between private banking and the Bank of England, as well as their common functions of receipt and investment, although it is unclear that private banking would have changed its nature during the eighteenth century had the restrictions upon joint-stock growth been removed.[1]

The records of early banking are sparse and uneven – where they exist – although the genealogy of this development seems fairly certain, even if the details of banking before 1700 are still unclear. Deposit banking traces its long-term origins to the scriveners of the late Elizabethan and early Jacobean periods and, later, to a group of goldsmith-bankers who assumed the position the scriveners lost. The expansion of London during the Tudor and Stuart periods drew the gentry to the capital, especially during the 'Season' and for the sessions of parliament. To support their temporary visits to London landowners began to divert a portion of their rents in and near London, as well as the profits of their stock sales at the London markets, into the hands of depositaries, who agreed to act as agents in their clients' affairs. From their rather simple functions as cashiers scriveners began to act as loan brokers on behalf of their clients. Moneylending was the first of the functions recognisable as banking. Over the long period of this development the growth of banking may owe much to bill-discounts (when inland bills came into general use during the 1650s), although the records of such activity do not yield clear evidence, and the problem of bullion transport to and from London during this period is likewise unexplored.

The scriveners' expertise in conveyancing gave them a practical legal knowledge their clients trusted. 'Scriveners' law', as their critics termed it, was contract law, acquired from writing and registering indentures. From this notarial tradition emerged the greatest of the money-scriveners, Sir Robert Clayton, and his partner, John Morris, who, from 1660 to 1685, succeeded in integrating within banking practice the mortgage in fee as large-scale security in loan transactions. Goldsmith-bankers also came to play a more specialised role as moneylenders in the private market, where their clients were landowners. When Dudley North returned to London from Turkey, he was approached by several goldsmiths on the Royal Exchange who offered to receive and pay his money, without giving him interest. He rejected their offers, being himself a merchant with his own methods of receipt and disbursement. Only when he retired from the City to the country did he find the cash-keeping facilities of the bankers attractive and, more particularly, their skills in mortgage investment and abilities to handle the legal and financial aspects of freehold trusts.[2]

Deposits of bankers with landowning clients outside London often followed an irregular, if predictable, pattern of receipt and withdrawal. In the seventeenth century this course is described in detail for the years

1646 to 1685 in the records of the firm of the money-scrivener, Robert Abbott, and, following his death in 1658, in the papers of his successors to his business, Robert Clayton and John Morris. Their deposits peaked in late summer during the Smithfield markets, and later when the Michaelmas rents came due, although rents might continue to dribble in later in the year from delinquent tenants. Disbursements were heaviest during the spring and summer months when clients were resident in London. Throughout the year they might instruct their bankers to pay various tradesmen's bills.[3] Often a portion of their deposits were earmarked for investment, usually in mortgages. The suggestion is that these bankers aligned their other functions along a pattern of seasonal credit. Timed-deposits and notes bankers issued may well have been structured to tide them through the period when their reserves were low.

In the eighteenth century the same problem of irregular cash-flow is described in the letter-book kept from 1730 to 1734 by the goldsmith-banker John Ewer who was located at the Golden Unicorn, Pall Mall. His name does not appear in Hilton Price's lists of bankers, and the only record of his business in his letter-book, where he recorded copies of correspondence and, occasionally, financial instruments he posted to his clients. Ewer's bank dealt in negotiable receipts, probably on a smaller scale than other larger establishments, and in several instances he suggested that his rates and fees were cheaper than his competitors. On 10 August 1732, Ewer wrote to his client Col. John Gordon in Dublin, asking him not to remit to him any money in the future through Drummond's bank, whose rates were expensive.[4] In another instance he chided a client for buying his lottery tickets from another banker, as Ewer's rates for this service were lower than others. His clients Col. John Gordon and Aspinwall and Wogan held accounts also with Andrew Drummond, and Ewer struggled to find a place alongside this large enterprise.[5]

Ewer's customers included English officers stationed in Ireland, where he dealt with agents to the British army, men like John Wayte, an agent to Col. Pearce's regiment at Dublin. Through the soldiers, their agents and quartermasters there extended a network of intermediation to London, where another series of men handled the London affairs of these men. At each stage the middleman demanded his commission. In 1732 Ewer wrote to Wayte that the numbers of agents in London had contracted, as certain colonels had devised a plan of paying a small sum of money to men in the capital to do the work of agents, who kept the greater profits in these transactions to themselves.[6]

Ewer issued his own notes and discounted the notes of other bankers, as well as bills of exchange. No mention of cheques appears in his correspondence. The amount of actual cash Ewer received from his military clients was small, it seems. In November 1733 he wrote to Sir Roger Bradshaigh that he had received his son's quarter salary,[7] and it is possible that this banker accepted other military salaries from soldiers stationed in or near London. In Ireland, however, it was the custom for agents to receive soldiers' pay and to act as their financial agents there and abroad, when Ewer served as their London correspondent. John Ewer wished to receive soldiers' pay directly by establishing himself as an agent to the army. In the summer of 1731 he sent John Wayte in Dublin the king's warrant entitling Henry Janssen to a captain's half-pay on the establishment of Ireland, together with Janssen's affidavit delegating Ewer as his agent.[8] The following month he instructed Wayte to prepare a scheme to receive the half-pay of other officers, which may refer to the entire regimental pay at their disposal.[9] Such commissions offered bankers opportunities to charge small commissions for their services and to hold soldiers' deposits for their own use until they demanded its recall.

Ewer complained to his clients of his cash-flow problem, which was a variation on the seasonal cycles of the Abbott, Clayton and Morris enterprise. When the gentry left town in early autumn, at the end of the 'Season', they depleted their cash reserves on deposit in Pall Mall. In October 1731 Ewer urged Thomas Saunderson to repay his overdue loan. The town was empty, and 'I can less spare the money than at another time', he wrote.[10] In December of the following year he complained that 'this is a season ... men in our business commonly are in want', for after the exodus of landowners, with their cash, London merchants commonly settled their yearly accounts at this time.[11] Had he acquired commissions to receive in England the pay from the British establishment of English soldiers stationed abroad, Ewer's control of capital would have been less subject to the rhythms of country and City cycles.

As it was, shortage of cash determined the process by which Ewer negotiated inland bills. Most of the letters Ewer wrote during this period about his banking business concern bills, negotiated often in multi-party transactions. When the instrument was drawn upon a merchant in London, Ewer had the responsibility of collecting the bill and placing the cash to his client's account. The chain of endorsements made bill collection risky. In 1731 Ewer discounted John Stephenson's bill drawn on John Haddock of Tooley Street, Southwark, but endorsed to Edward Fitzgerald. Ewer paid Fitzgerald £15 but could not then locate Haddock.[12] In another instance, the banker demanded payment of a bill from a man who sent him a counter-bill, made upon his drawee.[13] Because his cash was short, Ewer ordinarily refused to offer credit upon the bills he received unless his clients had sufficient funds to cover the delay and risks of collection. But it is clear that his clients used bills drawn against their accounts much as they would cheques, which might explain why Ewer made no reference to those negotiable instruments in his letters. Upon instructions of their clients, they then remitted bills to Ewer, drawn upon London merchants trading in Ireland. Ewer discounted these bills and placed the cash to the account Wayte held with him.[14] In the course of the process Wayte drew against his account with another series of bills, used in this instance as cheques. When the transaction involved Irish money, Ewer charged Wayte exchange fees, commissions and postage.

This equilibrium of assets to liabilities suggests Ewer was a small-scale banker. At the same time it is difficult not to believe that the larger banks with landowning clients, such as Martin's, Hoare's and Child's faced the same problem of seasonal fluctuations with their deposits. With a large clientele greater variation would follow. Not all the gentry with London bank accounts would spend a period in town to reduce their reserves, and for those who did attend the 'Season', not all would exhaust their accounts, especially if they had instructed their banker to invest a part of this capital. The greater the number of services a banker offers his clients, the less his operation is a simple cash-keeping facility.

Drummond's Bank traces its origins to 1717, when Andrew Drummond established himself as a silversmith in Whitehall. His work in silver, and gold also, lasted until at least 1737, but his banking operations began soon after he opened his doors and did not proceed directly from his work in fashioning specie. According to the bank's historians, it was the deposit account opened 28 September 1717, by John Gordon, agent, that gave Andrew Drummond his first working capital as a banker.[15] As the name implies, Gordon was a Scot, and the early ledgers include names familiar to the northern nation. Following the Act of Union of 1707 many Scots came south to London, and Andrew Drummond served his clients' needs on both sides of the border.

Drummond's work in gold and silver is documented in special ledgers, to 1737. The source of the bank's business appears in an unbroken series of clients' accounts (to 1815), interspersed with profit and loss accounts. No correspondence survives in the bank from this period. Turning the folios of the ledgers, one is impressed with two considerations. First, the number of single-client accounts developed especially after 1725. If the stable conditions following the South Sea Bubble crisis attracted individual clients to Drummond's doors, the bank before that time appears not to have solicited its business from individual patrons. Second, both before and after 1725, it was not any specific Scots connection which swelled the bank's coffers. The lion's share of Andrew Drummond's business was concerned with men who, like John Gordon, were colonels or agents of regiments of the British army, and their business with Andrew Drummond followed directly the military reforms of George I.

This connection with military finance may well have come from Andrew Drummond's relation John Drummond, a merchant in the Low Countries during Marlborough's wars. The Duke of Chandos relied heavily on John Drummond's services, and later he became a client in Andrew Drummond's bank.[16] At any rate, direct army connections promoted the rise of Andrew Drummond's bank in its earliest stages. In 1717 parliament reduced the standing army by 10,000 men and in the following year disbanded five dragoon regiments and six foot regiments and placed the officers on half-pay. The end of the War of the Spanish Succession, together with the recent fear that the army would align itself with Jacobites both reinforced traditional suspicions of a standing army. The new king, himself a military man and anxious to use English forces for his plans in Germany, was determined to reform the army as a means of increasing its efficiency. By reducing the discretionary income and range of financial action of the officers, a new system of finance made the officers accountable to the government's pay officers.[17]

The lieutenant-colonels and colonels were the key figures in the system. They might delegate all or a part of the finances of the regiment to agents, men like William Robert Adair in Pall Mall, or other agents like John Wayte who lived closer to the troops. When the soldiers' pay, the subsistence per diem, reimbursement for uniforms and weapons were received in London from the Pay Officers, they might then act as their own bankers to the regiments. Or they might turn to other men, like Andrew Drummond and John Ewer to receive their money on deposit in London and draw upon it as their needs arose.

The descriptive entries in Drummond's early ledgers are disappointingly brief. The 1726–27 Drummonds registered accounts for the 'Fourth Troop of Guards' and 'Colonel Anstruther's Regiment', 'Colonel Samuel Horsey & Co.', 'Colonel Negus & Co', which are certainly agents' accounts. The colonels, Robert Gardner and Robert Munro, and the captains, John Rutherford, James Ogilvy and Alex Wilson also held accounts with the bank at this time, and the volume of business documented in each account is great enough to suggest strongly that these were agents' accounts also, rather than personal ones. In the following years (to 1760) the names recurring in Drummond's ledgers are William Adair, Maynard Guerin, Captain Thomas Levett, John Moody and Patrick Low, and these accounts far outshadow the other clients of the bank.[18]

Entries in the ledgers are disappointingly brief, making it impossible to know with any precision how the system of agents returns and withdrawals defined the cash-flow of Andrew Drummond. The seasonal cycles of deposits and disbursements in Ewer's bank would not appear to define Drummond's operation, where the traffic was constant throughout each year. The volume of bills discounted expanded over the years. At the same time, Drummonds, before 1760, rarely did business in long-term loans. In each annual accounting period the loans granted during one year were all set to be repaid during the same term. From 1733 to 1735 the bank loaned £55,840, while during the same period it discounted bills on its clients' accounts for £49,192. Like Ewer's, Drummond's maintained a large capital balance by granting only short-term loans to meet its heavy volume of discounts. During the years 1746–50 the bank negotiated loans for £82,887 and reduced its discounts following the 'Forty Five' to £38,032. Gradually the bank acquired more of an aristocratic clientele. By reducing the dependence the discounts of army agents made upon its lending capital, Drummond's acquired a longer use over its deposits. Its connections with the Treasury and its responsibility for paying contracts abroad brought many naval and army officers to the bank. Thus in the course of the eighteenth century Drummonds advanced beyond the simple cash-keeping operations of its foundation and overcame the problem of banking constructed exclusively on discounts.[19]

Like Ewer's and Drummond's, Hoare's began as a goldsmith-bank. In 1673 Richard and James Hoare took over the foundation of Robert Tempest, the Golden Bottle in Cheapside. Their cash book, kept from August to December 1678 describes the character of the new operation: the banking business of the firm amounted to £25,135. 4. 0, while profits from its goldsmith operations brought in only £531. 15. 0. In 1690 the bank moved its site from Cheapside to Fleet Street and ceased the practice of its former days of paying interest on its clients' deposits. The Hoares offered their customers a range of services, which included investing their deposits in governmental loans, stock shares and mortgages. Richard Hoare established correspondents in the country to allow his customers to cash their clients' cheques there.[20]

By the beginning of the eighteenth century Hoare's had acquired a specialised clientele of landowners who required an agent, in this case the bank, to act as a middleman in their purchase of securities. Sir Richard Hoare defined his expertise as an investment agent in a letter he wrote in 1704 to his client Sir Nathaniel Curzon:

> East India Bonds either on the old or new company, and tallys on several funds; as to the bonds, you know, Sir, that they must be sold at the Exchange. When you shall have occasion for the money, the [East India] Company never paying money but when they think convenient. As to tallies, it will be next to an impossibility to get that sum on one fund that will be free from the danger of coming upon a deficiency, but I will take care to get tallies on such funds and payable at such times so you shall not come within any danger of the deficiency but you must make an allowance either for bonds or tallies so that you will not make above £4-10-0 per annum. You may be assured I will use my best endeavours to have it done the most for your advantage.[21]

From 1701 to 1730 the bank did extensive business selling Exchequer receipts, three per cent annuities, lottery tickets, stock shares in the Bank of England, South Sea Company, East India Company, African Company, as well as malt orders.[22]

Ewer's, Drummond's and the Fowler-Rocke enterprise (later, Gosling's) all sold the same securities to their clients. It was Hoare's money-lending facilities which distinguished it from those other banks. The Hoares negotiated loans for their clients at the same time they placed their own capital out in loans. Correspondence to and from the Hoares and their clients reveals something of the brokerage process the bank played in its mortgage loans. On 22 June 1704, Sir Richard Hoare asked Sir Thomas Pelham that if he was willing to lend Lord Strangford £9000 upon mortgage, he would send him the estate particular the bank had prepared for the security.[23] This implied that a form of assessment had been made to determine the long-term value of the security. In another example, negotiations for a mortgage floundered when legal counsel advised Hoare's lenders that the security in question was defective. The bank's lawyers inspected the legal writings and prepared the contracts. Lawyers for all parties to the loan evaluated their proposals. The process took about a month before the loan was sealed at the Golden Bottle. The Hoares held all the legal writings to their clients' loans before the principal and interest was paid in. Without these papers, the borrower would find it difficult to mortgage the lands already secured. Lender and borrower could not settle the loan without the defeasance included in the writings. The bank's custody of the legal writings contributed to its control of the credit process.[24]

Throughout the eighteenth century Hoare's continued to grow. Selected maximum and minimum deposit balances after the Bubble show that the bank's deposits sank sharply only in 1746, 1762, 1783, 1788 and 1797, and these reverses were only temporary.[25] The practice of the bank's clerks before 1771 was to enter in the ledgers money lent upon mortgage as 'mortgage bond' or 'money lent upon interest'. Mortgages became the bank's primary investments. When the loan principals were paid into the bank, they were registered as credits in the ledgers along with other cash assets.

	Clients' Principals Repaid[26]	Percentage of Total Cash Assets
1725	£184,397	73
1735	£224,790	90
1745	£266,613	87
1755	£766,064	93

With the predictable cycle of its deposits, the bank regulated its loans accordingly, in a way that gave Hoare's a stable pattern which saw little change.

The stock of Gosling's bank passed through several families when Sir Francis Gosling bought into the foundation in 1742 and established the beginning of his own family's connection with the Three Squirrels in Fleet Street. Gosling's was unique in its commercial clientele, especially the bookselling trade. Sir Francis Gosling's father Robert Gosling I was a prominent publisher and stationer. The merging of this commercial tradition with the goldsmith-bank of Abraham Fowler, James Rocke, John Simpson and Samuel Bennett gave the bank a bridge with the business world, which Joslin found unique in London banking practice.[27]

Robert Gosling's (1684–1741) publishing career changed dramatically in 1717 when Elizabeth Nutt sold him half-interest to the patent she and her late husband owned to print the laws of the realm. Traditionally the king's printers enjoyed the privilege of publishing the current laws and statutes of the realm. Gosling's interpretation of the patent was challenged when his range of publications began to include collections of old laws, law reports, abridgements and legal commentaries. Before his death he published, printed, sold and distributed at least 477 separate titles, including 44 individual editions of parliamentary statutes, 192 legal treatises and dictionaries, 46 editions of law reports and a miscellany of religious, historical, literary and classical titles. Lords, MPs, lawyers, judges and other sections of the carriage trade all came to Gosling's shop near the Old Bailey for their books.

Gosling did a brisk business supplying other book dealers in London and the provinces, extending credit and discounting bills in this connection. His banking business has so far gone unnoticed. No accounts survive describing this activity, and there is no reason to believe that his banking business rivalled the success of his publishing enterprise. He issued at least three forms of banker's notes (in 1733 and 1735). More significant, perhaps, is new evidence relating to Gosling's role as a loan broker. In 1713 one of his clients asked him if the £160 he had placed on deposit had been invested in a mortgage. 'I can't imagine why you should not promote what you take to be very much your advantage in placing out your money to a more beneficial account.' For this client Gosling redeemed another mortgage, and in the process had the lands surveyed. In another instance, *c.* 1720, while acting on behalf of two parties to a mortgage, he paid £3. 15. 0 for a survey of an estate. Later he made a trip north with two other men to inspect and appraise the timber on the property. When the writings pertaining to the transaction were signed, Gosling was present in Wallop and Romsey when mortgagor and mortgagee agreed to the terms he had arranged. In another transaction in 1733, Gosling arranged a mortgage between a Mrs Lawrence and a Mr Russell, preparing all the preliminaries of credit and arranging all the writings of the conveyances and their registration. These skills in mortgage credit extend beyond the simple form of small-scale moneylending ordinarily associated with merchants.[28]

The family's publishing business came to an end in October 1742, when Francis Gosling auctioned the plates and stock of his father. At the same time he bought a share in the Three Squirrels, thereby merging the family's banking enterprise with a goldsmith-bank. From 1728 until the early 1750s the bank in Fleet Street served its clients primarily by purchasing stock shares for their portfolios, with moneylending as a minor adjunct to this business. The bank's loan book from 1728 to 1752 recorded a total of £8902 repaid in principal and interest, an average of only £371 per year. After 1752 the business of the bank changed, as its moneylending facilities superseded its services as a broker in stock shares. During the next 24-year period Gosling's loaned £58,701, or an average of £2445 per annum. In 1777 Sir Francis and his son Robert Gosling II acquired all the stock shares in the bank. Under their leadership during the next 12 years the bank loaned £73,658, or an average of £5666 per annum. Thus, not only did the bank increase its moneylending facilities, it changed from a small-scale loan establishment to one offering large-scale loans, strongly suggesting an orientation to mortgage security.[29]

Drummond's, and to a lesser extent, Ewer's, appear to represent in their clientele a type of military banking unfamiliar to the seventeenth-century experience of the goldsmiths and the scriveners. The large-scale, though short-term, loans Drummond's negotiated almost exclusively until the 1750s suggest they were secured with assets other than land. Hoare's seems to fit the same model of investment less precisely, with its orientation to mortgage investment. That Hoare's and Drummond's (after 1750) were able to offer a variety of investments to their clients does not upset the general practice that each bank was a specialised operation, and the tendency of Drummond's and Gosling's to seek more and more clients who were landowners recalls a striking similarity between Georgian banking and its Stuart roots. On the one hand bankers realised profits from the fees and commissions they charged as stock and loan brokers and bill-discounters. The fee-based nature of their business is more apparent in the records than the more intriguing matter of how these men held the use of their clients' reserves to their own advantage. Rates and commissions are linked to fee-based profits, while use is linked to the length of time between the receipt and disbursement of deposits. Presumably bankers desire that their deposits remain on hand as long as possible, that they might use their cash to their own advantage, commonly for short-term loans. The process of bill-collection is fraught with delay, to the banker's disadvantage, as the correspondence of John Ewer indicates. Services bankers rendered in purchasing stock shares might have been given upon credit, rather than taken only after sufficient capital was deposited to clients' accounts. Where loan records do survive, no distinction is apparent between the loans banks negotiated as brokers on behalf of their clients and loans made in the names of bankers and expropriated from their clients' deposits. Malachy Postlethwait understood the importance social difference of clients meant to bankers manipulating their deposits. Traders were in the habit of depositing large sums with bankers but rarely did they leave this money on deposit for long. Landowners, on the other hand, withdrew portions of their deposits which they then replaced with rents, 'when it follows one banker will lend out 9/10 and another cannot afford to lend 1/2'.[30] The course the banks reviewed here followed was to seek a variety of clients, each with his own peculiarities of deposit and withdrawal, as well as the demands each placed upon their bankers' servics. In both its deposits and investments Georgian banking acquired a stable base.

University of North Carolina
at Greensboro

NOTES

I wish to acknowledge the advice and help of Professor L.S. Pressnell, Mr Brian Cooper (Drummond's Bank), Mr Ken Roberts and Mr G.F. Miles (Gosling's Bank), Mrs Arabella Stuart-Smith (Hoare's Bank), and National Science Foundation Grant #SES-8411703.

1. D.M. Joslin, 'London Private Bankers, 1720–1785', *Economic History Review*, 2nd Series, Vol. 7 (1954), pp. 167–86, and 'London Bankers in Wartime, 1739–84', in L.S. Pressnell (ed.), *Studies in the Industrial Revolution Presented to T. S. Ashton* (London, 1960).

2. Roger North, *The Life of the Honourable Sir Dudley North, Knt.* (London, 1744), p. 148.
3. Frank T. Melton, *Sir Robert Clayton and the Origins of English Deposit Banking, 1658–1685* (Cambridge, 1986), pp. 47–52, 182–5.
4. Westminster City Library. Manuscript Acc. 796, John Ewer to Col. John Gordon, 10 Aug. 1732.
5. Ibid., John Ewer to the Duchess of Hamilton, 28 Aug. 1731.
6. Ibid., Same to John Wayte, 17 June 1732.
7. Ibid., Same to Sir Robert Bradshaigh, 3 Nov. 1733.
8. Ibid., Same to John Wayte, 12 June 1731.
9. Ibid., Same to same, 1 July 1731.
10. Ibid., Same to Sir Thomas Saunderson, 21 Oct. 1731.
11. Ibid., Same to the Duchess of Hamilton, 9 Dec. 1731.
12. Ibid., Same to John Stephenson, June 1731.
13. Ibid., Same to Alexander Ross, 4 Nov. 1731.
14. Ibid., Same to John Wayte, 14 Aug. 1731; same to John Gordon, 17 Aug. 1731.
15. Hector Bolitho and Derek Peel, *The Drummonds of Charing Cross* (London, 1967), p. 29.
16. Ibid., pp. 21–3.
17. Charles Dalton, *George the First's Army 1714–1727* (London, 1910–12), Vol. I, pp. xxxviii, xlvi–xlvii; Alan J. Guy, *Oeconomy and Discipline. Officership and Administration in the British Army 1714–63* (Manchester, 1985), pp. 8, 12, 13, 58, 59, 143–6, 148, 162–8; Alan J. Guy, *Regimental Agency in the British Standing Army, 1715–1763: A Study of Georgian Military Administration* (Manchester, 1980).
18. Drummond's Archives, Banking Ledger 1726–1727, *passim, et seq.*; Dalton, op. cit., Vol. I, pp. 115, 154, 168, 191, 241.
19. Bolitho and Peel, op. cit., pp. 70–73.
20. *Hoare's Bank. A Record 1673–1932* (London, 1932), pp. 15–18; Hoare's Archives, I.G.5 (1).
21. Hoare's Archives, Letters to customers 1701–6: Richard Hoare to Sir Nathaniel Curzon, 9 Sept. 1704.
22. *Hoare's Bank. A Record 1672–1955* (London, 1955), pp. 22, 23, 24–5.
23. Hoare's Archives, Letters to customers 1701–6: Richard Hoare to Sir Thomas Pelham, 22 June 1704.
24. Ibid.: Richard Hoare's letter, 15 Feb. 1705.
25. *Hoare's Bank. A Record 1672–1955*, op. cit., p. 85.
26. Hoare's Archives. Constructed from the 'B' ledgers, 1725–33, 1734–42, 1743–51, 1752–60.
27. *The History of Gosling's Branch. Barclays Bank 19 Fleet Street*, London (London, n.d.), pp. 1–2.
28. Frank T. Melton, 'Robert Gosling, Publisher and Banker', in *The Economics of the Book Trade* (London, 1985), pp. 27–39.
29. Gosling's Archives. Constructed from the Profit and Loss ledgers, 1728–1789.
30. *An Universal Dictionary of Trade and Commerce* (London, 1774), *sub* 'Banking'.

THE BUSINESS OF MIDDLEMAN IN THE ENGLISH POTTERY TRADE BEFORE 1780

By LORNA WEATHERILL

> China-men. This Business is altogether shop-keeping, and some of them carry on a very considerable Trade .... They usually employ a Stock of 500l and often more.
>
> (*General Description of all Trades*, 1747)

I

The inland trades and the businesses of middlemen in general have not been neglected by historians but there continue to be considerable gaps in our understanding of the mechanisms of trading and the ways in which producers and consumers were influenced by the sales networks that gradually developed to accommodate increasing quantities of many different kinds of goods in the home market.[1] In many ways the most enlightening accounts of these mechanisms are those that look most closely at a trade or locality.[2] This article illustrates the importance of internal trade in the seventeenth and eighteenth centuries by studying the trade in earthenware and china, household durables that were typical of many others finding their ways into the homes of people of middle rank at the time.[3] Considerable insight into the ways that consumption, production and trade were closely bound together is gained through showing how pottery was traded from producers in a few parts of the country to the final consumers.

This was a time of rapid expansion for the pottery industry and changes in consumer behaviour throughout these years had resulted in wider markets and a powerful demand for both earthenware and china from all parts of the country. Changes on the production side, in the technology, organisation and location of the industry, had resulted in very rapidly increasing production, especially in the late seventeenth century and after about 1750. In the 1680s the workforce was under a thousand, by the 1720s it had increased to about 1,500. By 1780 it was about 5,500 of which 4,000 were in the largest centre of production in North Staffordshire and a further thousand in several other centres in the north of England. Imports of oriental chinaware, amounting to between one and two million pieces a year, were also landed in London and initially sold at the East India Company's auctions there.[4]

Concentration of production in a few areas, and concentration of imports through London, meant that a well-organised trade on a large scale was essential to sustain the growth of both production and consumption. The businesses that developed to undertake this trade and the mechanics of dealing are the main subject of this essay but it begins with a brief outline of consumer demand for pottery before 1780 to show that the home market was extensive by 1780 and had grown markedly during the previous century.[5] It also ends by showing that the sales network was crucial to the growth of the industry and to the health of individual businesses within it.

II

During the eighteenth century many people in Britain came to expect to own a much wider range of furniture and household goods. These changes, along with others in diet and clothing, were widespread in society and dated back into the seventeenth century. For instance, ownership of looking-glasses grew substantially amongst people who had sufficient resources to leave probate papers and they were recorded twice as often in a sample of inventories in 1725 as they had been in 1685.[6] Changes of this kind occurred in the ownership of many goods; clocks were in nine per cent of these inventories in 1685 and in 34 per cent in 1725. Earthenware and china were to be found amongst the domestic utensils of middle-rank households and they too were recorded more frequently in 1725 than previously, as Table 1 illustrates. This shows a gradual expansion in the proportions of 'middling' households owning earthenware and it also shows that there was still considerable scope for expansion in 1725. The extraordinary growth in ownership of china amongst the London freemen (represented by the inventories of the Court of Orphans) is also notable, for even in these very wealthy households china was virtually unknown in the 1670s but had become a normal household possession before the 1720s.[7]

The market for earthenware and china in the early eighteenth century was also geographically and socially widespread. Earthenware was found in all areas, although it was recorded in higher proportions of the inventories sampled from Lancashire and Kent than elsewhere as Table 4 illustrates. Ownership of china was concentrated in London and the North-East of England, although it was recorded in all the areas examined by 1725. The social distribution of ownership is indicated in Table 2, which distinguishes different groups of people who left inventories according to a combination of occupation and status. Of particular importance in outlining the market for pottery, and the resulting patterns of internal trade, is the observation that earthenware was widely used by 1725, for by then it had become normal equipment in many kinds of household, although it continued to be relatively unusual in the poorer rural households of husbandmen. Of course, the information derived from probate inventories only applies to the middle ranks of society and no conclusion should be drawn about the behaviour of labourers from the small numbers of their inventories shown in Table 2. Ownership of china was still concentrated in the gentry, professional and commercial classes in 1725 although, as these groups of people were widespread and numerous

TABLE 1

PERCENTAGE OF INVENTORIES WITH EARTHENWARE, CHINA AND ITEMS USED FOR HOT DRINKS, 1675–1725

	Inventories from Eight English Dioceses				Inventories from the Orphans' Court, London			
Date	Number of Inventories	Earthenware %	China %	Utensils for hot Drinks %	Number of Inventories	Earthenware %	China %	Utensils for hot Drinks %
1675	520	27	0	0	50	64	4	2
1685	520	27	1	0	50	56	10	0
1695	497	34	2	1	50	58	30	8
1705	520	36	4	2	50	72	48	48
1715	455	47	8	7	50	90	74	78
1725	390	57	9	15	50	88	80	96
All	2902	37	4	4	300	71	41	39

Sources: A quasi-probability sample of 2,902 probate inventories from eight dioceses in England: see note 6 for details. A similar sample of 300 inventories made in the Court of Orphans in the City of London, see note 5.

in most parts of Britain, this does not mean that the market was narrowly confined and there was also considerable scope for expansion.

By the middle of the eighteenth century the industry was catering for a wider range of domestic needs than ever before, suggesting that the basic kinds of patterns observed using evidence from inventories continued after 1725 and the markets served by the industry continued to be in the middle ranks of society and geographically widespread. Pottery made and imported before 1780 (as afterwards) was very varied, but largely served the needs of different kinds of households for practical and decorative utensils; earthenware, and even china, was only very rarely ostentatious. Their uses were closely associated with two important new developments, as vessels for hot drinks and (rather later) as tableware, although it was also used for a wide range of other purposes. Tea, coffee and chocolate had been introduced into Britain as exotic drinks in the mid-seventeenth century and by the mid-eighteenth century drinking them had become an established part of the normal behaviour of the middling and upper classes in Britain, although this behaviour did not spread to the lower ranks until later.[8]

The recording of utensils and furniture associated with the new hot drinks in the sample of probate inventories is also shown in Table 1. This therefore indicates the early development of the habit and its likely

TABLE 2

FREQUENCIES WITH WHICH EARTHENWARE, CHINA AND UTENSILS FOR HOT DRINKS WERE RECORDED IN A SAMPLE OF PROBATE INVENTORIES FROM EIGHT PARTS OF ENGLAND, 1675–1725

Status or Occupation	Number of Inventories	Earthenware	China	Utensils for Hot Drinks
		%	%	%
Gentry and Professional	160	43	6	6
Yeomen: large farmers	952	33	1	1
Husbandmen: small farmers	332	28	0	1
Craft trades	459	43	4	4
Dealing trades	452	49	10	10
Labourers[1]	28	43	4	0
Widows & Spinsters with no Occupation	217	33	4	2
Unknown Occupation or Status	302	30	6	7
All	2902	37	4	4

Sources and Notes: 1. There are too few labourers' inventories to be representative of all labourers in the population.

See note 6 for details of the sample.

The distinction between the groups is based on those often used to categorise the social order at this time, although they are not without problems. See D. Cressy, 'Describing the Social Order of Elizabethan and Stuart England', *Literature and Society*, Vol. 12. (1976), pp. 29–44.

impact on the pottery trade. Here, there was remarkably rapid change in the early years of the eighteenth century and by 1715 they had become a normal part of the equipment of the wealthy households of the London freemen, although they continued unusual amongst people elsewhere, especially in rural areas. As far as the trade in pottery was concerned, the importance of this is considerable, for there was no substitute for pottery in making and serving these progressively more popular hot drinks. Production in the first half of the eighteenth century was closely associated with, although not confined to, providing a variety of vessels for the tea-table.

Tableware was a later development on any scale, and its use was related to numerous changes in the living standards and domestic behaviour of families in the middle ranks. But production of these wares developed more slowly, for many families continued to eat in very simple ways, used a few pewter or wooden vessels and had no practical need for elaborate sets of pottery tablewares.[9] Even so, the market for pottery expanded notably before 1780, especially amongst the upper and middle classes and the development of internal trade in earthenware and china was part of the response to these developments.

III

It is not easy to trace internal trade in any commodity because things could be manufactured, transported and sold in quite complex ways without any official notice being taken of them, with the result that internal trade can remain hidden from direct and easy observation. It is, however, possible to reconstruct some elements of the trade, and the businesses involved in it, by tracing dealers, merchants and shopkeepers from three kinds of evidence; first, the ledgers of the producers themselves, second, insurances and advertisements that refer to dealers, and third, lists of dealers in trade directories. When these are taken together they give some considerable insight into the businesses of the dealers and the organisation of the trading networks over the whole country, including Scotland, although the trade here did not develop fully until after 1780, so Scottish dealers are not included in the table.

Both Table 3 and the flow chart in Diagram 1 are based on this evidence and are therefore reconstructions that look at the organisation and structure of the inland trade in different ways. The table shows how many dealers were recorded in different places before 1780. It shows where the businesses of the dealers were located and is therefore indicative of static elements in the trade. The diagram shows some of the kinds of trading relationships between different kinds of dealers and is therefore indicative of the dynamic elements in the trade.

The dominant position of London in the pottery trade is evident from both ways of seeing it, for well over a third of the dealers were located in London and many of the trading networks focused on the capital.[10] The rest of the dealers were scattered throughout the other market centres of England, so that the largest concentration after London (Bristol) had far fewer dealers, 32 as compared to 190. The extent of this concentration was much greater than even this table indicates, for the businesses in London were more specialised than those elsewhere, for those in the provincial centres often sold glass and earthenware alongside other things, like ironware and grocery.

In London the most important dealers, known as chinamen, specialised in the sale of imported china. They were, as we shall see, extremely innovative in developing techniques for selling their wares and they also operated on a very large scale. For instance, in 1756 and 1757 two chinamen advertised that they had 100,000 pieces for sale each; one of them priced the plates at 11s. a dozen, so that this one advertisement could have represented a stock of £4,500 and even if each piece were valued at as little as 6d., they were advertising stock worth £2,500 each.[11] Insurances also suggest very large stocks, especially as one insurance

TABLE 3

DEALERS IN CHINA AND EARTHENWARE IN ENGLAND BEFORE 1780

Place	Number of Dealers
London	190
Bristol	32
Liverpool	28
Newcastle on Tyne	20
Norwich	14
Hull	8
Bath	7
Manchester	6
Cambridge	5
North Staffordshire	9
84 other towns in England with 1–4 dealers each	120
unknown or unclear	80
	519

For comparison with Scotland see Weatherill, 'Marketing English Pottery in Scotland', p. 23: the only dealers recorded there before 1780 were in Edinburgh (9) and Leith (2).

Notes and Sources: References to dealers and customers from the sources were entered in a manual card index and the total counted from this. Other information thus listed was used in the text.

1. *Sales ledgers of producers*

Stoke Museum, ceramic mss. collection. Sales ledgers of Jonah Malkin, 1747–54; John Wedgwood, 1755–71.
Staffordshire R.O. Account Books of John Baddeley of Shelton, 1759–1772, D 1788 v 99 – v 101.
B.M. Department of Medieval and Later Antiquities, Bembrose Papers, Small ledger relating to Derby Porcelain Co. 1769–70, no catalogue number.
India Office Library, Home Misc. Series, Sales of China, 1715–1725, Vols. 10–14.

There are a number of later ledgers, which are not used in this article, but which give similar data, see Weatherill, Thesis, Chapter 11; Keele University Library, Wedgwood Accumulation, Ledgers 1790–1816, no catalogue numbers; Stoke Museum, Ceramic Mss. Collection, Sales Ledger of John Wood, 1777–1800, no catalogue number; Royal Doulton Ltd., Minton Ms., Sales Ledgers, 1796–1815, Nos. 1322–4.

2. *Directories*

Kent's London Directory (1736).
The Intelligencer or Merchant's Assistant (1738).
Mortimer's London Directory (1763).
Bailey's British Directory, 4 vols. (1783–84).

3. *Handlist of Insurances*

E. Adams, 'The Bow Insurances and Related Matters', *ECC Trans.*, ix (1973), pp. 67–108; 'Ceramic Insurances in the Sun Company Archives, 1766–1776', *ECC Trans.*, x (1976), pp. 1–38.

4. *Advertisements and miscellaneous other sources*

Guildhall Library, London, Glass-Sellers' Company Records, ms. 5556, Agreement with John Dwight, May 1676, which has 37 signatures of dealers.

F. Buckley, 'Potteries on the Tyne and other Northern Potteries during the eighteenth century', *Arch. Aeliana*, 4th series, iv (1929), pp. 68–82.
F.E. Burrell, 'Some Advertisements of Ceramic Interest', *ECC Trans.*, v (1960), pp. 176–9.
J.E. Nightingale, *Contributions Towards the History of Early English Porcelain* (Salisbury, 1881, reprinted E.P. Publishing, 1973).
W.J. Pountney, *The Old Bristol Potteries* (Bristol, 1920).
A. Toppin, 'The China Trade and Some London Chinamen', *ECC Trans.*, iii (1935), pp. 37–56.
S. Smith, 'Norwich China Dealers of the Mid-Eighteenth Century', *ECC Trans.*, ix (1974), pp. 193–211.
B. Hillier, 'Two Centuries of China Selling', *ECC Trans.*, ix (1973), pp. 2–15.
B. Watney, *Longton Hall Porcelain*.

DIAGRAM 1

A FLOW CHART TO ILLUSTRATE LINKS IN THE DISTRIBUTION NETWORK FOR POTTERY AND PORCELAIN IN THE EIGHTEENTH CENTURY

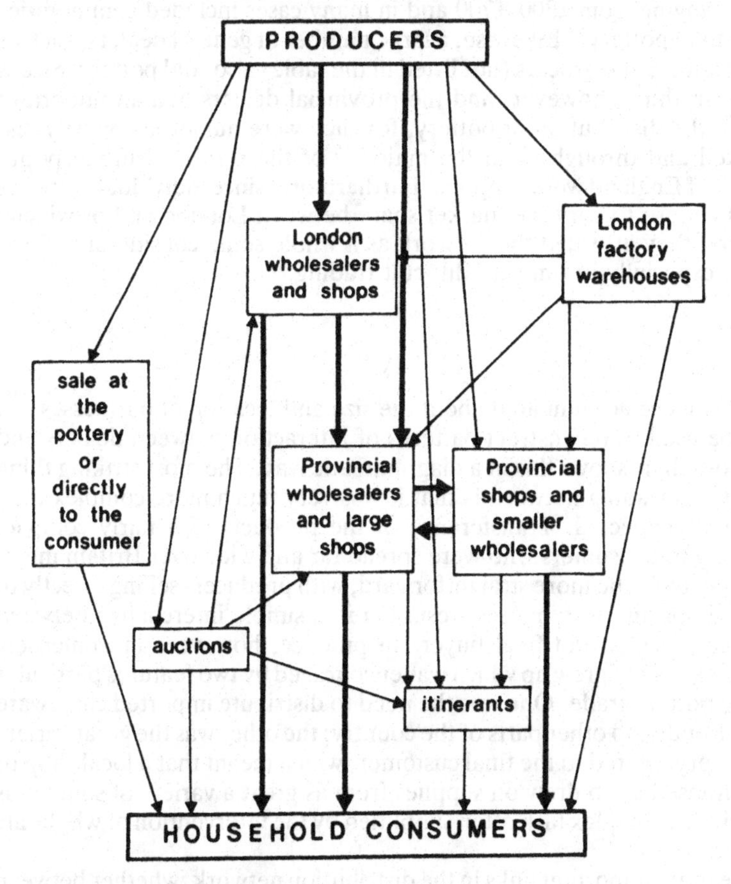

Sources: See the text and those listed with Table 1

is likely to understate the value of the business; the well-established partnership of Akerman and Scrivenor insured stocks for £3,000 in 1770 and 1772 and Charles Vere of Fleet Street (a chinaman since the 1740s) for £2,000 in 1770.[12]

General stoneware and earthenware dealers in London worked on a comparable scale by the time the trade was well established in the mid-eighteenth century, with insurance valuations for stocks between £300 and £3,000.[13] These were large even in comparison with the largest producers of the time; the Bow porcelain factory used about £12,000 in fixed and working capital at its zenith in the 1750s, of which £3,000 was stock in the warehouse and £1,100 stock in the factory itself. The larger earthenware producers even in the 1770s had stocks of lower value; the Turners insured their warehouse stock for only £1,000 in 1770 and Wedgwood and Bentley's stock in the Newport Street warehouse was insured for £3,000 in 1771.[14]

The provincial businesses were on a smaller scale, with insurances of stock ranging from £300–£700 and in many cases included commodities other than pottery.[15] Likewise, a large number of general dealers, such as ironmongers and grocers (not listed in the table) also sold pottery. Size is not everything, however, and the provincial dealers had an important role in the distribution of pottery, for they were numerous, widely distributed and through them the majority of the rural and urban populations of England were supplied. Furthermore, since individual potteries could choose to vary the market share between London and provincial dealers, they afforded the network as a whole some considerable flexibility, especially in times of difficult trading.

IV

The evidence accumulated about the size and location of businesses can also be used to reconstruct patterns of interaction between dealers and the flow chart shows this in a diagrammatic way. The most striking thing about this trading network is that it was very much more complex than might be expected. Transference of the products of a fairly compact industry to consumers who were spread far and wide over Britain might be expected to be more straightforward, with producers selling directly to local shops and warehouses, resulting in a simple interchange between producer, seller and final buyer. In practice, however, an immensely complex system grew up which was encouraged by two features particular to the pottery trade. One was the need to distribute imported chinaware from London to other parts of the country; the other was the great variety of pottery offered to the final customer, which meant that a local shop or warehouse had to draw on supplies from as great a variety of sources as possible, a complex task often simplified by the intervention of wholesale dealers.

The more important links in the distribution network, whether between dealers and producers or between different kinds of dealers, are indicated in the diagram by heavier lines. The most significant trade was from producers to larger dealers, especially those in London, followed by inter-trading between dealers and especially from the large dealers in London to those in the provinces; the trade from larger dealers in the provinces to other dealers there was also significant, although involving smaller individual transactions.

As early as the seventeenth century there was some trade from producers to large dealers and there is even some evidence for large-scale trading in some of the early coarseware products. For instance, North Staffordshire butter pots were widely distributed to farmers and butter factories in the North Midlands, and two potters managed to double the price of the output in 1682 by buying all the butter pots made in that year in Burslem, suggesting a concern with buying on a large scale.[16] Dealers were also likely to have operated in North Devon, in connection with a well developed trade between the potteries there and the east coast of North America.[17]

There certainly were general earthenware and stoneware merchants at work in London in the later seventeenth century, although the evidence is indistinct, coming mostly from the records of the Glass-Sellers' Company, which in October 1675: 'appointed a committee and to treat and agree with the Pottmakers ... and agreed with the Pottmakers concerning rates and prices of Earthenwares'.[18] The fate of any such agreement is not known, but the London delft potteries were the largest in the country at the time, with workforces of up to fifty. They probably sold through dealers, for the potteries were in Lambeth and Southwark at some distance from the main commercial centres, and they do not appear to have had retail showrooms.[19] The Glass-Sellers' Company also entered into two contracts with the earliest stoneware pottery at Fulham in 1676 and 1677; in these the prices, wares and conditions were fully outlined and 37 signatures were attached, presumably of dealers who were to stock these wares.[20]

By the mid eighteenth century the trade of the general earthenware dealers was well established and also much better documented, so that the scale and complexity of some individual businesses can be traced. Thus James Abernethy, 'merchant' of Leadenhall Street, London, had wide-ranging business contacts; he was in partnership with Richard Addison at the Hermitage delftware pottery at Wapping in the 1760s; he dealt in lead; he was in partnerships with other merchants, including John Livie and Weatherby and Crowther, who themselves were involved in glass production and with the porcelain factory at Bow; he was evidently interested in the development of the trade in fine earthenware and especially in coloured glazed wares, and clearly knew makers of these in Staffordshire and Liverpool; he bought china from John Baddeley in 1761.[21] Then there was William Strapham of Thames Street amongst Baddeley's larger customers; his stock was insured for £1,000; he may, unusually, have had a relative acting as an agent in North Staffordshire, for a Joseph Strapham was listed as 'merchant and factor for all kinds of earthenware' in Stoke in 1784, the only such entry.[22]

Some of the larger dealers in the main provincial centres, such as Newcastle, Liverpool and Bristol, had functions akin to those in London. They were a varied group. John Dunbibin, for instance, was involved in delftware production in London and Liverpool in the 1750s and 1760s; he was clearly a dealer in Liverpool in the 1760s, trading extensively with North Staffordshire potteries, sometimes through the agency of Josiah Wedgwood; his business seems to have been in financial difficulties and he was evidently bankrupt in 1761 although he continued to trade.[23] Robinson and Rhodes were specialised dealers who enamelled early Wedgwood and Leeds cream wares; they bought white ware, and an advertisement of 1760 specifically says that they enamelled English and foreign china.[24]

The factory warehouses in London are better documented than many other outlets and, for this reason, have received disproportionate attention notably in McKendrick's account of Wedgwood.[25] They were not, however, numerous and can best be seen as attempts by some producers (especially those who made china and high quality earthenwares) to enter the London markets. It is hard to generalise about them. At one end of the spectrum were the provincial china producers, notably Lowestoft, Longton Hall and Derby, who came to some kind of agreements with dealers to act as their agents, possibly in return for using the name of the factory.[26] In these cases it is clear that the warehouse was not closely controlled by the factory and it was possible for the warehouse to trade with other producers. Thus the Longton Hall warehouse (closed 1761) also received wares from John Wedgwood in the 1750s, and this kind of agency seems to have been a common way for the smaller provincial china producers to develop a London outlet, at least before 1770.

The most important warehouse of all was that of the Bow factory, opened at Cornhill in 1753. A few surviving accounts show that most of this company's output was sold there.[27] Advertisements specified that it was for both wholesale and retail trade, although there was also a brief attempt to have a retail showroom in St. James's Street, 'for the convenience of Nobility and Gentry' in 1758. The Worcester factory had a similar warehouse in Aldersgate Street from 1756, 'for the better accommodation of Merchants and Traders . . . where they may be supplied every day'.[28]

A few producers of high quality earthenware had London warehouses before 1780, including Wedgwood, Spode and Turner. Wedgwood himself mentions that the idea of a showroom in London was suggested to him by some visitors to Burslem in 1765 (the Duke of Marlborough, Lord Gower, Lord Spencer and others). 'The Gentlemen . . . wonder I have not a Warehouse in London where patterns of all sorts I make may be seen.' He had already, five days before, written to his brother for advice about having someone in London to show patterns and take orders. His idea then was on the modest scale of renting two back rooms in an unfashionable quarter.[29] In the end Wedgwood was more ambitious, and came to channel most of his sales through the warehouse and made little use of the dealers. The warehouses set up by the other makers of fine quality earthenwares were different from Wedgwood's, so they need not be seen as copying Wedgwood, nor need Wedgwood be seen as leading. Spode, for instance, opened a warehouse in Foregate Street, Cripplegate in 1778 but it was quite independent of the factory, for it was a separate venture by Spode II, only under the direct control of the Stoke business for a few years in the 1790s after the death of Spode I. Not only did it trade in Spode wares, but in the wares of other producers, nor did the Spode factory sell exclusively to it.[30]

The bulk of production was distributed by dealers and the factory warehouses were not numerically important. This calls into question the framework of McKendrick's discussion of Wedgwood's contribution to the development of the sales techniques of the earthenware industry as a whole, for he does not stress that such warehouses were unusual. The markets served by the English porcelain factories were broadly similar to those served by the highest quality earthenwares in which Wedgwood, Spode and others specialised, and it is entirely appropriate to find Wedgwood gradually adapting known methods, but entirely inappropriate to interpret Wedgwood as a leader in this respect.

The London chinamen were undoubtedly the most important entrepreneurs in developing the sales network and associated sales techniques, not because they distributed the bulk of the products of the growing home industry but because their activities confirmed concentration on London and large-scale operation; in addition they probably introduced up-market sales techniques and a few of them may have encouraged the production of china in England.

The trade in imported chinaware became established from the 1690s, when simple chinaware became available in larger amounts, alongside many other attractive products from China and the rest of the Far East. There is little direct evidence about how the trade of chinamen developed in the early eighteenth century and only three of the 45 merchants who bought china at the East India Company sales in the early 1720s have been identified from other sources and only two were listed in the earliest London directories ten years later.[31] Members of the Glass-Sellers' Company probably became involved for, of 37 dealers of the company who entered an agreement with John Dwight (a maker of fine stoneware) in May 1676, four can be traced as chinamen before the middle of the eighteenth century, which is a remarkable continuity, considering the length of time and the nature of the sources. In one case, Robert Farrar, the business lasted through the eighteenth century and eventually (and uniquely) transferred to china production in North Staffordshire in the 1790s, when the trade in imported china declined.[32]

The chinamen had immense significance in the development of the home industry because they confirmed a distribution network centred on London, which could eventually absorb the products of the home industry. Before about 1745 the chinamen dealt in imported china alone, but in the late 1740s several English porcelain manufactories were set up. The exact role of established chinamen in the sale of home produced china cannot be traced because sales ledgers have not survived; there are, however, advertisements which refer to both foreign and home china. Thomas Williams of the 'Chinese Warehouse of Curiosities' in the Strand sold, as well as foreign china, 'an Assortment of all the Porcelain Manufactories in England . . .'. He was also, for a short while, a 'factor' for the Derby Porcelain Company.[33]

Some large chinamen certainly bought the fine stonewares and earthenwares that were so important to the growth of the pottery industry in the second half of the eighteenth century; Thomas Lawton of Wapping was one such, with a very large and complex business by the late 1760s. From 1765 he was called a 'chinaman, potter and glass-seller' and in the late 1760s his business expanded from an insurance valuation of £2,400 in January 1765 to £6,500 in January 1767.[34] He was an important customer of John Baddeley in every year that is covered by the accounts of this potter (1759–71); he took, for instance, a tenth of Baddeley's output in 1770 which was a relatively high proportion to go to one dealer. Yet many of the chinamen, and especially those with shops in the West End, probably continued to specialise in imported chinaware until the import trade collapsed in the 1790s.

Chinamen also pioneered wholesale and retail sales techniques, some of which were taken up by the English china producers and, later, by the earthenware manufacturers. Many of the sales ideas that Wedgwood discussed with his partner Bentley were already used by the London chinamen, and were not new to the trade as a whole. The early eighteenth-century china shops had a reputation as fashionable lounges in which curious and high-priced items were displayed in an appealing way. Some of the china auctions of the 1750s and 1760s were attended by the 'nobility and gentry', who bid for their own lots of high quality wares.[35] China shops were concerned to have the right ambience in their showrooms and the advertisements for the warehouse in the Strand of Thomas Williams make this clear, for it had separate rooms for the retail trade, with a door into Spring Gardens, 'by Desire of several Ladies and Gentleman'.[36] Techniques of this kind were developed well before the beginnings of Wedgwood's enterprises in the 1760s.

In some other retail trades, the idea of marking the exact price on the goods was a novel one, treated with suspicion and hostility even in the late eighteenth century.[37] Pottery, china and glass are not strictly comparable, for they lent themselves more readily than other commodities to exact pricing. One of Wedgwood's ideas was to fix the prices in the retail warehouse, but this too was already done by china dealers by the 1750s. The short-lived Bow retail warehouse on the Terrace in St. James's Street advertised, in 1757, 'the real Price marked on each Piece, without abatement', and there are other similar advertisements for

Chelsea and Worcester.[38] Whether this was done in the earlier eighteenth century cannot be known because there is no similar evidence. Likewise, it is not possible to obtain a detailed insight into the motivations of the chinamen, for they have not left the kind of discursive evidence that is available about Wedgwood, but by the time Wedgwood entered the market in the 1760s, the chinamen had had over 70 years of experience in dealing with this up-market product. This does not belittle Wedgwood's achievement in identifying the potential of such techniques for the sale of his different kinds of ware, but it does show that the environment in which he worked was complex and he should be seen as adopting techniques for his ornamental wares which had already been developed for china dealing.

The large dealers, whether in London or elsewhere, obtained most, if not all, of their supplies (except for imported china) from the producers. By the time of the earliest sales ledgers it is clear that the mechanics of the trade were already established. Dealers could write for their orders, giving detailed comments about their requirements, their trade and their problems. Manufacturers do not seem to have been expected to send unsolicited orders and it is likely that regular customers ensured that their suppliers were willing to deal with them.[39] This correspondence was probably supplemented by travellers before the 1760s and there is internal evidence in John Wedgwood's sales ledger (1758–70) that someone, possibly his partner and brother, Thomas, made regular journeys to collect debts, although these were not the same kind of regular journeys made by the travellers of the late eighteenth century.[40]

The large dealers also visited producers in North Staffordshire and elsewhere in the normal course of their business. This too was well established by 1780, but the origins and development of these links are obscured by lack of appropriate evidence much earlier in the century. The kinds of journey can be seen from a few advertisements; William Beloe of Norwich visited North Staffordshire in the 1770s to maintain his connections with manufacturers and in 1783 he advertised that he was 'lately returned from Staffordshire with a very large and Elegand Assortment'.[41] Likewise, William Absolon of Great Yarmouth advertised in 1784 that 'He has lately laid in a fresh Assortment from the best Manufactories'.[42] Somewhat earlier, in 1769, William Hilcoate of Newcastle on Tyne, who made cream-coloured earthenware as well as being a dealer, advertised that he 'is just returned from the South where he has purchased from the best Manufactories a large assortment'.[43]

Correspondence and personal visits of this kind also had a more general significance, for it was through these personal contacts that the trade was knitted together into a framework of people who knew one another and who could discuss and influence the development of the industry. It was along these lines within the distribution networks that information about new products and consumer preferences could be channelled. The surviving evidence on this is not extensive but there are references in correspondence to the types of wares preferred by particular customers, or in particular localities, and it seems that the makers were responsive to such requests.[44]

The other series of links in the network illustrated by Diagram 1, that had tremendous significance for the trade, were those between the larger dealers, especially in London, and other dealers, especially in the provinces. The London warehouses acted as entrepots for provincial dealers, who visited them in much the same way that they visited the producers, but here they could acquire a much wider range of goods than from any individual producer. Thus Elizabeth Studwell of Norwich advertised in 1783 that 'she is just returned from London ... with a fresh assortment of china, glass and Staffordshire Ware', a combination that she could not have acquired in any other way.[45] Again, the Bow warehouse (1753–62) advertised, in papers in Derby, Birmingham and probably elsewhere, that it was 'for the convenience of all Customers both in Town and Country'.[46]

The habit of relying on London dealers was consolidated by the need to acquire imported chinaware at the East India Company auctions, and in this sense the china trade had an important influence over the development of the network as a whole, for it firmly encouraged an already existing tendency for concentration on London. Provincial dealers certainly visited London dealers to buy chinaware, although the best examples come from the better-documented second half of the eighteenth century, with the growth of advertisements in the provincial press. In 1762 a Bristol dealer advertised various kinds of china, which were 'the best of the kind that could be purchased in London'.[47]

The provincial dealers were also encouraged by the possibilities of visiting the East India Company sales in person; in the Dublin business of the Elers brothers, for instance, one of the partners stayed in London in the 1710s and 1720s in order to attend these sales. Somewhat later, William Beloe of Norwich advertised, in 1783, that he had just received chinaware from the sales and a Bristol shop said, in 1778, that 'the said shop is supplied every week with a new assortment from the East India Company's [and other] warehouses in London'.[48]

The London dealers also pursued their trade into the provinces and did not rely exclusively on being visited by provincial dealers. There were, for instance, auction sales of Bow and foreign china in Norwich in the 1750s and 1760s, which were organised by auctioneers from London and, at least in part, intended for the 'trade'.[49] A London dealer opened a shop in Bristol in 1765 for the duration of the fair there to sell foreign and London wares.[50] Whether this kind of visiting was widespread is impossible to say from the limited evidence, but it does seem more likely that dealers would normally have visited London, or sent their orders.

The dealers who had contacts with London in this way varied from the larger dealers in the main centres, to shopkeepers in a large number of smaller towns. And, of course, all these dealers, large and small, could also obtain wares directly from a variety of producers in different parts of the country, as well as from larger dealers and from each other.

It is clear that specialist shops for earthenware date back to the seventeenth century, and were already able to offer a much wider choice of pottery of different kinds than could otherwise be bought from one place. Shopkeepers' inventories show a wide range of wares, from ordinary cooking pots, to decorated vessels and new types of pottery.[51] In this respect shops both in the provinces and London enhanced knowledge about different types of wares from an early date, and saw themselves as providing a service to customers. In 1691 the Glass-Sellers' Company asserted that glass and earthenware were sold by shopkeepers, 'in all Cittys, Townes & Corporate Market Townes and boroughs and allmost in all villages in England'.[52] This was clearly exaggerated, but they also made the point that shops could judge when the pottery was properly made and were 'persons of judgment in these commodities'. The correspondence a century later in the Wedgwood archives shows retailers pursuing a similar line and taking care over the wishes of their customers.

It would be interesting to know in more detail how shops functioned and how goods were displayed and purchases encouraged, both in London and the provinces. There was a close relationship between wholesale and retail trading, as in many other trades and even very small shops often had a wholesale function as well. Some insight into the appearance and nature of shops in a large provincial centre is suggested by S. Smith's detailed study of Norwich, where there were several shops and warehouses on prime sites in the central shopping and market streets, some of which even had glass windows suitable for display from at least the 1750s. Pottery was also sold in the market and there were auction sales in inns in the town.[53]

Few skills were needed by china and earthenware shopkeepers, and these were mainly concerned with matching sets and understanding qualities, rather than with any of the more complex skills needed in drapery and grocery. Dealers in pottery ordered, or received, crates of 'sortable' wares which contained pottery that had not been made up into sets. The shopkeepers and wholesalers matched sets of ware, a skill which became more important as customers came to require matching sets, especially when manufacturers' quality control over colour and size was imperfect.

A few dealers undertook decoration and something is known of them through the interest of collectors in such unusual wares. They bought both imported chinaware and home-produced wares 'in the white' from a number of producers and decorated it, often with local scenes or coats of arms. The best known example is the dealer-decorator, James Giles of Cockspur Street in London, who decorated porcelain and glass from several producers, as well as selling some finished wares before 1774. In the provinces, William Absolon decorated pieces with local scenes in Yarmouth but in other respects seems to have functioned as a normal wholesale and retail dealer. He obtained supplies from the major manufacturers.[54]

The larger provincial dealers fulfilled a role in redistribution to other traders similar to that of the London dealers, but on a smaller scale. The details of the advantages of this trade were spelt out in a later advertisement by a Plymouth dealer, Dickens and Warwick, which is worth quoting at length because it explains how small pottery shops were able to stock a range of wares and some of the problems in doing this. These points were equally applicable to the period before 1780 and the business of Dickens and Warwick itself probably dates from the early 1780s. They advertised, in 1823:

> they have lately purchased in the Manufactories some considerable stocks of goods, comprising a general assortment of china and earthenware which they are enabled to offer at manufacturers prices ... Dickens and Warwick have always on hand large quantities of cream colour and dip't ware of every sort: also Sunderland brown, and yellow glazed, and Bristol stone ware. To those who are aware of the frequent delays in the canal conveyance from the Staffordshire Potteries, the difficulty of procuring shipment from Liverpool to the smaller ports in the West of England, and the great uncertainty of sea-passage, it is needless to explain the advantages of prompt supplies of goods; a single purchase from Dickens and Warwick will be sufficient to convince of the facility with which they can make up an assortment of goods from various manufactories, without delay, and in a much less number of packages than the buyer could possibly procure from the Potteries.[55]

The network of dealers, whose interactions are illustrated by the flow chart, was largely established before 1750, with complex trading arrangements between larger and smaller, London and provincial dealers of various kinds. That it was a well-developed system stands out if it is compared with the trade in Scotland. Here, even in the late eighteenth century, the links in the web of relationships were straightforward, with little evidence for inter-trading between dealers. The Edinburgh dealers do not seem often to have sold to trade customers and commercial relations remained simple; in Scotland as a whole the dealers were mainly retailers, who bought directly from the producers and sold directly to their final customers.[56]

There were a number of other trading links which did not have such long-term and fundamental significance, yet are worth consideration because their existence is indicative of the variety within the inland trades at this time. Pottery was sold directly from the potteries themselves, with the disadvantage that consumer choice was limited to the products of one pottery and as the industry became more diversified this mattered more. The sales ledgers of the mid-eighteenth century show that by that time few sales were made to individuals from the more developed potteries, so that examples of direct selling tend to be from the late seventeenth or early eighteenth centuries. One nice instance is of James Morley, who advertised (*c.* 1690–1700) 'at ye Pot-House in Nottingham' a wide range of stonewares on an illustrated trade card, apparently aimed at private buyers, for it makes no reference to trade terms or discounts.[57]

Auction sales were also an early technique, by which new products were introduced or stocks cleared off, especially by early china factories. It was a strategy which became progressively less necessary as the main trading networks became established, and the china factories gradually adopted other techniques at the same time. Auctions were not held at all by the makers of fine earthenware and stonewares, on which the expansion of the industry was based after 1760 and none of them were like those held in the cloth trade later in the eighteenth century in London, where the aim was to sell as large a volume of goods as quickly as possible and at as low a price as possible.[58] Auctions in the pottery trade were especially important to the English china factories before about 1760, possibly influenced by the way in which imported china was auctioned by the East India Company. By 1780, with the growth of the sales network, they had become much less important.

There was a much longer continuity in the various activities of itinerant dealers. Urban hawkers seem to have existed in the seventeenth century. The Glass-Sellers' Company complained of them in the 1690s and asserted that they, 'go about streets from house to house to sell to and furnish those houses with glasses and earthenware'. Their assertions that the trade was not necessary can be taken as the standard grievance of shopkeepers against market and itinerant dealers.[59] Nearly a 150 years later, Mayhew took a statement from a street seller of crockery in London, suggesting very long continuity in this kind of outlet. In this case, and in Swift's ironical *Directions to Servants*, the integration of crockery dealing into a wider network of street trading is hinted at because both accounts refer to, 'that execrable Custom got amongst Ladies, of trucking their old Cloaths for *China*'.[60]

Itinerant dealers also served an essential role in distribution to rural areas remote from shops, and they were often the final link in a long chain of distribution. In the early part of the period under review they could have contributed to the dispersal of knowledge about new products. Nicholas Blundell in Lancashire, for example, bought his early china from a travelling salesman in 1710 but made later purchases from dealers in Liverpool.[61] They were often associated with fixed traders and, in many cases, complemented the retail trade, so that there were shops and dealers who specialised in supplying them with wares. Paul Jackson advertised, in 1775, that 'Hawkers from Northumberland and Cumberland may be supplied at his shop' in Newcastle on Tyne.[62] Travelling dealers could also buy their wares at the potteries and many of them visited North Staffordshire in order to do so. When a pottery in Derby closed in 1779, its wares were auctioned and the advertisement specified, 'This earthenware will be sold in different lots and is well worth the notice of Pot-Carriers .... No less a quantity than two horse loads will be sold to one person'.[63]

It is, however, important not to overstress the significance of the itinerant trade, especially after the end of the seventeenth century. Some writers have done this, possibly because itinerants lived more colourful lives than the fixed dealers, and writers aiming at collectors of pottery have tended to be more interested in them than in the more important, large-scale dealers.[64] In addition, the influential contemporary account of the industry in Burslem in the 1680s by Dr Robert Plot implied that 'cratemen' were the most important sales outlet; they '... carry them at their *backs* all over the Countrey'.[65] Unfortunately, this comment has been taken, by some writers, to apply to the eighteenth century as well. As the dealers became more numerous, with retail outlets in many towns, the need for travelling pottery salesmen became much less.

V

What importance did the various sales outlets and the network as a whole have? There are several different ways of looking at this question; there were relationships between expansion of production and the adequacy of the network; different supply conditions influenced ownership patterns in different parts of the country, it is also possible to compare the impact of different sales policies on the fortunes of individual producers.

Sales outlets and transport facilities seem to have been adequate to sustain the growth of the industry and do not seem to have inhibited expansion at any time. The role of the distribution networks during two periods of rapid growth, one in the late seventeenth century, the other after 1740, was a supportive one. In the late seventeenth century the traditional outlets of the industry multiplied and, as in production, there do not seem to have been new departures, but rather growth was based on existing businesses and ideas. The main discontinuity was the renewed impetus to concentration on London brought about by the trade in chinaware and the growth in the important businesses of the chinamen. The second phase of growth began after a clear upturn in the late 1740s, so that the industry expanded by about 70 per cent by 1760 and a further 60 per cent in the next 20 years. The sales networks were already there and the network itself expanded and diversified. By 1780 there were specialist dealers in all parts of the country and many general tradesmen stocked pottery on a smaller scale. The single most important change had happened before the industry entered its renewed phase of growth; this was the extension of the network to accommodate imported china in the early eighteenth century. Even here there was continuity with the past through the involvement of the Glass-Sellers' Company.

The strength and appropriateness of the way the trade had already developed by 1780 can be seen from the fact that it continued to function in the same kinds of ways, but on a larger scale, into the nineteenth century. The foundations were already laid and the increased output after

1780 continued to be distributed along the existing channels and there is no evidence that manufacturers gave up their marketing activities, or that they gave up production, to concentrate on selling, as they did in the more complex Lancashire cotton trades.

Regional variation in the frequencies with which pottery was recorded in the sample of inventories is suggestive of the impact of the trading networks on consumer choices. There were, of course, many influences over the ownership of these and other household goods but the patterns shown in Table 4 indicate that the supply of goods, especially those whose trade was strongly concentrated on London, could influence the extent to which these goods were available in different places. So that ownership of china, which was only available from London at this date, was greater in the places with a well-developed trade with the capital. The north-east of England stands out in this respect and there were concentrations of other kinds of goods here too. The trade link was that household and other goods were shipped as part of the return trade for coal, salt and manufactured goods. Likewise, northern Kent sent bulky agricultural produce to London, with a return trade in household and other goods. The more remote or land-locked areas of the north-west received supplies less easily and those to Carlisle went through Newcastle. The supply conditions were different for earthenware in that it was manufactured in several parts of the country and the trade had not centred on London as early as 1725. The predominance of Kent, Lancashire and London can partly be seen as a result of ease of supply but this is not the only explanation because it was widely made in the north-west midlands, and occurs infrequently there in inventories.[66]

At a different level, the importance of the network can be encapsulated in the experiences of two china factories in the 1750s, and this also emphasises that any producer's sales strategies have to be appropriate to the products made and the markets served. But this contrast illuminates the inter-relationships between production and marketing.

The Bow china factory (*c.* 1748 to 1769) was commercially successful, at least before about 1763, whereas that at Longton Hall (1751–61), in spite of considerable aesthetic success, went from one financial crisis to another.[67] Not all of the contrast in commercial success can be attributed to differences in their use of the sales networks, for there is other evidence of inadequate management and production problems at Longton Hall and, of course, Bow was more favourably sited near its main markets in London. But of great significance were the important links with the distributive trades in the Bow partnership, for the glass and china dealers, John Weatherby and John Crowther were involved from the beginning.[68] By contrast, Longton Hall was a much smaller enterprise and the partners seem mainly to have been concerned to invest capital. There is not much evidence of technical and other expertise, and the factory seems to have been in continuous financial difficulties even from the beginning, although some of the reasons for this was that they probably tried to make ware of too high a quality. There was only one working partner, who was

TABLE 4

REGIONAL VARIATIONS IN THE OWNERSHIP OF EARTHENWARE, CHINA AND UTENSILS FOR HOT DRINKS IN A SAMPLE OF INVENTORIES, 1675–1725

Locality	Number of Inventories	Earthenware %	China %	Utensils for Hot Drinks %
London Freemen[1]	300	71	41	39
London	367	41	12	15
North-East England	325	26	10	3
North-East Kent	390	58	3	6
Cambridgeshire	390	32	3	2
South Lancashire	390	75	1	1
Hampshire[2]	260	13	0	0
North-West Midlands	390	17	0	1
North Cumbria	390	23	2	0
All	2,902	37	4	4

Sources and Notes: 1. Orphans' Court inventories are included to contrast with the main sample, see note 5.
2. 1715 and 1725 are missing from this diocese, so the figures for china and utensils for hot drinks are misleading in comparison with the other localities.

See note for details of the sample. See also Lorna Weatherill, *Patterns of Consumption in Britain, 1670–1750* (forthcoming, 1986), Ch. 9.

probably more talented on the technical side than as a salesman, although work done by collectors and archaeologists on the site suggest production problems as well.

These rather different factories used the sales networks in different ways. The Bow partnership entered the London market at an early stage and tried to set up an appropriate sales outlet through their own warehouse in Cornhill by 1753, within a few years of beginning production, possibly influenced by the experience in the china trade of Weatherby and Crowther. Chronologically the decline of Bow and its eventual sale to Duesbury of Derby coincided with the end of this partnership when Weatherby died in 1762. Longton Hall does not seem to have tried to penetrate the London market until it was too late, expecting customers to come to the remotely sited factory and failing to make full use of the network of dealers in the provinces. Even in the late 1750s ware was still advertised for sale at the factory, although some attempts were by then being made to have an outlet in London, for in 1758 there was a warehouse or agency of some sort there. But when the factory closed in 1760, due to unresolved financial problems, there was a great deal of unsold stock (90,000 pieces) which was eventually auctioned at Salisbury, for reasons which are not at all apparent. The differences between these two producers certainly supports McKendrick's general point that producers needed a good sales policy to succeed; it also points towards the possibilities for variety because those potteries whose records have survived – Turners, John Wedgwood, Baddeley, Josiah Wedgwood and, later, Spode and Minton – all used the available resources in different ways. Josiah Wedgwood chose to sell in a very unusual way, in that he concentrated far more than most on the development of his own warehouses in London and elsewhere. The others more or less used the sales networks available.

VI

The mechanics of the pottery trade were complex and the middlemen fulfilled a vital role in the development of the industry. There were, however, things that they did not do, for they were a separate part of the trade and the functions of dealers and producers were, although mutually interdependent, different. The merchants, with very rare exceptions, did not become involved in production and they did not invest in production, either directly or through allowing credit to their customers; in fact producers allowed credit to dealers, which resulted in a considerable and necessary investment in trade debts, especially in the growth sectors after 1750.[69]

There was both continuity and change over the period examined here, for the network became larger, more dense and more sophisticated. There were few shops and dealers in the seventeenth century, serving the small market of a small industry, there were no advertisements, no travellers, no sales ledgers and only a little china and delftware to be redistributed from London. By 1780 the trade had apparently changed out of all recognition. Yet there was continuity in that each change, growth or innovation was based on something that had happened before, or it was encouraged by some already existing tendency; concentration on London was encouraged, in the first half of the eighteenth century, by the way that china was imported into London and distributed elsewhere. The idea of a factory warehouse grew gradually out of the experiences of the china dealers and manufacturers. The increases in the numbers of dealers in the later eighteenth century continued an already existing trend.

Inter-relationships within the whole trade can also be seen from the details in this study. Each part was separate and can be looked at in its own terms. Production grew in response to many technical, entrepreneurial and other stimuli. The domestic and personal behaviour of individuals in their homes underwent many economic and social changes. They came to drink quite different beverages, with the concomitant need for special utensils; they laid their tables differently and appreciated decorated things of all kinds. To the extent that these were social changes, they were independent of the technical capacity of producers. Yet they were closely associated, for without appropriate household demand, there would have been no production; without production (as well as imports of china) there would have been no way of translating changing social behaviour into changing material culture. The businesses and motivations of middlemen were also separate but they were essential links between the parallel, but different, needs of householders and potters. The mechanics of the trade – the businesses, the travellers, the letters, the shops – bound producers, traders and consumers together into a composite whole. A consumer society would not have been possible without them.

University of St. Andrews

NOTES

1. The classic still remains R. B. Westerfield, *Middlemen in English Business, 1660–1760* (1st ed. 1915; reprint Newton Abbot, 1968); J. A. Chartres, *Internal Trade in England, 1500–1700* (London, 1977); T. S. Willan, *The Inland Trade* (Manchester, 1976); D. Alexander, *Retailing in England During the Industrial Revolution* (London, 1970).
2. Margaret Spufford, *Small Books and Pleasant Histories* (London, 1981), especially Ch. 5; Margaret Spufford, *The Great Re-clothing of Rural England: Petty Chapmen and their Wares in the Seventeenth Century* (London, 1984); Joan Thirsk, *Economic Policy and Projects* (Oxford, 1978); M. M. Edwards, *The Growth of the British Cotton Trade, 1780–1815* (Manchester, 1967); S. I. Mitchell, 'Urban Markets and Retail Distribution, 1730–1815' (D. Phil., Oxford, 1975).
3. I am grateful to Professor Fisher's seminar at the Institute of Historical Research of the University of London for comments on an early version of this article. I am also indebted to Professor T.C. Smout for suggestions and encouragement. Some of the data was collected using grants from the SSRC and the 27 Foundation. See also Lorna Weatherill, 'The Growth of the Pottery Industry in England, 1660–1815' (Ph.D., London University, 1981) and 'Marketing English Pottery in Scotland, 1750–1820: A Study in the Inland Trade', *Scottish Economic and Social History*, Vol. 2 (1982), pp. 18–4.
4. Lorna Weatherill, 'The Growth of the Pottery Industry in England, 1660–1815', *Post-Medieval Archaeology*, Vol. 17 (1983), pp. 15–46; K. N. Chaudhuri, *The Trading World of Asia and the East India Company, 1660–1760* (Cambridge, 1978), pp. 406–10 and 385–406.
5. Weatherill, 'Growth', pp. 30–32. There was an export market for pottery, although this does not seem to have been very large before the end of the eighteenth century. It is not possible to compare the amounts recorded in the customs ledgers with other estimates of the size of the industry because ways of calculating the size of the industry are not compatible with the units used by the customs. Also the customs ledgers list glass with earthenware until 1814. It is best to see it as an industry aiming at the home market before 1780 although there were some exports. These seem to have been organised by merchants at the ports, although a few manufacturers dealt in the overseas markets directly, especially after 1780.
6. Commentary on the sample of probate inventories is based on a sample that I have taken as part of a research project entitled, 'Consumer behaviour and material culture, 1660–1760'. I have taken a sample of 65 inventories from eight dioceses in England (Carlisle, Durham, London, South Lancashire, East Kent, Cambridgeshire, Staffordshire and Winchester) at ten-year intervals, beginning in 1675. I have noted the recording in these of about 25 household goods, including pottery and items used in making and drinking tea, coffee or chocolate. This is not the place to rehearse the problems with the sample and the conclusions that can be drawn from it, but these observations are introduced here to give precision to the context in which the trade in pottery developed.
7. The inventories made in the Court of Orphans in London were sampled in the same way as those from the English dioceses, only I took 50 per decade because they were less varied, London Record Office, Inventories of the Court of Orphans.
8. Tea drinking is widely referred to, but there is no satisfactory account of who exactly

drank it and under what circumstances. There is a useful survey in G. Scott-Thomson, *Life in a Noble Household, 1641–1700* (London, 1965 edn.).

9. It is surprisingly difficult to trace the links between the use of pottery at table and eating habits, although such a link seems very likely. See Weatherill, 'Thesis', pp. 312–16.
10. There was not a strong bias to London in the sources used, except in the seventeenth century; most of the evidence taken for the table purported to cover the whole country.
11. J. E. Nightingale, *Contributions Towards the History of Early English Porcelain* (Salisbury, 1881, reprinted London, 1973) hereafter called *Contributions*. This is a curious collection of newspaper advertisements and sales catalogues; a few advertisements unknown to Nightingale have been found since. He searched the London papers, *Public Advertiser* and *General Evening Post*. These advertisements were in *Public Advertiser*, 22nd March, 1756 and May 1757, Nightingale, *Contributions*, pp. xiv and lxiv.
12. Guildhall Ms. 11936, Vol. 202, No. 290979, 9 Nov. 1770 and Vol. 212, No. 307078, 17 Jan. 1772; Vol. 202, No. 290932, 7 Nov. 1770. Charles Vere probably sold other commodities as well, for his trade card of 1762 specified tea, chocolate, snuff, fans and glasses, 'wholesale or retail'. He eventually became a banker and died in 1789, leaving a considerable estate. See A. Toppin, 'The China Trade and Some London Chinamen', *English Ceramic Circle Transactions*, Vol. 3 (1935), p. 49 and plate xxi.
13. Guildhall Library, London, Ms 11936, Vol. 112, No. 150132, Wm. Strapham, Queenhithe, 24 Dec. 1755, potter and dealer in glass, stock £500; Vol. 181, No. 253130, Wm. Strapham, Queenhithe, 13 Jan. 1768, potter and dealer in glass, stock £1,000; Vol. 135, No. 179068, Thos. Backhouse, Queenhithe, 21 Nov. 1760, dealer in earthenware, stock £500; Vol. 144, No. 195410, George Yard, 13 Jan. 1763, stock £700; Vol. 137, No. 181603, Jn. Dunbibin, Southwark, 10 March 1761, dealer in glass and earthenware, stock £800; Vol. 206, No. 297480, Thos. Bacchus, Upper Thames Street, 9 May 1771, dealer in china, glass and earthenware, utensils and stock £3,000; Vol. 212. No. 308603, Andrew Abbott and Wm. Clapham, Theobald Row, 6 March 1772, Staffordshire warehousemen, utensils and stock £500; Vol. 216, No. 314548, Wm. Banks, Lombard Street, 6 Aug. 1772, dealer in china, glass and earthenware, utensils and stock £500; Vol. 218, No. 319491, Mary Findon, St. John Street, 16 Dec. 1772, fruiter and potter, earthenware stock £50.
14. Lorna Weatherill, 'Capital and Credit in the English Pottery Industry', *Business History*, Vol. 24 (1982), pp. 243–58; Guildhall Ms. 11936, Vol. 198, No. 286041, 25 June 1770; Vol. 210, No. 304306, 30 Oct. 1771; Ms. 7252, Vol. 3, Nos. 31533 and 31534.
15. Guildhall Library, London, Ms. 11936, Vol. 204, No. 296533, James Bell, Newcastle on Tyne, 12 April 1771, merchant, paperstuff and stoneware £700; Vol. 171, No. 23840, John Berry and Robert Pyke, Liverpool, 17 Oct. 1766, dealers in nails and earthenware; £300; Vol. 172, No. 242282, John Feaston, Liverpool, 29 Jan. 1767, mugg merchant, £100; Vol. 181, No. 254538, 23 Jan. 1768, dealer in earthenware, £200; Vol. 204, No. 296664, 16 April 1771, dealer in earthenware, £500; Vol. 122, No. 161092, Joseph Flower, Bristol, 4 Feb. 1758, dealer in earthenware, £600; Vol. 171, No. 239258, William Graham, Liverpool, 4 Nov. 1766, dealer in earthenware, £300; Vol. 178, No. 25087, Thomas Statham, Liverpool, 11 Nov. 1767, dealer in earthenware, £200; Vol. 206, No. 298529, Parker, Lickbarrow and Gaworth, Liverpool, 18 June 1771, dealers in earthenware, £500 in 5 warerooms; Vol. 230, No. 339018, Thomas Mills, Edinborough, 17 April 1774, merchant, china and glass in shop, £500.
16. Stafford Record Office, Trans Q/SR, 1682 no. 12; F. Redfern, *History of Uttoxeter* (London, 1865), p. 274; L. Weatherill, *The Pottery Trade and North Staffordshire, 1660–1760* (Manchester, 1971), pp. 76–7.
17. C. M. Watkins, 'North Devon Pottery and its Export to America in the Seventeenth Century', *U.S. National Museum Bulletin*, Vol. 225 (Washington, DC, 1960), pp. 19–59.
18. Guildhall Library, Ms. 5556, 'Glass-Sellers' Company Court Minutes', 23 Oct. 1673.
19. A very full description of a pottery at Montague Close in the 1690s does not include a warehouse or shop, although it did have a separate counting house and other specialist rooms. Public Record Office, London, C5/149/49, 18 Jan. 1692/3, Answer of Henry

Makinfield.

20. Guildhall Library, Ms. 5556.
21. Abernethy's name occurs in a large number of records because of the complexity of his business contacts. Keele University Library, Wedgwood Accumulation, correspondence from James Abernethy to Josiah Wedgwood I, 1762/3, 5-30541-30548 and 5-4000-4025; *Mortimer's Directory* (1763) lists Addison and Abernethy in Wapping and consignments were sent there by Baddeley in 1761; Baddeley lists the business as Abernethy and Livie from 1765/8 in his sales ledgers, Stafford Record Office, D1788 v99 and v100; *Public Advertiser*, 24 June 1760, announces the dissolution of a partnership with Weatherby and Crowther, in F. E. Burrell, 'Some Advertisements of Ceramic Interest', *English Ceramic Circle Transactions*, Vol. 5 (1962), p. 179, hereafter called 'Advertisements'; Guildhall Library, London, Ms. 11936, Richard Addison and James Abernethy insured utensils and stock for £2,000 and the mill for £300 at the Hermitage pottery, 7 Oct. 1761, Vol. 139, No. 185063; Abernethy and Livie insured stock, utensils and mill for £4,800 on the 6 Feb. 1764, Vol. 153, No. 206684; it is not known when this delft pottery closed, but Abernethy is called a merchant in insurances of 1770 and 1771, Vol. 197, No. 281722 and Vol. 204, No. 295125.
22. *Bailey's British Directory* (London, 1784); Guildhall Ms. 11936, Vol. 112, No. 150132, 24 Dec. 1755, stock insured for £500, including glass; Vol. 181, No. 253130, 13 Jan. 1768, utensils and stock (including glass), £1,000; he was also mentioned in the account books of John Wedgwood and John Baddeley.
23. Dunbibin had wide contacts; Mortimer's, *London Directory* (1763) lists him in Southwark as a potter, and he was in a partnership with John Latham, Daniel Dunbibin and Samuel Dunbibin (his son in London) in Liverpool in the 1760s. Guildhall Library, Ms. 11936, Vol. 150, No. 205220, 20 Dec. 1763, stock and utensils, £500; Vol. 173, No. 241690, 16 Jan. 1767. The insurance gives no detail but utensils and stock were insured for £1,000. The most accessible file of letters from Dunbibin is collected in Liverpool Public Library, 942 ENT/1. No references have been found in the bankruptcy papers in the Public Record Office, London.
24. Leeds Intelligencer, 28 Oct. 1760; D. Towner, 'David Rhodes – Enameller', *English Ceramic Circle Transactions*, Vol. 4 (1957/9), pp. 3–13; Robinson gave up his partnership with Rhodes in 1764 and Rhodes eventually went to London as an enameller for Josiah Wedgwood from 1768 to 1777.
25. N. McKendrick, 'Josiah Wedgwood. An Eighteenth Century Entrepreneur in Salesmanship and Marketing Techniques', reprinted in E. M. Carus Wilson (ed.), *Essays in Economic History*, Vol. 3 (1962), pp. 353–79; N. McKendrick, 'Josiah Wedgwood and the Commercialisation of the Potteries', in N. McKendrick, J. Brewer and J. H. Plumb (eds.), *The Birth of a Consumer Society* (London, 1982), pp. 100–145.
26. G. Godden, *The Illustrated Guide to Lowestoft Porcelain* (London, 1969), pp. 5–6. Clark Durnford had an agency in 1770, see B. Watney, *Longton Hall Porcelain* (London, 1957); *London Evening Post*, Oct. 1758; Guildhall Library, Ms. 11936, Vol. 126, No. 164994; for Derby, *Public Advertiser*, 28 Jan. 1758, in Nightingale, *Contributions*, p. lxx.
27. British Museum, Department of Ms., Add. Ms. 45.905.
28. *Public Advertiser*, 20 March 1756, Nightingale, *Contributions*, p. lxxv; a general survey of Worcester, H. Sandon, *Worcester Porcelain, 1751–1793* (London, 1969).
29. Keele University Library, Wedgwood Accumulation, Josiah Wedgwood to John Wedgwood, 2 Aug. 1765, 25-18087 and 7 Aug. 1765, 25-18090; also Ann Finer and G. Savage, *The Selected Letters of Josiah Wedgwood* (London, 1976), p. 37.
30. L. Whiter, *Spode* (London, 1970), pp. 206–9.
31. These were William Eamson of Cheapside and Shewell, Andrews and Company. The third was a partnership of two brothers, John and David Elers, who had tried to make stoneware at Vauxhall and in North Staffordshire. They seem to have given up these ventures to concentrate on dealing, with John in Dublin and David in London as an agent; the best account of this complex business is in R. Edwards, 'London Potters, 1570–1719', *Journal of Ceramic History*, Vol. 6 (1974), pp. 60–62. Full references to the sources are listed with Table 1. One problem with early listings is that they rarely give

any details of the businesses of the merchants, as the later ones do, which makes tracing a full list of particular trades difficult.

32. Guildhall Library, Ms. 5556; R.G. Haggar, 'Miles Mason', *English Ceramic Circle Transactions*, Vol. 8 (1972), pp.183–98; the business came into the hands of Miles Mason, who married Ruth Farrar, who had inherited it. This was a unique case of a dealer turning successful manufacturer.
33. *Public Advertiser*, 11 Feb. 1758; *Public Advertiser*, May 1757; Nightingale, *Contributions*, p. lxiv; F.A. Barrett and A.L. Thorpe, *Derby Porcelain, 1750–1848* (London, 1971), pp.21–3.
34. Guildhall, London, Ms. 11936, Vol. 153, No. 207022; Vol. 157, No. 228655 and Vol. 172, No. 241514.
35. B. Hillier, 'Two Centuries of China Selling', *English Ceramic Circle Transactions*, Vol. 7 (1968), pp. 7–8; Nightingale, *Contributions*, p. xc.
36. *Public Advertiser*, 28 Jan. 1758, Nightingale, *Contributions*, pp. lxx–lxxi; *Mortimer's Directory* (1763).
37. D. Alexander, *Retailing in England during the Industrial Revolution*, pp.173–4.
38. *General Evening Post*, 20 to 22 Dec. 1757, in Nightingale, *Contributions*, p. xlviii (Bow); *General Evening Post*, 16 Jan. 1752, in F.E. Burrell, 'Advertisements', p.77 (Chelsea and Worcester).
39. The only large collection of orders before 1780 is in Keele University Library, Wedgwood Accumulation, catalogued under the name of the writer.
40. It is doubtful if representatives visited customers regularly twice a year as Nightingale's travellers did, see A.H. John, 'Miles Nightingale – Drysalter', *Economic History Review*, 2nd series, Vol. 18 (1965), pp.157–8; A.R. Mountford, 'John Wedgwood, Thomas Wedgwood and Jonah Malkin, Potters of Burslem', (unpublished M.A., Keele, 1972).
41. *Norfolk Chronicle*, 12 July 1783, in S. Smith, 'Norwich China Dealers in the Mid-Eighteenth Century', *English Ceramic Circle Transactions*, Vol. 9 (1974), p.199.
42. *Norwich Mercury*, 10 July 1784, in A.J.B. Kiddell, 'William Absolon, jnr. of Great Yarmouth', *English Ceramic Circle Transactions*, Vol. 5 (1950), p.55.
43. *Newcastle Journal*, 4 March 1768, F. Buckley, 'Potteries on the Tyne and other Northern Potteries during the Eighteenth Century', *Archaeologia Aeliana*, 4th series, Vol. 4 (1927), p.78.
44. Keele University Library, Wedgwood Accumulation; there are files of letters from dealers, indexed under the names of the dealer, and many have some comment on preferences. 'Never fail to send me your Newest patterns and Lowest prices'. (Abernethy to Wedgwood's, 3 Aug. 1763, 5-30548); 'the Gentry now seem to prefer that pattern (green edged ware)'. (Joseph Harris to Wedgwood's, 23 April 1782, Moseley papers); 'take great care in choosing the Bordered Ware as much alike in color and painting as can be' (Van Veldhyson to Wedgwood's, 22 March 1782, Moseley Papers).
45. *Norfolk Chronicle*, 22 March 1783, in S. Smith, 'Norwich China Dealers', pp.200–201.
46. *Aris's Birmingham Gazette*, 5 March 1753, in E. Adams, 'The Bow Insurances', p.77; *Derby Mercury*, 9 March 1753, in Nightingale, *Contributions*, p. xiv.
47. *Felix Farley's Journal*, 22 Dec. 1762, in W.J. Pountney, *Old Bristol Potteries* (Bristol, 1920), p.225.
48. *Felix Farley's Journal*, Sept. and Nov. 1778, in W.J. Pountney, *Old Bristol Potteries*, p.99.
49. These were often held in an inn, Wrench's Court. One, at least, was quite large, having 5,000 pieces in 1761, S. Smith, 'Norwich China Dealers', pp.206–8.
50. *Felix Farley's Journal*, 19 Jan. 1765, in W.J. Pountney, *Old Bristol Potteries*, p.229.
51. Three provincial shopkeepers' probate inventories are known, two are reproduced in full in D.G. Vaisey and F. Celoria, 'Inventory of George Ecton, Potter of Abingdon, Berks., 1696', *Journal of Ceramic History*, Vol. 7 (1974), pp.13–42, the originals are in the Bodleian Library, Oxford; also Lincoln Record Office, probate inventory of Richard Hargrave, March 1720/21, Wills 0. 2019.
52. British Museum, Sloane Ms. 857, No. 82.

53. S. Smith, 'Norwich China Dealers of the Mid-Eighteenth Century', *English Ceramic Circle Transactions*, Vol. 9 (1974), pp. 193–211.
54. J. Howell, 'William Absolon of Great Yarmouth', *English Ceramic Circle Transactions*, Vol. 10 (1980), pp. 314–33; R. J. Charleston, 'A Decorator of Porcelain and Glass – James Giles in a New Light', *English Ceramic Circle Transactions*, Vol. 6 (1967), pp. 292–316.
55. *Pigot's Directory* (1823).
56. L. Weatherill, 'Marketing English Pottery in Scotland, 1750–1820; A Study in the Inland Trade', *Scottish Economic and Social History*, Vol. 2 (1982), pp. 32–4.
57. Bodleian Library, Oxford, Douce Portfolio 139 (283). It was possibly a specimen pull for a trade card *c.* 1690–1700. See A. Oswald and R. G. Hughes, 'Nottingham and Derbyshire Stoneware', *English Ceramic Circle Transactions*, Vol. 9 (1974), pp. 140–89.
58. M. M. Edwards, *The Growth of the British Cotton Trade*, pp. 151–4.
59. British Museum, Sloane Ms. 857, No. 80 (N.D. – 1690s), 'Petition of the Company of Glass-Sellers to the House of Lords'.
60. J. Swift, 'Directions to Servants', (1745), in H. David (ed.), *The Prose Works of Jonathan Swift*, Vol. 13 (Oxford, 1959), p. 57.
61. F. Tyrer and J. J. Bagley (eds.), 'The Great Diurnal of Nicholas Blundell of Little Crosby, Lancs.', *Record Society of Lancashire and Cheshire*, Vol. 110 (1968), p. 262, he bought two dishes and two bowls for £1 4s. 0d. in 1710; Vol. 112 (1970), p. 260 for purchases in Liverpool in 1719.
62. *Newcastle Chronicle*, 12 Aug. 1775, Buckley, 'Advertisements', p. 79.
63. *Derby Mercury*, 7 April 1780; there is an account of this pottery in D. Towner, 'The Cockpit Hill Pottery, Derby', *English Ceramic Circle Transactions*, Vol. 6 (1957–59), pp. 254–67.
64. See, for instance, B. Hillier, 'Two Centuries of China Selling', *English Ceramic Circle Transactions*, Vol. 7 (1968), pp. 2–15.
65. R. Plot, *The Natural History of Staffordshire* (Oxford, 1686), p. 123.
66. These generalisations are fully documented in Lorna Weatherill, *Patterns of Consumption in Britain, 1670–1750* (London, forthcoming 1986/7).
67. The evidence about Bow and Longton Hall is very scattered and has been found by writers interested in collecting the wares produced. H. Tait, 'The Bow Factory under Alderman Arnold and Thomas Frye (1747–1759)', *English Ceramic Circle Transations*, Vol. 5 (1963), pp. 195–216; E. Adams, 'The Bow Insurances and Related Matters', *English Ceramic Circle Transactions*, Vol. 11 (1973), pp. 67–108, this corrects some points about the partnership. For Longton Hall, the original partnership papers have been found and the site excavated, B. Watney, *Longton Hall Porcelain*, pp. 52–64; H. Tait and J. Cherry, 'Excavations at the Longton Hall Porcelain Factory', *Post-Medieval Archaeology*, Vol. 12 (1978), pp. 1–29.
68. This dealing partnership dated back to the 1730s and Weatherby and Crowther seem to have tried, in the early 1740s, to interest more than one producer in North Staffordshire in the idea of making china. Their activities are, of course, very poorly documented, but they turn up again and again in advertisements, partnerships and sales accounts in the middle of the eighteenth century, giving the impression of all pervasive interests. Some of their activities are reported in P. Bembrose, 'Newcastle under Lyme: Its contribution to the growth of the North Staffordshire pottery industry, 1650–1800' (M.A. thesis, Keele University, 1973); A. R. Mountford, 'Thomas Briand – A Stranger', *English Ceramic Circle Transactions*, Vol. 7 (1969), pp. 87–99.
69. L. Weatherill, 'Capital and Credit in the English Pottery Industry', *Business History*, Vol. 24 (1982), pp. 243–58.

THE TRADING AND SERVICE SECTORS OF THE BIRMINGHAM ECONOMY 1750–1800

By ERIC HOPKINS

The term 'Industrial Revolution' has been in use in this country for about a hundred years, and still serves as a convenient short-hand expression for the manifold economic and social changes of the late eighteenth and early nineteenth centuries. Its shortcomings as a comprehensive description of economic change are well known, of course, and even among the initiated its repeated use may still help to emphasise industrial change at the expense of commercial change.[1] Yet as industry grew, commercial activity was directed not only to the sale of the increasing flood of manufactured goods, but also to meeting the needs of the expanding urban population, especially the need for housing, foodstuffs, and consumer goods, together with the wide range of professional, cultural, and leisure facilities which characterise urban life.

How far in fact the physical expansion of any one town was due to industrial growth, and how far it was caused by growth in the tertiary sector, is very difficult if not impossible to determine. There is general agreement among historians that trading and services were important but, so far, the argument has been conducted in very general terms, for example, analysing the constituent elements of the service sector under separate heads, or discussing the economic significance of service sector expansion in largely theoretical terms.[2] More oblique approaches have laid emphasis on the importance of commercial entrepreneurship, or have indirectly stressed the importance of retailing by postulating a consumer revolution in the second half of the eighteenth century.[3] A recent study has examined the extent of urban retailing in Cheshire.[4] What has been missing so far has been any investigation into the development of the trading and services sector of the larger industrial towns during the onset of the Industrial Revolution. The purpose of this article is to enquire into this aspect of economic growth in Birmingham in the second half of the eighteenth century – that is, to consider the evidence for growth other than in the well-known metal industries of the town. These industries constituted the economic heart of Birmingham, of course, but too often they have been allowed to monopolise the economic scene, to the exclusion of all other activities which cannot be subsumed conveniently under the heading of metal manufacture. Robert Southey's famous remark that every man he met in Birmingham stank of train oil and emery certainly suggested that he must either have directed his enquiries too narrowly to the metal industries, or not have had a very discriminating sense of smell as between one man's occupation and another's.[5] In fact, large numbers of men, women, and children were employed other than in the town's metal workshops in the early nineteenth century. The term 'trading and service sector' which is used here is employed so as to include principally building, retailing, transport of all kinds, the professions, entertainment and sport, cultural services and domestic service.

The general expansion of industry in Birmingham in the second half of the eighteenth century is well-established. Indeed, a substantial expansion was already in progress before the mid-century. Population increased rapidly from 1700 onwards, and it has been calculated that in the next 50 years it at least trebled and possibly quadrupled, and this at a time when the population of England and Wales increased by only 14 per cent. Only Sheffield can match the growth of Birmingham in this period, its population rising from less than 3,500 in 1700 to 12,001 in 1757. Building in Birmingham reached a peak in the years 1746–50, and was on an unprecedented scale.[6] In the second half of the century, industry continued to expand up to the outbreak of war against France in 1793, particularly in the toy, button-making, and brass manufacturing branches.[7] No doubt this expansion was facilitated by the improvement in turnpike and canal services, the latter improving not only the distribution of manufactured goods, but also making a vital contribution to industrial prosperity by reducing the cost of coal transported from Black Country pits and used in the town's furnaces. Birmingham was therefore at the height of industrial activity by the early 1790s, house-building booming to an extraordinary degree in the 1780s. It was said that the rate of building doubled after the conclusion of the war against the American colonists in 1783, and that whole streets were being erected, a complete street being built in less than two months. Hutton, the Birmingham historian, suggested that 'perhaps *more* are erected here, in a given time, than in any place in the whole island, London excepted'.[8] By this time Birmingham was acquiring fame as (in Burke's words) the 'toyshop of Europe', and also as the most important industrial town in the country outside London. One of the earliest national directories described it as 'deservedly considered the first manufacturing town in England', and one which was 'esteemed the second at present in England, for population and extent'; while Arthur Young went somewhat further in 1791 by calling it 'the first manufacturing town in the world'.[9]

Much of the building which took place was in the form of industrial premises or housing for industrial workers. Additional accommodation was also required for business premises, particularly in the food and drink trades, the clothing and furnishing trades, and for the professional services provided by doctors and lawyers. Increasingly Birmingham was becoming a regional centre which was made more accessible than before by the improvement in communications. The development of the canal system meant that Birmingham became the centre of the national network of inland waterways.[10] Thus Birmingham offered a wide range of services for an extensive area, both as a marketing centre for the manufactures of the Black Country and beyond, and as a centre for professional and cultural services. As Professor Wise has put it, 'a regional capital was in course of emergence'. This was not only in the industrial and commercial sphere for Birmingham's meat markets were also of great importance for farmers in the surrounding districts.[11] Any assessment of economic growth in Birmingham in the second half of the eighteenth century must therefore take into account an important amount of activity not associated directly with its own purely industrial expansion.

The problem, of course, is to locate sources which give an acceptable indication of this activity. Trade directories have shortcomings which are well known. Quite apart from the basic question of degrees of accuracy, the categories of occupations in directories may vary from edition to edition, and especially from one publisher to another. Again, the change in the numbers in any one trade do not necessarily indicate a change in the importance of the trade concerned; for example, a decline in the numbers of firms may be accompanied by an increase in the size of the remaining individual firms. However, having said all this, the numerous directories for Birmingham in the period 1760–90 nevertheless may be said to bear witness to the importance of trade in these years. Commercial expansion was naturally related closely to industrial expansion, each contributing to the other's growth, and as part of this growth there developed the building trades and the provision of foodstuffs, clothing, drink, books and stationery, legal and medical services. A start may be made with *Sketchley's Birmingham Directory* (3rd edition), 1767, which supplies the following information:

Building		*Woodworking Trades*		*Foodstuffs*	
Masons & bricklayers	20	Cabinet makers	12	Bakers	50
		Carpenters	9	Butchers	32
		Joiners	26	Grocers	50

Clothing		*Drink*		*Druggists*	*Booksellers*	*Printers*
Hatters	9	Publicans	294	11	7	7
Drapers	26	Malsters	32			
Milliners	10					
Peruke makers	54					
Shoemakers	47					
Tailors	64					

Attorneys	*Apothecaries & Surgeons*	*Others*	
21	20	Excisemen	7
		Gardeners	14
		Professors of the Polite Arts (mostly schoolmasters)	21

In addition, two important categories – factors and chapmen (20), and merchants (38), indicate the importance of middlemen, and of the export trade.[12]

In themselves, these figures are not especially significant, and indeed, they may occasionally be misleading: for example, Boulton & Fothergill, a leading firm of button-makers, are included by the compilers among the merchants, not the button manufacturers – a reminder that Matthew Boulton was engaged in exporting both his own and the goods of others as well as manufacturing. Yet trades and callings other than in the metal trades are as numerically important in the directory as many of the metal trades themselves. The number of drapers and mercers (26) is larger than the number of edge-toolmakers (10) – and the directory considers Birmingham to be the first town in the country for edge-tools – while there are more shoemakers (47) and tailors (64) than there are gun and pistol-makers (35) and brass-founders (32). It will be objected, of course, and quite rightly, that simple comparisons of this kind can give no indication of relative importance in terms of numbers employed or output; but the purpose at this stage of the argument is rather to draw attention to those parts of the local economy which are not directly concerned with the major metal-working industries of Birmingham, and to emphasise again that such industries cannot grow in isolation, and must be able to call on a variety of other services if they are to house, feed and clothe their workers, and market their products. Moreover, the continuing importance of some of the key non-manufacturing sectors is seen in the way in which they increased between 1767 and 1788. This is to be observed in particular in professional services, in the food trades, in furnishing and clothing fabrics, and (above all others) in the numbers of merchants and factors:

	1767	1788
Professional services		
Surgeons*	20	27
Attorneys	21	26
Food Trades		
Butchers	32	67
Bakers	50	66
Grocers and druggists	61	70
Drapers and Mercers	26	38
Merchants and Factors	38	133

* the 1767 figure includes apothecaries.

Sources: Sketchley's Birmingham Directory (3rd edition), 1767, and *Pye's Directory*, 1788.

By the early 1790s, according to the *Universal British Directory*, the number of bakers had risen further from 66 to 85, and the number of butchers from 67 to 86. The most common trade listed in this directory for Birmingham was that of victualler.

A survey of Birmingham insurance policies by the Sun Insurance Company of London in the year 1765 helps further to establish the relative importance of the manufacturing to the non-manufacturing sectors of the local economy.[13] The 76 policies were all of a modest size, the largest being for £2,000, taken out by William Welsh, Joseph Williamson, and John Startin, toymen and ironmongers of Snow Hill, who insured their warehouse for £250 and their stock for £1,750.[14] Eight policy-holders took out policies for sums amounting to £1,000 or more and, of these, three were not in the metal trades – Henry Venour and Abel Humphries, drapers, insured their house and stock for £1,500; Edward Ruston, druggist, insured his property and stock for £1,000; and William Harrold, draper, insured his stock and dwelling house in Moor Street for £1,500.[15] Of the 21 policies issued for premiums between £500 and £1,000, 11 were to the non-metal manufacturing sector, the majority being haberdashers, hosiers, cabinet makers and joiners.

A noteworthy feature of many of the policies, taken as a whole, is the provision for the insurance of small house property. Although details of the process of house building of the time are not known (for example, who were the actual builders, how much building land cost, what return on capital could be expected), it is still clear that the construction of new dwellings must have been on a very extensive scale. Further, it appears that house ownership was probably spread over a large number of owners, some of them manufacturers, others not. Thus, Charles Thompson, a corkscrew-maker, took out three policies (£800, £500, £500) covering 36 houses in all, together with three shops, stables and brewhouses.[16] Another policy-holder, Edward Thomson, a buckle-maker, insured as follows:[17]

Dwelling house	£200
Household goods	£80
A warehouse	£50
Stock therein	£50
A large shop	£50
House adjoining	£150
Another house	£170
Another house	£100
Two other houses	£150
	£1,000

The inclusion of house property in this way is not only an indication of the usual practice of the time of buying houses as a safe form of investment, but also again emphasises the importance of economic activity other than in manufacturing. Investment in housing was not confined to the more substantial policy-holders. Two bricklayers, Henry Gough and James Day, were also owners of houses. Gough insured four houses for £220, and a further four houses (let to a button-maker, chain-maker, butcher, and nailer) for £170. Day insured 11 houses and a school house, their values ranging from £65 to £15.[18] It may well be that these two bricklayers were really jobbing builders, and it is evident that neither house building nor homeownership was confined to the larger capitalist. Certainly the acquisition of land or buildings was popular with those seeking both security in investment and steady profits. William Hutton remarked in his journal for 1769, 'The purchase of land was a delight, a study, a profit. I have acquired by it more than £10,000. We saved this year £479.'[19] As a stationer and bookseller, Hutton was certainly not above supplementing his income by property deals when the housing market was so prosperous.

Of course, an investigation of policies issued in a period of only one year can be no more than a snapshot of insuring activity. Many larger insurers will inevitably be missing, and even those who are caught in the net may be insuring only part of their property. There was no Sun policy issued in 1765 to Matthew Boulton who had just completed his Soho works, costing (he claimed) £10,000. Nor was any policy issued at the time by the other well-known, but smaller, London company, the Royal Exchange, which in fact had very few Birmingham policy-holders. At the other end of the scale, Joseph Tirebuck of the Windmill Inn took out a small policy of £300 (£100 on his house, £100 on his household goods, £100 on his stables) but without cover for his stock, which might have been dealt with in a previous year. There is the further consideration that some manufacturers might have thought that their machinery or other fixtures and fittings were not subject to any great risk from damage from fire, and were simply not prepared to pay the necessary premiums. A survey of a longer period than one year will not get round the last difficulty, but at least widens the scope of the trawl and improves the chance of netting the bigger fish.

Thus, a review of policies covering the years 1777 to 1786 certainly provides some interesting additional information. In the first place, amounts insured above £2,000 are no longer exceptional, whereas in 1765 £2,000 was the maximum sum insured. In 1778 William Taylor, John Richards and Claude Johnson, button- and toy-makers, took out a policy for £7,000, and in 1783 William Taylor and John Richards took out another policy for £6,200.[20] But larger sums were not confined to button manufacturers. Bernard Sheppard, a mercer and draper, was given cover for £5,000 in 1778; another firm of drapers, Richard Peyton and George Cockle, took out a policy for £3,000 in 1781, while in 1786 a haberdasher, James Dicker, had two policies, one for £4,200 and one for £4,000 (perhaps one a replacement for the other).[21] In this ten-year period, therefore, more valuable properties were being insured than in 1765.

In the second place, although the largest policies were taken out by the button makers, the largest *group* of insurers were the mercers, drapers and haberdashers. Clearly, their stock was especially susceptible to damage from fire or flood, and had to be insured accordingly. Of the 115 policies for amounts of £1,000 or above, roughly two-thirds were issued to non-manufacturing insurers, this group including insurers denominated merchants or factors. Of the 303 policies for amounts of £500 and above, between a half and two-thirds every year were again taken out by non-metal industry insurers (see Table 1). They included insurers in the building and furniture trades; in the food trades (victuallers, grocers, bakers, butchers); in the clothing and soft furnishing trades (drapers, mercers, milliners, peruke-makers, breeches-makers, haberdashers, hosiers, shoemakers); in the beer, wine and spirit trades (innkeepers and brewers). Policies were also taken out by booksellers, stationers, and bookbinders; druggists and surgeons; and attorneys. When the whole range of policies is reviewed, it can be seen that well over half the policies fall into the trades and services sector.

The nature of the evidence makes it impossible, of course, to quantify exactly the division between the manufacturing element (more specifically, the brass-founders, button- and toy-makers, and the gunsmiths) and the rest. As noted earlier, some factors combined both industrial and commercial functions by employing outworkers and marketing their products, but for the purposes of this analysis they have been treated as non-manufacturing. Yet the impression is inescapable that at least half of Birmingham insurers over the period 1777–86 were not directly engaged in manufacturing. Or to put the same point another way, alongside the growing metal industries of the town there was an equally important trading and service sector which was vital to the development of Birmingham industrial society.

However, it may be questioned whether the policy evidence for Birmingham may not be distorted in some way so as to give an undue prominence to the non-industrial sector. It is instructive, therefore, to investigate the issue of policies over the same period in Manchester, Sheffield and Liverpool, and to compare results with Birmingham; see Table 2. Of these three towns, Manchester was a booming industrial centre by the 1780s. The number of policies taken out was rather larger than in Birmingham, and the number of policies for £1,000 and over was getting on for three times as great, with one quite extraordinarily large policy issued in 1786 to Robert Peel and associates, calico printers and merchants, for £61,000.[22] The most prominent group of insurers, as one would expect, were calico printers, manufacturers of various kinds of cloth (check, fustian, woollen, cotton, silk, linen, velvet), and dyers. Nevertheless, merchants, victuallers, warehousemen, grocers, timber merchants, and drapers were important groups, and collectively they accounted for between a third and a half of all policyholders.

Sheffield is perhaps a better town for comparison with Birmingham, because of its similar industrial organisation based on small workshops; but the number of policies over the ten-year period is markedly less than for Birmingham (well under half as many), and the policies of £1,000 and over considerably fewer. In this town, the typical manufacturer was a cutler, of course, but non-industrial policy-holders are again an important element, accounting for about half of all policy-holders.

TABLE 1

SUN INSURANCE COMPANY POLICIES ISSUED TO BIRMINGHAM INSURERS 1777–86

	1777	1778	1779	1780	1781	1782	1783	1784	1785	1786	Totals
Policies issued	72	70	94	72	90	66	33	49	73	74	693
Policies											
(i) below £500	42	42	48	38	43	34	18	35	52	38	390
(ii) £500–£900	18	13	26	24	30	23	8	10	16	20	188
(iii) £1,000 & and above	12	15	20	10	17	9	7	4	5	16	115
Trades & Services policies											
(i) in range £500 and above	23	14	27	20	30	23	10	6	12	20	185
(ii) over whole range	44	39	52	36	54	41	15	24	38	43	386

TABLE 2

SUN INSURANCE COMPANY POLICIES ISSUED IN BIRMINGHAM, MANCHESTER, SHEFFIELD AND LIVERPOOL, 1777–86

Birmingham

Year	<£999	>£1,000	Trades & Service Sector	Total
1777	60	12	44	72
1778	55	15	39	70
1779	74	20	52	94
1780	62	10	36	72
1781	73	17	54	90
1782	57	9	41	66
1783	26	7	15	33
1784	45	4	24	49
1785	68	5	38	73
1786	58	16	43	74
	578	115	386	693

Manchester

Year	<£999	>£1,000	Trades & Service Sector	Total
1777	44	16	23	60
1778	38	34	24	72
1779	32	15	17	47
1780	37	23	30	60
1781	37	25	25	62
1782	26	26	25	52
1783	24	18	17	42
1784	22	14	16	36
1785	63	67	46	130
1786	102	81	72	183
	425	319	295	744

Table 2 (contd)

Sheffield

Year	<£999	>£1,000	Trades & Service Sector	Total
1777	35	5	20	40
1778	35	12	19	47
1779	40	1	18	41
1780	32	6	20	38
1781	28	4	18	32
1782	24	4	11	28
1783	4	0	2	4
1784	11	1	9	12
1785	9	5	6	14
1786	24	1	13	25
	242	39	136	281

Liverpool

Year	<£999	>£1,000	Trades & Service Sector	Total
1777	64	21	38	85
1778	48	16	39	64
1779	43	20	33	63
1780	55	19	29	74
1781	54	19	34	73
1782	48	18	24	66
1783	27	14	19	41
1784	22	6	13	28
1785	44	13	24	57
1786	31	11	18	42
	436	157	271	593

Lastly, because Liverpool was not an industrial town in the same sense as the three other towns, in the event it proved impossible to make a useful comparison between the manufacturing and non-manufacturing elements, but the proportion of policies in the service sector to the total number of policies is just on a half: very similar to the figure in Sheffield, and not much different from the figure for Birmingham. The nature of the Liverpool policies is interesting. They covered a wide spectrum, ranging from mariners, boat builders, sail makers, and ship's chandlers to a surprising number of gentlemen and widows, with merchants emerging clearly as the group holding the largest policies. The largest policy of all was for £21,600, taken out by the merchant John Sparling, and there were 13 policies in all for sums of £5,000 and above: a testimony, one might think, to the mercantile wealth of the town. As in the other towns, carpenters, joiners and cabinet makers are noticeable, and so are grocers and drapers, although in rather smaller numbers than might be anticipated.

This comparison of Birmingham policy-holders with policy-holders in the three other fast-growing towns does not yield any very striking results, but it does establish that the proportion of non-manufacturing policies to the whole number issued in Manchester and Sheffield was not markedly different from the Birmingham figure; Sheffield is clearly the closest to Birmingham. It may be, of course, that in both towns there were many small firms which in this period still did not think it necessary to take out insurance, so that the total of insuring manufacturers is very much under-represented; but it must be reiterated that the point of the exercise is not severely statistical, but rather to emphasise the importance of those parts of the local economy not based on metal manufacture. Given this limited objective, it is suggested that the point is well made by a survey of the insurance data.

In what other ways may the importance of the non-metal sector be demonstrated? The most obvious comparison to be made is that between industrial and mercantile growth. As might be expected, no figures are available to show the increase in either domestic trade in Birmingham or in Birmingham exports for the second half of the eighteenth century. Nevertheless, there is enough qualitative evidence to illustrate the importance of both in this period. Foreign trade was of special importance to the larger Birmingham businessmen, particularly to those engaged in the toy trade. In 1759 it was claimed that this trade amounted to about £6,000,000 per annum, of which some £5,000,000 was exported.[23] This is almost certainly an exaggeration, but the letter books of Boulton & Fothergill, a leading firm of buttonmakers, show that the firm traded widely in Europe, with customers in Holland, France, Germany, Italy, Switzerland, Austria and Turkey.[24] In 1767 Matthew Boulton observed that 'more than half the letters we receive are wrote in the German language'. About this time his partner John Fothergill spent two years in Europe extending their trade contacts.[25] It is commonly said that by concentrating on goods which were valuable in relation to their size and weight, Birmingham gained world-wide markets before most other inland centres.[26] Hutton himself emphasised the importance of foreign trade for Birmingham, 'for the West Indies, and the American world, are intimately acquainted with the Birmingham merchant; and nothing but the exclusive command of the East India Company over the Asiatic trade prevents our riders from treading upon the heels of each other in the streets of Calcutta'. He added further 'To this modern conduct of Birmingham in sending her sons to the foreign market, I ascribe the chief cause of her rapid increase'.[27]

By 1812 the great importance of Birmingham's foreign trade was again being stressed, this time by witnesses before the Committee of the House of Commons appointed to consider petitions against the Orders in Council. It was then stated that 'Our trade to the United States of America would be about equal to what we call our home trade, England, Ireland and Scotland'. It was also claimed that about two-thirds of Birmingham manufacturers depended on foreign markets, the home market accounting for about a third of total sales.[28]

However, it is probable that earlier on in the 1760s and 1770s Birmingham's export trade was still only modest in extent. The national exports of non-ferrous metals and manufactures rose only slightly after 1762, then remained steady before declining during the War of American Independence. Only when peace returned in 1783 was there an improvement in the figures (mirrored, interestingly enough, in the numbers of policies issued in Table 2), and then a rapid increase towards the end of the 1780s. The same applies to exports of wrought iron and hardware.[29] Of course, all this is only suggestive: Birmingham's overseas trade did not necessarily conform to the national trends of the time, and in any case it is likely that a proportion of Birmingham's exports was smuggled abroad, avoiding official statistics altogether. All the same, the impression persists that Birmingham merchants' hopeful expectations of booming foreign markets in the earlier period were not always fulfilled. Boulton is a case in point: in 1782 he remarked of a traveller for the firm who had visited Russia and Poland, and had secured several thousand pounds' worth of orders which were never paid for, 'it is the same old story, a lack of remittances from abroad'. But by the beginning of the next century, there is no mistaking the importance to Birmingham of the export trade, and the evidence given in 1812 may not be far from the truth in rating it above the home trade.

It still remains a reasonable proposition that the home trade must have played a major part in the middle decades of the eighteenth century in the greatly increased economic activity in Birmingham. It has recently been argued that there was a consumer boom in England in the eighteenth century, and that 'in the third quarter of the century that boom reached revolutionary proportions'. It has further been suggested that the Birmingham toy trade was 'arguably the characteristic consumer industry of the commercial revolution'.[30] Certainly the button trade prospered in the 1780s, riding high on the fashionable demand for large buttons on tailcoats, breeches buttoned to the knee, and gaiters buttoned throughout their length. Marketing techniques became more sophisticated with the increasing numbers of middlemen or factors. In his evidence before the House of Commons in 1759, John Taylor, the leading Birmingham button manufacturer of the time, remarked on the mercantile chain stretching from the workshop to the village shop 'The master workmen sell to the factor, the factor to the merchant, the merchant to country dealers or shopkeepers in the large towns, who sell to the shop keepers of inferior rank in small towns and villages'.[31] Matthew Boulton is well known for his elaborate selling methods and direct promotion of his wares in London and elsewhere,[32] and indeed it has been argued that his concentration on selling was to the detriment of the efficient working of the Soho Manufactory.[33]

As the volume of trade increased, banking facilities also improved. Early in the eighteenth century, these services were provided by the more substantial tradesmen. According to Hutton, 'about every tenth trader was a banker, or retailer of cash. At the head of whom were marshalled the whole train of drapers and grocers'.[34] The importance of drapers and grocers in the business life of Birmingham has been noticed earlier on. They were the leading retailers in the growing towns of the time, and were relatively highly capitalised, both in the form of starting capital and in the substantial holding of stocks.[35] It is not surprising that Hutton gave them pride of place in his reference to informal banking. In 1765 the first Birmingham bank was set up by John Taylor, the button maker, and Sampson Lloyd II, the ironmaster, with a starting capital of £8,000. In 1770 they set up a further establishment in Lombard Street, London. In their first ten years the firm is supposed to have made annual profits averaging 45 per cent on capital, while in the 20 years from 1780 to 1800, the rate of profit on an augmented capital of £30,000 rose from about 16 per cent to 25 per cent. By the 1790s Taylor & Lloyd had been joined in the banking field by Coate's, Goodhall's and Spooner's banks. It has been estimated that by the end of the eighteenth century, the West Midlands had approximately one bank for each 12,000 inhabitants – a greater banking density than London, which had one bank for each 17,000.[36] Hutton himself seemed to think banking an excellent career for anyone aiming at financial and social success: 'I have seen a miserable cooper, not worth the shavings he made, place his son to a banker, and *his* son became a rich *banker*, a *member* and a *baronet*'.[37]

Another indication of the increase in commercial activity in the Birmingham area in the second half of the eighteenth century is to be found in the great improvement in transport services, and especially in coach services rather than the better-known canals, which carried raw material for industry and building materials rather than purely commercial traffic. In 1767 it appears that there was still only one regular London coach, running three times a week, together with two fly services. By 1785 the number of London services had jumped to six, while the total of all services to all parts was 28, running from seven inns. The speed of the London to Birmingham coaches also increased. Whereas in 1752 it took two days in summer and three in winter to complete the journey, in 1782 it took only 19 hours in summer and 22 hours in winter.[38] A newspaper report in July 1782 claimed that the journey was actually being accomplished in only 14 hours, but this must have been exceptional.[39]

Other indications of the growth of trade include the setting up of a Court of Requests, or small debts court, in 1752 for the recovery of debts of under 40 shillings. By a local act of parliament, 72 commissioners were appointed, three to constitute a quorum. The court sat every Friday morning, and if Hutton is to be believed, there were as many as 80 to 100 cases brought before it each week.[40] Bankruptcies were not uncommon, and disagreements over contracts and articles of partnership were sometimes taken to the London courts. Exchequer Bills and Answers of the period contain a number of cases stated by Birmingham orators (complainants), together with defendants' answers. They include bills presented by button-makers, bankers, japanners, and brass-founders. The causes of complaint were various, and might, for example, be based on the disputed distribution of a trader's estate; but differences over partnerships were rather more common. Thus, in 1798 William Brett and James Cole, button-makers, had ended their partnership and were at odds over the disposition of their machinery, valued at £1,430, consisting of lathes, figuring machines, presses, stamps and other articles.[41] These cases are a salutary reminder of the legal aspects of manufacturing and trading, and help to explain the increasing numbers of lawyers in Birmingham after 1760.

It must also be remembered that Birmingham businessmen were keenly aware of the need to act together in promoting their own commercial interests. They were not slow to lobby the House of Commons from time to time, as in 1759, over the bill to prohibit the export of buckle chapes, and again in 1798, appearing before the Committee of the House appointed to examine the decline in the copper trade. In 1812 the strongest representations were made to the Committee considering petitions against the Orders in Council. In 1783 they set up their own Chamber of Commerce, which became part of the London General Chamber of Manufacturers. Representations were also made to the government in 1785 on a number of matters, including Pitt's Irish trade proposals (Samuel Garbett, the chairman, twice waited on the prime minister), and again in 1786 on the Eden Treaty with France.[42] Local bills were also presented to set up their own Assay Office in 1773, and for the erection of a public proof house for guns in Birmingham in 1813. Employers were active in the passing of a succession of improvement acts in 1769, 1773, 1801, 1812 and 1828, giving powers to commissioners which were directed as much to the efficient working of the markets and goods traffic as to the improvement of the health of the inhabitants.[43] Thus, the importance of commercial considerations is again apparent.

Lastly, something should be said perhaps about the leisure activities of Birmingham in the second half of the eighteenth century. It is true that the town had no resident, leisured class at this time, and cannot be compared with London, Bath or York in this respect. Birmingham was never a so-called gentry town. All the leading residents were manufacturers, merchants, shopkeepers, publishers, bankers, physicians, and so on, all engaged in earning a living. Jane Austen makes her character Mrs Elton (always sensitive to the low connections of others) remark in *Emma* (published 1815), 'They came from Birmingham, which is not a place to promise much, you know, Mr. Weston. One has no great hopes from Birmingham. I always say there is something direful in the sound.' Certainly no one went to live there for pleasure. Yet it would be wrong to think of Birmingham as an intellectual desert – the existence of the Lunar Society is a sufficient disproof of this – and the leaders of the community were not simply interested in making profits to the exclusion of all else. In fact, there was a good deal of middle-class social activity centred on the theatre, clubs, assemblies, libraries and concerts. The first playhouse was opened in Moor Street in 1740, being replaced by another in King Street which gained its royal licence in 1807. Clubs were numerous, and took various forms: the best-known political clubs were at Freeth's Coffee House and at Joe Lindon's Minerva Tavern, while the freemasons established two lodges, known after 1784 as St. Paul's and St. Alban's. The Bucks copied the freemasons, while the Bean Club provided a meeting place for both the manufacturers of the town and the local landowners – another illustration of Birmingham's role as a regional centre. Weekly assemblies were held at the Royal Hotel, Temple Row. As for libraries, the Birmingham Library was founded in 1779, splitting in 1795 into the New and Old Libraries, the latter having 437 members. There were also eight or nine commercial libraries by 1800. The famous Birmingham triennial music festivals began in 1768 as a means of raising money for a general hospital. By the end of the eighteenth century the festival was making a profit of up to £3,000 from a three-day programme of music and a ball.[44]

Working-class leisure was enjoyed on a lower intellectual level, although this did not exclude attendance at the theatre in the gallery or pit.[45] The number of wakes (holidays lasting three or four days) seemed to have increased in 1750 and 1751 when in addition to the ancient wake in Deritend, two new wakes were begun, Bell Wake and Chapel Wake. These wakes were the occasion for much eating and drinking, cruel sports such as cock fighting and dog fights, and lewd sexual antics such as nude races. There were also two ancient fairs, in the Spring and in the Autumn. Most employers closed for a few days at Easter, Whitsun and Christmas, and also for stocktaking (Boulton & Fothergill took stock at Christmas). St. Monday, of course, was very firmly established, and a great occasion for heavy drinking.[46] The most important centre for working-class leisure activity was the public house, which was also the home of the large number of working-class clubs of many different kinds – building clubs, male and female sick clubs, watch clubs, clothes clubs, and (for the more serious-minded) debating societies. According to a mid-nineteenth century authority, the number of friendly societies registered with the Justices of the Peace amount to 213 in the period 1830–47, with a membership of at least 30,000. These more superior associations met once a month and held an annual dinner.[47] Thus, in spite of lengthy working hours, an important part of working class life (particularly of the lives of the better paid and more regularly employed) was given up to leisure pursuits.

In concluding this general survey of trading and service activities, some reference must be made to domestic service, one of the most important occupations in the town. Numbers engaged in this occupation at the end of the eighteenth century are not known, but 50 years later in 1851 domestic service was still the second largest occupational group in the country as a whole, and in Birmingham domestic servants were in that year nearly twice as numerous as either the button-makers or the brass-founders, and about three times as many as the gunsmiths.[48] It does not follow necessarily that a similar proportion of domestic servants was employed in 1800, but it seems unlikely that it would be very different; and it must be remembered that in addition there were pockets of personal service to be found elsewhere, as in the inns, and especially the coaching inns with their clerks and bookkeepers, waiters, porters, boots, ostlers, and stable boys.[49] Still other groups providing a more or less personal service in or about the house included grooms, coachmen, charwomen, washerwomen, and gardeners.

To sum up: since the eighteenth century the growth and prosperity of Birmingham have been based on the skills of its working people in the metal trades. The expansion of the metal industries in the second half of the eighteenth century is fundamental, of course, to the phenomenal development of the town; but this could not take place without a corresponding expansion of the trading and service sector. Hence the need for the building programme, the expansion of retailing, the network of factors and merchants, the speedier and more frequent coach services, the provision of banking and legal facilities, local newspapers, and so on. These developments were all closely linked. Obviously there is no question of discrete growth, but rather of each development being both a response and a trigger; industry, commerce and services grew in symbiotic relationship.

Of the many aspects examined, the housing boom and the increase in retailing stand out as having especial importance in the growth of the trading and service sectors in Birmingham. As regards the former, details are tantalisingly few; but enough has been said to indicate the scale of building after 1750, climaxing in the 1780s, and giving employment to numbers of bricklayers, slaters, glaziers, carpenters and simple labourers. As for retailing, the expanding population required more and more butchers, bakers, grocers, tea dealers, and a myriad of small-scale provision sellers and victuallers. A mass of petty traders operated in the street markets, where many and probably the great majority of working purchases were made.[50] Middle-class demand for clothing and furnishing fabrics is illustrated by the increased numbers of tailors, breeches-makers (listed separately from tailors in the later directories), mercers and drapers. In the late 1780s the shop tax levied in Birmingham was over twice the whole sum levied for the county of Cheshire.[51] By the early nineteenth century, a central shopping area was well established in the Bull Ring, New Street and High Street. All the houses in High Street were occupied as shops (save one house lived in by Mr Taylor, the banker), these houses trebling in value because of their use for retailing. One woollen draper, William Allin, having found his rent advanced over only a few years from £30 p.a. to £120 p.a., purchased the property for £3,000 and was then obliged to pay out £1,000 in repairs because the property was so old and decayed. He claimed that if it had not been used for trade, he would not have given £500 for it. Yet the premises were quite small: they consisted only of the shop (15′ × 12′), a small closet behind the shop used for keeping books, and four other rooms above. The yard was only 8′ × 9′, enclosed by high walls, with no outlet to the street, so that all deliveries had to be made through the shop. Premises as modest as these were evidently valuable if in a good position for trade.[52]

Exactly how important the housing, trading and service sectors of Birmingham's economy really were by the end of the eighteenth century as compared with the metal manufactures is clearly impossible to determine. In any case, it has been pointed out that it is not possible to separate the two growth areas completely: some leading manufacturers such as Matthew Boulton were expert salesmen of their own goods, selling direct to the public without always employing factors.[53] Nevertheless, the range of sources examined make it reasonable to assume that trading in particular constituted an extremely important part of local economic activity. Moreover, industrial prosperity was heavily dependent on a buoyant foreign trade, so that when foreign markets declined, Birmingham industry became very depressed. Thus the war with France which began in 1793 was regarded as ruinous to trade, and as a consequence it was said that the quantity of goods made in 1799 was no more than half what had been made in 1791. The result was a crop of bankruptcies, widespread unemployment and a severe, albeit temporary loss of population of some 4,000 souls.[54] It can scarcely be denied, therefore, that the trading and service sector was of major importance in Birmingham at this time.

It may be going too far, nevertheless, to suggest that this element in a town's economy played just as great a part in rapid urbanisation as industrial specialisation; or to assert, more specifically, that urban retailing 'was arguably as crucial for the growth of the new industrial centres as was technological innovation'.[55] In the case of Birmingham, technological innovation was noticeably absent in the period 1750–1800, and steam power was used on only a very minor scale before the 1830s. Consequently it cannot be claimed that the new technology was a primary cause of the great urban expansion of the second half of the eighteenth century; although the extended use of an improved hand technology based on the stamp and the press must have contributed to industrial growth in the middle decades of the century. However, it is quite clear that industrial growth in Birmingham began well before the classic period of the Industrial Revolution, and the urbanisation of Birmingham was accordingly different from the development of cotton towns based on the new spinning technology. It would seem somewhat dangerous to generalise too widely on the relationship between urbanisation, technological innovation and the trading and service sector, and equally hazardous to single out retailing as being as important to urban growth as technological innovation. The Birmingham evidence cannot be used to support either suggestion.

It is therefore better to see the advance of the trading and service sector in Birmingham as being within a broad spectrum of undifferentiated economic growth based primarily on the metal trades, but owing much at the same time to Birmingham's position as a regional capital distributing foodstuffs, manufactures and services over a wide area of the West Midlands. Dr Money has rightly said that the economic and social history of Birmingham was not set apart by any drastic discontinuity from the past; but his further contention that Birmingham and the West Midlands 'cannot advance any single obvious claim to significance in the affairs of the nation in the late 18th century' is surprising and surely open to question.[56] Not only was the Black Country iron industry revolutionised by the use of mineral fuel for smelting and by Cort's puddling and rolling process, making it the second largest area for iron production in the country by the early nineteenth century, but Birmingham itself became the first industrial city in Europe, well before Manchester; this certainly appears to give Birmingham a claim to significance in the affairs of the nation in the late eighteenth century.[57] In the remarkable century-long expansion of the town, industry, trade and the service sector marched together. It is true that it is difficult to demonstrate quantatively the contribution made by the trading and service sector to the growth of Birmingham's economy as a whole, but on the basis of the evidence discussed here there can be no doubt that it formed a substantial element.

University of Birmingham

NOTES

1. For a useful discussion of the implications of the phrase and the problems arising, see Allan Thompson, *The Dynamics of the Industrial Revolution* (London, 1973), especially Chapter I; M. Fores, 'The Myth of a British Industrial Revolution', *History*, 66 (1981); A.E. Musson, 'The British Industrial Revolution', *History*, Vol. 67 (1982).
2. R.M. Hartwell, *The Industrial Revolution and Economic Growth* (London, 1971), Ch. 10, 'The Neglected Variable: the Service Sector'; M. A. Katouzian, 'The Development of the Service Sector: A New Approach', *Oxford Economic Papers* (1970), pp. 362–82; T. Weiss, 'Urbanisation and the Growth of the Service Workforce', *Explorations in Economic History*, Vol. 8 (1971), pp. 241–58.
3. N. McKendrick, 'An 18th Century Entrepreneur in Salesmanship and Marketing Techniques', *Economic History Review*, 2nd series, Vol. 12 (1960), and 'Wedgwood

and Thomas Bentley: An Inventor-Entrepreneur Partnership in the Industrial Revolution', *Transactions of the Royal Historical Society*, Vol. 14 (1964); Neil McKendrick, John Brewer and J.H. Plumb, *The Birth of a Consumer Society* (London, 1982).

4. Ian Mitchell, 'The development of urban retailing, 1700–1815' in Peter Clark (ed.), *The Transformation of English Provincial Towns 1600–1800* (London, 1984). Retailing in the eighteenth century has not as yet been given much specialised attention, but see Alison Adburgham, *Shops and Shopping 1800–1914* (London, 1964); Dorothy Davis, *A History of Shopping* (London, 1966); D. Alexander, *Retailing in England during the Industrial Revolution* (London, 1970).
5. Robert Southey, *Letters from England* (London, 1807), quoted in B.I. Coleman (ed.), *The Idea of the City in 19th century Britain* (London, 1973), p.34.
6. C.W. Chalklin, *The Provincial Towns of Georgian England* (London, 1974), p.259; C.M. Law, 'Some notes on the Urban Population of England and Wales in the 18th century', *The Local Historian*, Vol. 10 (1972).
7. It is not the intention here to rehearse the evidence for industrial expansion in Birmingham in the second half of the eighteenth century, but see Conrad Gill, *History of Birmingham*, Vol. I (London, 1952), the Victorian County History for Warwickshire, Vol. VII, 'The City of Birmingham', and M.J. Wise, *Birmingham and its Regional Setting* (Birmingham, 1950), which give good general accounts. See also W.H.B. Court, *The Rise of the Midland Industries 1600–1838* (London, 1938), and the introductory chapters in G.C. Allen, *The Industrial Development of Birmingham and the Black Country, 1860–1927* (revised edition, London, 1966).
8. B. Faujas de St. Fond, *A Journey through England and Scotland to the Hebrides in 1784* (Glasgow, 1907), Vol. II, pp.348–9; W. Hutton, *History of Birmingham* (4th edition, Birmingham, 1809), p.71.
9. *The Universal British Directory* (1790–98); Arthur Young, *Annals of Agriculture* XVI (London, 1791), p.532.
10. See generally Charles Hadfield, *The Canals of the West Midlands* (Newton Abbot, 1966); VCH for Warwickshire, Vol. II, pp.33–4. W.T. Jackman, *Development of Transportation in Modern England* (London, 1962 edition) remarks rather quaintly that 'Birmingham was becoming the Kremlin from which canals radiated in all directions', p.370.
11. M.J. Wise, 'Birmingham and its trade relations in the early 18th century', *University of Birmingham Historical Journal*, Vol. 2, 1949–50; and *Birmingham and its Regional Setting* (Birmingham, 1950), p.180.
12. Broadly speaking, the term 'merchant' was used for firms trading abroad, while 'factors' traded at home: Nemnich, *Account of Birmingham* (Birmingham, 1802), p.104. However, while a factor was usually a wholesaler or middleman (see J. Drake, *Picture of Birmingham* (Birmingham, 1825), p.17, who describes the factor travelling the country with his samples), he might also be a co-ordinator of manufacturing processes in a number of small workshops, who would then sell either to a retailer or direct to the public.
13. London Guildhall Library, Sun Insurance Registers, MS/11936/158, Vols. 157–164.
14. Policy no. 218160, dated 27.3.1765.
15. Policies no. 221138, dated 28.6.1765; no. 223851, dated 23.8.1765; and no. 227190, dated 18.11.1765.
16. Policies no. 220802, dated 22 June 1765; no. 220803, dated 22 June 1765; and no. 220804, dated 24 June 1765.
17. Policy no. 217052, dated 12 Feb. 1765.
18. Policies no. 221313, dated 2.7.1765; no. 226998, dated 13 Nov. 1765.
19. Llewellyan Jewitt, *The Life of William Hutton* (London, 1872), p.184.
20. Policies nos. 399886 and 480543. The information in this and subsequent paragraphs relating to Sun Insurance policies is based on print-outs from the Social Science Research Council Survey Archives for these policies for the period 1777–86, the computer data being obtainable from the University of Essex, Wivenhoe Park, Colchester, Essex, CO4 3SQ. The help of Mr Ralph Bailey, University of Birmingham, in preparing the print-outs is gratefully acknowledged.

21. Policies nos. 404049, 451792, 96002, and 98018.
22. For some indication of the scale of this policy, see the analysis of policies issued in 1780 contained in Table 2 of L.D. Schwarz and L.J. Jones, 'Wealth, Occupations and Insurance in the late 18th century: The Policy Registers of the Sun Fire Office', *Economic History Review*, 2nd series, Vol. 36 (1983). The largest policy in this list is for £47,400, issued to a firm of brewers in Pimlico.
23. Journal of the House of Commons, 20 March 1759.
24. See for example, Boulton Papers, Boulton & Fothergill Letter Book, 1757–65.
25. Boulton Papers, ibid., and M. Boulton Copy Letter Book, 1766–68, letter 10 July 1767.
26. VCH for Warwickshire, Vol. VII, p.91.
27. Hutton, op. cit., 2nd edn., 1783, p.70.
28. Minutes of the Select Committee on Petitions against the Orders in Council, 1812, pp.10, 25, 27.
29. B.R. Mitchell and Phyllis Dean, *Abstract of British Historical Statistics* (Cambridge, 1971), p.294; Elizabeth Schumpeter, *English Overseas Trade Statistics 1697–1808* (Oxford, 1960), pp.25, 26; François Crouzet, 'Towards an Export Economy: British Exports during the Industrial Revolution', *Explorations in Economic History*, Vol. 17 (1980); N.F.R. Crafts, 'British Economic Growth 1700–1831: A Review of the Evidence', *Economic History Review*, 2nd series, Vol. 36 (1983).
30. McKendrick, Brewer and Plumb, op. cit., pp.9, 69.
31. Journal of the House of Commons, 20 March 1759.
32. E. Robinson, '18th Century Commerce and Fashion: Matthew Boulton's Marketing Techniques', *Economic History Review*, 2nd series, Vol. 16 (1963).
33. Eric Hopkins, 'Boulton before Watt: the earlier career re-considered', *Midlands History*, Vol. 9 (1984).
34. Hutton, 2nd edn., 1783, p.83.
35. Ian Mitchell, loc. cit., pp.275, 277.
36. Humphrey Lloyd, *The Quaker Lloyds in the Industrial Revolution* (London, 1975), pp.169–71, 175, 209; Rondo Cameron (ed.), *Banking in the Early Stages of Industrialisation* (London, 1967), p.26.
37. Llewellyan Jewitt, op. cit., p.297.
38. *Sketchley's Birmingham, Wolverhampton and Walsall Directory*, 3rd edn. 1767; Pye's *Birmingham Directory, 1785*; W.T. Jackman, op. cit., pp.684, 690.
39. J.A. Langford, *A Century of Birmingham Life* (Birmingham, 1868), Vol. I, p.298.
40. Hutton, 2nd edn., 1783, p.99.
41. Exchequer Bills and Answers, E112/2022.
42. J.A. Langford, *A Century of Birmingham Life* (2nd edn., Birmingham, 1870), pp.316–17, 319, 330; G. Henry Wright, *Chronicles of the Birmingham Chamber of Commerce, 1813–1913* (Birmingham, 1913), pp.11–26; Witt Bowden, *Industrial Society in England towards the end of the 18th century* (New York, 1925), pp.168–9. On the lobbying necessary to obtain a renewal of Watt's patent, see Eric Robinson, 'Matthew Boulton and the art of parliamentary lobbying', *Historical Journal*, Vol. 7 (1964), pp.209–29. For the lobbying of the 1780s, see John Mackenzie Norris, 'Samuel Garbett and the Early Development of Industrial Lobbying in Great Britain', *Economic History Review*, Vol. 10 (1957–58), pp.450–60.
43. VCH for Warwickshire, Vol. VII, pp.324–7.
44. For a detailed account of clubs and musical and literary activities, see John Money, *Experience and Identity: Birmingham and the West Midlands 1760–1800* (Manchester, 1977), especially Ch. IV, V and VI.
45. George Davis, *Saint Monday, or Scenes from Low Life* (Birmingham, 1790), pp.9, 10.
46. George Davis, op. cit.; Douglas A. Reed, 'The Decline of St. Monday, 1776–1876', *Past and Present*, Vol. 71 (1976); Eric Hopkins, 'Working Hours and Conditions during the Industrial Revolution: A Reappraisal', *Economic History Review*, 2nd series, Vol. 35 (1982); Douglas A. Read, 'Interpreting the Festival Calendar: Wakes and Fairs as Carnivals' in Robert D. Storch, *Popular Culture and Custom in 19th Century England* (London, 1982).
47. R. Rawlinson, *Report to the General Board of Health... on the Borough of Birmingham*

(London, 1849), pp. 44–5.

48. The figures are – domestic servants, 8,359; button-makers 4,980; brass-founders 4,914; gunsmiths 2,867. There were three other groups closely associated with the figure for domestic servants but recorded separately in the printed Census Returns – cooks (346), housemaids (354), and nursemaids (413). It has been estimated that in 1861, 40 per cent of the 150,000 workers in Birmingham were in service occupations: E. P. Duggan, 'The Impact of Industrialisation on an urban labour market: Birmingham, England, 1770–1860' (unpublished Wisconsin Ph.D. thesis, 1972), p. 226. The national figure for trade, transport, public services, and the professions as a percentage of the total occupied population in Great Britain has been estimated for the same year as 38 per cent: Peter Mathias, *The First Industrial Revolution* (2nd edn., London, 1983), p. 224. See also François Crouzet, *The Victorian Economy* (London, 1982), p. 70.
49. For personnel employed in coaching inns, see Harry Hanson, *The Coaching Life* (Manchester, 1984).
50. Alexander emphasises the growth of retail markets in industrial towns where the numbers of street traders were very large and their contribution to urban distribution very important: Alexander, op. cit., p. 233.
51. The amount levied for Cheshire appears to be on average about £250 in the late 1780s: Mitchell, op. cit., p. 271; the amounts levied for Birmingham for the three years of the shop tax are – 1786–87, £475. 10. 2; 1787–88, £573. 16. 2; 1788–89, £524. 15. 4; Exchequer records, E182/1062, part I.
52. Select Committee on the Shop Window Duty, Minutes of Evidence, 1819 (528) ii, pp. 13, 16.
53. Hopkins, op. cit., pp. 47, 54.
54. Nemnich, op. cit., p. 98; Langford, op. cit., Vol. I, pp. 305, 308, Vol. II, p. 2; George Yates, *An Historical and Descriptive Sketch of Birmingham* (Birmingham, 1830), p. 72; Southey, loc. cit., p. 34.
55. Clark, op. cit., pp. 25–6, 278. However, there is no doubt that the proportion of those employed in the service sector (considered in the broadest sense) did increase markedly between 1750 and 1850. Hartwell estimates this increase to be from about 25 per cent to about 40 per cent: Hartwell, op. cit., p. 212.
56. Money, op. cit., p. 275.
57. It is still often stated that Manchester was the first industrial city – see, for example, D. A. Farnie, *The English Cotton Industry and the World Market 1815–1896* (Oxford, 1979), p. 21 – but this seems to be due to the failure of historians of eighteenth-century Birmingham to emphasise the extent of industrial expansion which occurred there well before the technological revolution in spinning took place. As already noted, the population of Birmingham grew very markedly in the first half of the eighteenth century, and was still larger by about 8,000 than the population of Manchester in the early 1770s.

MATTHEW BOULTON AND JOSIAH WEDGWOOD, APOSTLES OF FASHION

By ERIC ROBINSON

Boulton and Wedgwood were face and obverse of the same medal, and while Wedgwood declared that *Artes Etruriae renascuntur*, Boulton might just as well have claimed that *Artes Corinthiae resurgent*. Moreover this resemblance was explicitly recognized by the two men themselves and by others in their society. Thus, in a letter to Boulton of 1771, in which he referred to Boulton's project for mounting Wedgwood's vases in metal, Wedgwood said: 'You flatter me very agreeably with your desire to unite the powers of Corinth and Etruria.'[1] In the same letter Wedgwood had referred to a certain 'Mr Antipuffado' in the *Public Ledger* who was bracketing them together:

> If you take in the Public Ledger you'l see Mr Antipuffado has done me the honor to rank me with the most *stupendous genius's* of the Age and has really *set me up very clearly*. He talks too that he should not wonder if some enterprising Genius at Birmingham should be tempted to make *Roman medals*, and *tenpenny nails*, or *Corinthian Knives* and *Daggers* and stile himself Roman medal and Etruscan tenpenny nail maker to the Empress of Abysinnia.

Wedgwood similarly advised Bentley not to write in reply anything that would anger Antipuffado, 'for I think he will do us more good than any *real puff* we could have contriv'd, I am well pleased too that I am not cut up & mangled by the hands of a dull rogue.' Wedgwood continued:

> I should have no objection to the Public being acquainted *in some way or other* that I have not directly nor indirectly been concern'd in the publication of these or any other paragraphs upon the subject, except the advertisements with my name affixed to them. What you have been so kind to send me wo.^{d} be a very proper reply, but in my present way of thinking I wo.^{d} not repeat the word *puffing*. It wo.^{d} give me the idea of a person fretting and fumeing in repeat.^{g} a *pointed* word so often after another who had been abus.^{g} him; besides I wo.^{d} not methinks take such *direct notice* of any word or *mode of expression* made use of by Antipuffado but I have not time to consider or say much upon the subject at present & leave the whole to my dear fr.^{d} & beg he will do & say just what he thinks proper.[2]

Thus Antipuffado saw Boulton and Wedgwood as manifestations of a similar spirit of emulation in the age, and, if he had wished, he might have added the name of others who shared this spirit, for it is clear that, though

Wedgwood and Boulton have been singled out by modern commentators as the principal exponents of new techniques of salesmanship and as leaders of the fashion business in their separate fields, they were not the isolated figures that their own self-estimates tended to suggest. By understanding the spirit of these two men, however, we may begin to appreciate more fully the implications of fashion for commerce in the second half of the eighteenth century.

Almost from its beginnings the eighteenth century witnessed a striking increase in fashion-consciousness. The growth of the periodical press, the greater frequency with which periodicals of all sorts appeared, the growing international market in books and magazines all combined to spread the taste for innovations. Whereas in the seventeenth century the French court, the international centre of fashion, had been content to see its influence spread by the *Almanack Royal*, which appeared annually, or by the *Mercure Galant*, which was published once every six months, by the last quarter of the eighteenth century the French journals, the *Galerie des Modes*, the *Cabinet des Modes* and the *Magasin des Modes* were all appearing at frequent intervals and being read widely throughout Europe.[3] Even in the English fashion-journals, the rapidity of change became so marked that it has occasioned surprise to modern historians. Thus we are told that: 'The *Lady's Magazine* of March 1774 advises the wearing of small drop earrings, but by July it is so important to wear no earrings at all that the news is put into capitals'.[4]

The world of fashion was accordingly already international: it was promoted by the printed text and the colour plate, by *les fameuses poupées*, those elegant dolls dressed in the latest style which circulated from court to court, and had its devotees not only among the itinerant aristocrats of the Grand Tour but also below stairs among the footmen and the maids. In the *St. James' Chronicle* for 1763, for example, one writer makes fun of the tradesmen who ape their betters by wearing 'myriads of gold buttons, and loops, high garters, shoes, overgrown hats' and he even speaks of a smith in 'a coat loaded with innumerable gilt buttons'. Well might we say, with Alexander Pope, that 'the whole Heart was nothing else but a Toy-shop'.[5] Thorstein Veblen's world of conspicuous consumption was already in full flood and it is to that world that Matthew Boulton, a Birmingham button-maker, and Josiah Wedgwood, a Staffordshire potter, responded, along with a multitude of lesser-known men who breathed the same air. Birmingham and the Black Country, with their hundreds of small workshops, like the pot-banks of Staffordshire, were geared to the demands of a fashionable market having innumerable gradations determined by social status, by price and by national or regional taste.

II

Let us first examine how Boulton and Wedgwood reacted to the hegemony of France in so many areas of fashion. The whole of Boulton's *ormoulu* trade was conceived in a spirit of patriotic opposition to France which in the mid-eighteenth century had a total monopoly of this sort of manufacture, a monopoly similar to that which it had previously enjoyed in the manufacture of certain types of gilt buttons and buckles until the 1740s and 1750s. Boulton is even found warning his son about the insidious dangers of the Parisian world of fashion:

> There is some danger in a young Englishmans head becoming giddy by the pagentry of Courts & the Folly of Fashion for in proportion to the predominence of those things good sense & good taste dwindle although there is as much difference between the one & the other as there is between water Gilding & Solid gold. It seems to be agreed on all hands that Germany is the place to make a *Man* & Paris the place to make a *Man of Fashion* (i.e. a Gambler & a Rake).[6]

This seems an odd note to be struck by one whose business was fashion, but anti-Gallicanism was particularly strong in the English at this period and was reinforced by a puritanism among members of the middle classes which anticipated the prudery usually associated with the reign of Victoria. In Boulton's character such contradictions between commercial conduct and professed principle were not unusual. His feelings of business rivalry towards the French, however, may be demonstrated by a letter to the London jewellers, Woolley and Heming:

> we are not in the least envious at seeing any of our Countrey men endeavour to rival us, it is not them we mean to oppose, but the Paris Artists who certainly have hitherto rival'd us & all the world in Elegance & cheapness of such like Ornaments they have Chacers at half the price they work for in London they can Gild better & cheaper. So that we think they are not easily rival'd unless by the plan we have form'd the Essentials of wch are cheapness good taste & good execution.[7]

The catalogues prepared for the sales of Boulton's *ormoulu* at Christie's lay great stress upon the patriotic not to say mercantilist nature of Boulton's rivalry with French manufactures, and in his correspondence with aristocratic patrons he himself emphasises his desire to interest 'such of the Nobility and Gentry as are Judges & promoters of the endeavor *of british artists*'.[8]

His friend, James Keir, in helping to prepare the catalogues, commented: 'I have omitted mentioning that you are content to work without profit for the advantage of your Countrymen; because, in these days, such an instance of disinterestedness would not be credited, and if it was, would rather excite admiration of your generosity, than of your understanding'.[9]

Samuel Smiles in his life of Wedgwood quotes a letter from Wedgwood to Bentley in which the potter expressed a similarly nationalistic attitude: 'And do you really think that we might make a complete conquest of France. Conquer France in Burslem? My blood moves quicker; I feel my strength increases for this conquest. Conquer France by pottery ware!'[10] That such an assault by crockery and vases actually struck terror into the hearts of France is doubtful, but that Boulton's and Wedgwood's commercial rivalry with France was reinforced by military and commercial conflict between England and France and by mercantilist principles is beyond question. France was to be both emulated and invaded. Thus in 1767, while discussing with Boulton an approach made to Lord Cathcart, British ambassador to St. Petersburgh, to persuade him to promote the sale of Wedgwood's wares in Russia, Wedgwood proudly announced that Lord Gower was in the process of sending a large table service to Paris.[11] It is clear that to British manufacturers the chance of selling in Paris was like an opportunity granted to a Welsh tenor to sing at La Scala, Milan.

In England, the Low Countries, in the German principalities, in St. Petersburgh and in France itself, good taste was French taste, and a manufacturer of fashion goods ignored French standards at his peril. Both Boulton and Wedgwood managed, to a minor degree, to sell to French merchants but such success as they had was mostly in less expensive goods. Thus Wedgwood tried to persuade Eden to obtain some concessions in the duties on the import of certain species of earthenware into France, saying:

> that our manufacture may now, in the present situation of the English and French bear such a duty may be true to a certain degree; but how long has that been the case? It is within my memory that the earthenwares of France were superior to ours; the revolution, therefore, has been sudden, and its effects may be temporary; the same circumstances, whatever they have been, that turned the scale in our favour in this age, may, in the next, vary as much in favour of France.[12]

But for other countries the manufacturer had to learn to adapt his wares to the taste of the particular region. As Boulton informed Mrs Montagu, it was 'not necessary to attend to elegance in such articles of my manufacture as are destind for Siberia and America, or even some parts of Germany; but rather to the bad taste of those countrys and to adapt my self to every Clime'.[13] Even at home in England it might be desirable from time to time to suggest that French taste was not always beyond reproach. Accordingly Boulton told the Earl of Findlater:

> some of thes[e] said drawings will serve also to shew the difference between my Ideas of Ornament and those generally adopted by the French, yet I am far from being partial to my own – My dealings with the World are too general to permit it. I only wish to excell in the execution of that Taste which my employers most approve whether it be French, Roman, Athenian, Egyptian, Arabesk, Etruscan or any other, but in any and all of these I w.[d] have Elegant simplicity the leading principal whereas in my opinion such of the *Orfèvre* of the French as I have generly seen is *trop chargé*.[14]

Wedgwood too adapted his wares to different national markets. He told Bentley in 1772 that he was considering making his pottery of 'as bright a *Straw colour* as possible: This would be just the thing the Russians and some of the Germans want, and perhaps not a disagreeable change and *distinction* for our own Nobility and Gentry'.[15]

The hard commercial facts were that both Boulton and Wedgwood could not afford to rely solely upon the home market if they were to benefit from economies of scale. Although they both sold cheaper wares that reached the homes and affected the furniture and apparel of the middle classes, the fashion world was still the world of the palace, the chateau and the country-house, and since high fashion must always cater to the singularity of taste of its patrons, both men needed a wider clientele than could be provided at home. So Boulton told Lord Cathcart, the British ambassador to St. Petersburgh:

> one Country is not a large enough Markett for Commodities which can be bought only by Persons of Elegance & Fortune nay the demands of our Country wou'd scarce be sufficient to pay the Expences of making our original Models If I was to carry this branch of our Manufacture as high as my Ideas w.^{d} lead me.[16]

Only a few months earlier Wedgwood had complained to his partner:

> Seriously, we must either find some new markets, or new Warehouses, or turn off some of our hands, which I should be very sorry to do as they are not easily made for our purpose. Many of our Ships I see by the Papers are sailing for the East Indies, and never a Vase or Bass relief on board![17]

In the early stages of Wedgwood's and Boulton's friendship, one of the factors drawing them together was Boulton's more extensive knowledge of foreign markets. He and his father before him had traded to Italy and the Low Countries since about 1748, while Boulton's partner, John Fothergill, had been apprenticed in Königsberg and had been a traveller in France and Italy. It seems to have been Boulton that introduced Wedgwood to Lord Cathcart and thus opened up the possibilities of export to Russia.[18] In 1776 Fothergill told Wedgwood that Boulton 'having paid the Empress many compliments, both in Sculpture and Painting', their firm had considerable interest at the Court of St. Petersburgh and were proposing to replace the French in the gilt trade there. They were thinking of sending out their own agent and wondered whether Wedgwood would like to share his services.[19] According to Wedgwood, Boulton and Fothergill's *ormoulu* trade, most of which was abroad, was flourishing exceedingly, and in particular they had sold 200 Venus and Adonis clocks at 25 guineas a piece.

There seems to be in several of the pronouncements made by Boulton and Wedgwood a new tone, something unprecedented in the history of commerce both of Britain and of the world. While Wedgwood adopted his title, not altogether unserious, of 'Vase Maker extraordinary to the

Universe',[20] Boulton's vision of himself was parallel. His early statement to Watt that 'it would not be worth my while to make for three countries only; but I find it well worth my while to make for all the world',[21] is typical of other declarations by him both before and after 1769. In 1767 he told his agent in Italy, Wendler, that he wished to know the taste and the fashions of all the different parts of Europe since he wanted 'to work for all Europe in all things that they may have occasion for in Gold, Silver, Copper, Plated, Gilt, Pinchbeck, Steel, Platina, Tortoishell or anything else that may become an article of consequence'.[22] Twenty years later he was still speaking the same language:

> I think I shall publish in some of the German papers some account of my new Coining Machine which is one of the most ingenious, most Mechanical, & most philosophical I ever invented; & the most perfect & I doubt not but in time it will be adopted by *all the princes on Earth* who coin money.[23]

Wedgwood's correspondence with Bentley is salted with similar statements:

> I have lately had a Vision by night of some new Vases, Tablets &c with which Articles we shall certainly serve the *whole world*![24]

> The third plan is to begin in my new works upon the White ware Sir William Meredith has for some years past been advertiseing for me, and which the *WORLD* has so long and so *IMPATIENTLY* expected at my hands.[25]

> I hope to bring the whole in compass for your next Winters shew and ASTONISH THE WORLD ALL AT ONCE, For I hate piddleing you know.[26]

and in connection with his cameos that they would 'be fine enough to set the rings, and all the world will wear them'.[27]

Undoubtedly semantic problems sometimes arise in connection with these references so that we cannot always be certain whether the writer is referring to the geographical world or to the world of high fashion, *le beau monde*. For the manufacturer of fashion goods, however, it is the international world of high fashion which is his market so that for him, in one sense, *le monde* and *le beau monde* are synonymous. How far Boulton and Wedgwood represent aspirations shared by other entrepreneurs in their period, how far their statements are original to themselves, or how far the one infected the other are difficult questions, but there is an uncanny parallel between their statements both about this and about other matters.

III

In England itself the tone of fashion was largely set by London, although London in turn might be influenced by Paris. The London season, extending from October or November to Easter, was a phenomenon easily recognisable at least since the beginning of the seventeenth century. For the London season the Spitalfields silk-weavers produced each year their new designs,[28] and the Birmingham toy-makers their buttons, buckles, patch-boxes, snuff-boxes, chatelaines, watches, watch-seals, necklaces, ear-rings, hair-combs and a mass of other jewellery. Dr Evans' remark that 'the sequence of style can be better studied in the nineteenth-century in the ornaments set with less precious stones than in diamond jewellery' ought surely to be applicable to the eighteenth century also.[29] So far as the Birmingham and Black Country toy trade was concerned, it too 'was an age not of great movements in art, that might find fitting expression in the cost of previous materials, but rather of passing fashions that had their greatest influence on jewels that were frankly a part of dress'.[30] Buttons and buckles were produced in an almost infinite variety of materials, shapes and ornaments. Sketchley's *Birmingham Directory* for 1767 says of button-making:

> This Branch is very Extensive, and is distinguished under the following Heads viz. Gilt, Plated, Silvered, Lacquered and Pinchbeck, the beautiful New Manufacture Platina, Inlaid, Glass, Horn, Ivory, and Pearl: Metal Buttons, such as Bath Hard and Soft White, &c. there is likewise made, Link Buttons in most of the above Metals, as well as of Paste, Stones, &c., in short the vast Variety of sorts in both Branches is really amazing.

The greatest button-maker of the age was John Taylor, whom Wedgwood met around the same time that he first encountered Boulton, although Wedgwood thought Taylor to be a man of meaner spirit than Boulton. Taylor died in 1775 when the button craze was at its height but had already made a fortune of £200,000. It is estimated that the value of the weekly produce of buttons alone at his works was at one time not less than £800 a week. As early as 1762, the competition of Birmingham toy-makers for the London market was cut-throat. Fothergill told Boulton that a London jeweller, Cantrell, had been besieged by different button-makers who 'had been with him like so many Wolves for orders'.[31] Boulton was continually writing to London customers offering to match the prices of any of his competitors in buttons.[32] Care had to be taken to introduce the buttons early in the season if they were to sell well. Thus on one occasion Boulton wrote to Perchard, a London customer, about some buttons: 'we are sorry they were introduced so late in the Season as we doubt not but it would have been to our mutual advantage had they appear'd sooner'.[33] Novelty was the essence of this trade, so that Wedgwood's cameos were grist to the mill of the Birmingham button-maker, one among many of the variations that fashion demanded, but important in establishing a stronger link with the antique taste then prevailing.

The historian of jewellery is very severe on this cut-steel jewellery of the later eighteenth century, describing it as 'the nadir to which the jeweller's art sank in the century that saw the dawn of the Industrial

Revolution'.[34] However that may be, and one suspects that the reaction is not unaffected by the art historian's traditional suspicion of the machine-made object, Boulton's and Wedgwood's co-operation was capable of producing some very fine objects, such as a sword-hilt and a tiara in the Lady Lever Art Gallery. The idea of mounting cameos and intaglios seems to originate in a letter from Wedgwood to Bentley dated 1771:

> I mentioned bracelets, rings and seals to her [Mrs Francis Crewe, a fashionable beauty, friend of Fox, Burke, and Sheridan] with which she seemed much delighted, and to these I think we may add Gemms to be set in snuffbox tops, such as the Cupid and Psyche, &c. or a favourite head, and I finished some of these ready for the oven yesterday – For snuffboxes and Bracelets I mean.[35]

The attractions of these cameos were underlined in the Wedgwood and Bentley catalogue of 1779:

> Cameos and Intaglios
>
> These are exactly taken from the finest antique Gems. The *Cameos* are fit for Rings, Buttons, Lockets and Bracelets; and especially for inlaying in fine Cabinets, Writing-Tables, Bookcases, &c. of which they form the most beautiful Enrichment, at a moderate Expence; the Price of the Cameos, with *several Figures* being *ten times less* than any other durable Imitations that have even been made in Europe; and the Figures are much sharper than in those that are made of Glass.
>
> The Ladies may display their Taste a thousand Ways, in the Application of these Cameos; and thus lead Artists to a better Stile in ornamenting their Works.[36]

The appeals are to price, quality and fashion, to self-interest and self-esteem. The first Soho settings of these cameos as buttons were shown in Wedgwood's London rooms in 1772,[37] and in the winter of 1772 and the spring of 1773 Boulton bought more cameos for setting in vases, lockets and bracelets. Boulton and Fothergill at this period were doing a lot of work in tortoiseshell and some cameos were used in this way: 'we make very pretty Tortoishell Goods as Boxes, Instrument & Toothpick Cases inlaid in a new tho' Antique tast'.[38] Surprisingly, however, apart from one or two patterns in the Boulton pattern book[39] there appear to be no other recognisable references in the letter books of Boulton and Fothergill to these Wedgwood settings. Meanwhile, in 1772, Henry Clay of Birmingham began his *papier mâché* manufacture and Wedgwood had the idea of persuading him also to use the cameos. Four years later, in 1776, Wedgwood told Bentley:

> I told you I would endeavour to push the Cameos into a wholesale channel whilst I was in Birmingham, but I had very little time there. However, I mentioned to Mr Boulton, and Mr Clay the idea of suiting the Cameos for different Markets by making the Heads of

> their eminent Men – But they both told me that the French are so much superior to us, both in Paper and Tortoishell Boxes, that they have not much expectation in those articles (unless in very cheap paper Boxes) from any market where they have the French for their Rivals. So you must do what you can in this time with the French Box makers.[40]

Nevertheless Clay did set cameos in three sets of dressing-boxes. 1773 seems, in fact, to have been the boom year for these settings of cameos in cut-steel. In the week of 18 May 1773 Wedgwood supplied 50 dozen seals to Birmingham,[41] on the 7 June 1773 Soho was asking for more for setting in boxes, lockets, bracelets, etc.,[42] and in the same month there was a 'hue and cry' for them in Buxton,[43] so that the demand for them seemed very healthy. Other Birmingham toy-makers, besides Boulton and Fothergill, were setting the cameos during the same period so that it may be difficult, if not impossible, to determine which were made by Boulton. The trade went on at least until 1786 when Wedgwood was still trying to promote the trade with Boulton and Fothergill.[44] Despite our limited knowledge of the trade we can be sure that it lasted from 1772 to 1786 at the very least; that it was in part undertaken by Boulton and Fothergill and other Birmingham toy-makers, such as Boden and Smith; and that Wedgwood also sold cameos mounted by Boulton and Fothergill on his own account.[45] The cameos were copied by other toy-makers. One who tried to buy a complete set of them was told by Wedgwood that he 'must take care not to sell him a set of models for a *few shillings*, which had cost me, besides time & labor, more than *twice as many guineas*'.[46]

The good-tempered rivalry between Boulton and Wedgwood can be seen in the same letter where after telling Boulton that he was going to make some small improvement in cameo buttons and warning him not to 'run away with a little Hobby Horse which you saw your friend pleased with having got a stride upon', Wedgwood adds a postscript: 'I refus'd an offer the other day of making my fortune by being concern'd in a partnership for making steam engines, of a new improv'd construction, & by patent.'

The first hint of suspicion that Boulton might attempt to make ceramics in competition with Wedgwood occurs quite early in the correspondence between the two men. At the beginning of 1768 Boulton ordered from Wedgwood vases for mounting which Wedgwood did not like to refuse;[47] in November of the same year Wedgwood told his partner:

> Never give yourself any pain about Mr Watt or the blue-neck Vases you apprehend are travelling this way. We are far enough before our rivals, and when ever we apprehend they are *trading too near our heels*, we can at any time manage them better than Lord Bute can manage the Merchants – to compare great things with small.[48]

Wedgwood did not care to refuse co-operation with Soho for fear that Boulton would turn elsewhere, to Samuel Garbett, for example,[49] and since sometime that same year, perhaps July 1768, Cox, the jeweller, had visited Soho and reported that Boulton and Fothergill were buying vases from other potters and were proposing to manufacture black vases themselves.[50]

Once again fashion was the impetus. A craze for ornamental vases after the antique, prompted in general by the Grand Tour and sharpened by the rediscovery of Etruscan art, led to a demand for simple neo-classical forms. This demand was met not only by Wedgwood's Etruscan painted cases but also by the Blue-John vases of Matthew Boulton. The slighting remark made by Wedgwood to the effect that 'those customers who were more fond of show & glitter than fine forms & the appearance of antiquity wo^d^. buy Soho vases, and that all who could feel the effects of a fine outline & had any veneration for Antiquity wo^d^. be with us'[51] should not be accepted uncritically, as the Matthew Boulton Pattern Books in the Birmingham Reference Library suffice to show. Wedgwood, Boulton, Cox and others were all profiting from the same movement of fashion, and differed in materials rather than in design. It might also be pointed out that Boulton's ware would show off better by candlelight and Wedgwood's would be more telling by day. The contrast was parallel to that which has been observed in jewellery:

> Moreover, the development, both in England and France, of country-house life, which was sharply divided between relatively simple outdoor pursuits by day and the elegance of salon life by night, established a distinction hitherto unknown between jewels intended for daytime wear and those intended for display by candlelight.[52]

IV

Boulton and Wedgwood both used the London newspapers for series of planned advertisements, both obtained puffs from newspaper proprietors, both opened showrooms, and carefully cultivated the royal family, the aristocracy, ambassadors, architects, actors and actresses, and indeed anyone who could be of use to them. If Wedgwood had his Queensware, Boulton had his King's Vases. If Boulton employed Flaxman, then Wedgwood did likewise. If Boulton sold his goods by auction at Christie's then Wedgwood had a sale at Cobb's. Wedgwood took the idea of printed catalogues from Boulton, but he could no doubt have found others using the same method. Fashion was in the air, and salesmanship was becoming increasingly geared to the fashionable market. Boulton and Wedgwood both sought out '*lines, channels and connections*', not because they were being brilliantly original but because patronage was the normal system of the age. As Professor Perkin has well said: 'For those who lived within its embrace it was so much an integral part of the texture of life that they had no name for it save "friendship".'[53]

In this highly involved system of vertical relationships, fashion helped both to strengthen the hierarchical system of status and at the same time to persuade members of the middling classes and even of the lower orders that they could at least to some extent imitate their betters. At the apex of the social system and of fashion was the Court. All principal Court occasions created opportunities for fashion. Perhaps the most significant of all was Court mourning which took place as frequently as the very frequent royal deaths. In the Williamson letters for 1748–65 we read, concerning the death of Princess Caroline in 1758: 'Everybody that think themselves anybody wear deep mourning and at court all belonging to it chamois clothes', and on the death of of George II in 1760:

> My wife hath bought this morning 28 yards of crape for it is equally worn with bombazine and by people of the best fashion ... Note as the mourning is meant to be as deep as possible women's hats are plain black silk with crape round the crown with a bow-knot and their silk cloaks of the genteelest should be garnished at the bottom with ditto [hatband] crape, not with love ribbon .... On Sunday all the world is to be in black.[54]

For those who were dealing in black goods, such occasions were a splendid windfall: for others it was not so welcome as Boulton's partner, Fothergill, found when he tried to sell plated buttons in 1765 just after the death of the Duke of Cumberland,[55] or in 1772 when George III and Caroline mourned the death of the Dowager. On that occasion, Boulton wrote:

> The King and Queen sat up all last night with the Dowager and are under great afflictions at her death. It is supposed there will be 6 Weeks mourning and 6 weeks Second mourning. It will be a real mourning to many of the Silk Mercers and the Spittlefields Workmen and it will also be some disappointment to me in my new Buttons. The Play Bills were taken down again today and no diversions will be open next week.[56]

The Spitalfields silk trade seems to have been particularly vulnerable. Miss Rothstein tells us of a letter in the *Universal Spectator* for 24 April 1731 in which there was a long complaint about court mournings and the trouble they caused to the silk industry, because 'what new blacks are bought are generally Italian and Dutch manufactures to the discouragement of our own'.[57] The Spitalfields silk-weavers also petitioned George III in 1768 to reduce the period of Court mourning, and marched through London with bands and flags to a service of thanksgiving when the king agreed.[58] What was a loss to Boulton and to Spitalfields was a source of great profit to the makers of black satin shoes, black gloves, black scarves, black silk cloaks and black millinery in which there was even a large export trade to America.[59] Nor were the toy-makers of Birmingham slow to adapt to the same demand by producing black necklaces and earrings and other funereal toys. What applied at the level of royal mourning, also applied to the ceremonies of private families. When Sophie von la Roche visited England in 1786 she commented: 'The spectacle of a party of women riding through this radiant countryside in mourning, with bands of crepe on their hats, impressed us strangely, as in our own land mourning is discarded in the country'.[60] Thus it was not the nineteenth century alone which saw a growth in the market for funeral goods and it was not only in the nineteenth century that the Birmingham coffin-furniture trade, for example, saw a considerable expansion.

To revert, however, to the royal family, happier occasions there were also celebrated. Royal birthdays not only inspired the poets to Birthday odes,[61] but gave an impetus to other trades. Lady Mary Wortley Montagu wrote to Anne Justice on 3 February 1711 'a full Account of that Important Busynesses, Dresse, which is at present much talk'd off against the Birth night where every body is endeavring to outshine the other'.[62] These occasions were sometimes used by the Royal Family deliberately to stimulate domestic industry:

> Sunday, 11th August 1754, being the princess Augusta's birthday, the princess of Wales, and all the princesses, appeared in curious hats of fine thread needle-work, on book-muslin, to encourage the waring it, as it employs a great number of poor girls, who else would be burthensome to the public.[63]

Boulton and Wedgwood were therefore not pioneers in making profit from such royal occasions. At these times the fashion-magazines illustrated the dresses in engravings,[64] gentlemen bought gala suits[65] for which Boulton, for example, supplied special buttons to eminent leaders of fashion,[66] the ladies watched for the lead set by the *bon ton*, and to a greater or lesser extent these fashion-manifestations of the royal birthday are observable throughout the eighteenth century and to a much later period. If Wedgwood's use of 'Uniques' was, as McKendrick has said, 'entirely for their advertising value' and 'could never go into general production'.[67] Boulton's presents of buttons and buckles on royal birthdays were made with immediate commercial ambitions: 'many of our new buttons were wore at Court on the birthday and I believe we shall sell a large quantity'.[68] It was exactly the same intention as he expressed when he made similar presents unconnected with the Royal birthdays. In 1772 he felt that foreign competition was cutting back his export trade so that it was necessary to recoup on the home market, and he wrote to Lord Clermont:

> Hence we are induced to wish to extend our Sales in our own Country which can only be done by the Spirit of Novelty and the example of persons like you. We therefore take the liberty of laying before you a few new patt.^{s} which will not come to half the price of french gold thread Buttons and sh^{d} esteem it as a Singular fav^{r} if you w^{d} do us the honour of setting an example and promoting the wear of them amongst y^{r} friends – thus Fashion will be establish^{d} to the emolument of our own Country and particulary to y^{rs} &c.[69]

The same letter was sent to Sir Lawrence Dundas, the Hon. Henry Seymour, Lord Kerry, the Hon. Col. Charles FitzRoy, the Earl of Aylesford, Lord Milbourn, Viscount Beauchamp, Lord Mount Stuart, the Duke of Richmond, Lord Sefton, Sir William Bagot, Sir Harbord Harbord, the Count de Scarnassis, and the Count de Welderen.

But memorial jewellery was a fashion peculiarly strong in Britain,[70] a factor which Wedgwood and Bentley recognised when they declared in their 1779 catalogue that:

> We beg leave in this place to observe, that if Gentlemen or Ladies choose to have Models of themselves, Families, or Friends, made in Wax, or engraven in Stones, of proper sizes for Seals, Rings, Lockets, or Bracelets, they may have as many durable Copies of those Models as they please, either in Cameo or Intaglio, for any of the above Purposes, at a moderate Expence.[71]

Mrs Crewe had cameo heads of her sons made,[72] Richard Lovell Edgeworth a cameo head of his wife, Mrs Honora Edgeworth, and a few other cameos were clearly made for commemorative purposes of a personal rather than a public nature; the cameo was a more durable, and an aesthetically preferable, substitute for the silhouette. A greater part of both Wedgwood's and Boulton's work, however, was concerned with commemorating public occasions: royal birthdays we have already mentioned, but there was no event of any importance in the later eighteenth century that one or other of them did not celebrate with a piece of plate, a medal, a printed teapot or a cameo.[73] In 1776, Wedgwood, having visited Boulton and Fothergill, wrote to Bentley: 'They are now preparing a complementary Group with a proper Inscription, upon the death of the Grand Duchess. You see they have carried *into execution* what we have only *talked about*, and will proffit by it, so surely as Princes love flattery'.[74] Boulton's medals on the Otaheite expedition, the death of Marie-Antoinette and Louis XVI, the victory at Trafalgar, followed the same policy and ran parallel to Wedgwood's commemorative pieces.

The custom practised by both men of naming their wares after distinguished people – such as Wedgwood's Queensware, or Boulton's King's Vases, or Wedgwood's Devonshire flower-pots – was much more extensively practised in the same period by the dress-makers, milliners, and wig-makers. There was, for example, the Garrick wig,[75] the Rutland gown (named after the Duchess of Rutland), the Gordon handkerchief, the Spencer hat (named after Lady Charlotte Spencer),[76] Otaheite tippets,[77] Otaheite handkerchiefs,[78] the Robinson gown (named after Perdita Robinson), Werther, and even Lunardi, hats (named after the balloonists):[79] 'These balloon fashions are about their zenith and must soon burst and be forgotten'.[80] Tile-makers made blue-painted fire-place tiles with figures of the celebrated actors and actresses of the day, Garrick, Mrs Yates and others.[81] The theatre clearly had an immense effect upon fashion, then as now, and there is no reason to suspect that either Boulton or Wedgwood was particularly original in responding to it. It should be said, however, that Boulton, who was largely instrumental in securing a theatre for Birmingham and was a personal friend of Mrs Sara Siddons, probably knew the theatre a little more intimately than Wedgwood.

The openness of English society in the later eighteenth century can be seen from the pervasiveness of fashion-consciousness through the different ranks of society. Domestic servants naturally copied fashions first because they had access to styles and perhaps to rejected garments, but they were soon buying new clothes in the style of their masters and mistresses. Dr Evans speaks of a report from a smart English sea-side resort at the end of the century that: 'All are dressed alike, mistress and maid'.[82]

> The Ladies Maid well immitates
> The Mistress in the Fair o',
> The Footman with his Curling Irons
> To Buckle and Curl her Hair 'o'.[83]

The gradations of society were codified in 'a whole protocol' of shoe-buckles. They were made in every size and in every material from diamonds to paste, from gold to pinchbeck, and Boulton sold to all levels of society and to both men and women.

> The vanity of the great will ever be affecting new modes, in order to increase that notice to which it thinks itself exclusively entitled. The lower ranks will imitate them as soon as they have discovered the innovation .... The pattern is set by a superior; and authority will at any time countenance absurdity. A hat, a coat, a shoe, deemed fit to be worn only by a great grandsire, is no sooner put on by a dictator of fashions, than it becomes graceful in the extreme, and is generally adopted from the first lord of the Treasury to the apprentice in Hounsditch.[84]

Dress was the first area to show those 'present whims of the Town', which Henry Fielding defined as taste, but architecture, gardens, furniture, carriages and a thousand other matters in their own time-sequence eventually came to show themselves. The ritual of tea-and-coffee-drinking requires silver among the aristocracy but 'humble Staffordshire clay' for the middling classes, although the better sorts of china may be used to reflect the patterns of the hangings or even Wedgwood's black basalt to set off the whiteness of a lady's hands. At the beginning of the century, Pope wrote in 'The Rape of the Lock':

> Now, when declining from the Noon of Day,
> The Sun obliquely shoots his burning Ray;
> When hungry Judges soon the Sentence sign,
> And Wretches hang that Jurymen may Dine;
> When Merchants from th'Exchange return in Peace,
> And the long Labours of the *Toilette* cease –

The Board's with Cups and Spoons, alternate, crown'd;
The Berries crackle, and the Mill turns round;
On shining Altars of *Japan* they raise
The silver *Lamp*, and fiery Spirits blaze:
From silver spouts the grateful Liquors glide,
And *China's* Earth receives the smoking Tyde:
At once they gratifie their Smell and Taste,
While frequent Cups prolong the rich Repast ...

At the end of the century, the pattern had not changed, only more were sharing in the delights of Fashion than ever before, and men like Boulton and Wedgwood had themselves become household names. Only in the fuller context of the social history, however, can such men be adequately appreciated, and until we know more about the commercial activities of their precursors and contemporaries, we should be cautious in our estimates of their innovating abilities.

University of Massachusetts

NOTES

The intention of this article is to continue the discussion started by N. McKendrick, 'Josiah Wedgwood: An Eighteenth-Century Entrepreneur in Salesmanship and Marketing Techniques', *Economic History Review*, 2nd series, Vol. XII, No. 3 (1960), pp. 409–33 and E. Robinson, 'Eighteenth-Century Commerce and Fashion: Matthew Boulton's Marketing Techniques', *Economic History Review*, 2nd series, Vol. VXI, No. 1 (1964), pp. 39–60.

1. Wedgwood to Boulton, 19 Feb. 1771, Assay Office Library, Birmingham, hereafter contracted to AOLB.
2. Houghton Library, Harvard. Wedgwood to Wedgwood and Bentley, Great Newport Street, London, 11 Feb. 1771. This letter makes it clear that Wedgwood is unlikely to have been deterred, as Mr McKendrick suggests he was, from newspaper advertisement by Antipuffado's piece.
3. M. Braun-Ronsdorf, *The Wheel of Fashion* (London, 1964), p. 11.
4. J. Evans, *A History of Jewellery 1100–1870* (London, 1953), p. 174.
5. Alexander Pope, 'A Dream of a Window in His Mistress's Breast', *Guardian*, No. 106, 1713.
6. M. Boulton to M. R. Boulton, 8 June 1787, AOLB.
7. Boulton and Fothergill to Messrs. Woolley & Heming, 19 Jan. 1771, Boulton and Fothergill Letter Book 1771–73, AOLB.
8. Draft letter, 27 March 1771, for distribution to potential customers, Matthew Boulton Letter Book 1768–73, AOLB (my italics).
9. James Keir to Boulton, ? 1771, Keir Book, AOLB.
10. S. Smiles, *Josiah Wedgwood* (London, 1905 ed.), p. 148.
11. Wedgwood to Boulton, 19 March 1767, AOLB.
12. Wedgwood to Eden, 30 June 1786, in A. Finer and G. Savage (eds.), *The Selected Letters of Josiah Wedgwood* (London, 1965), p. 298.
13. Boulton to Mrs Montagu, 18 Jan. 1772, AOLB.
14. Boulton to the Earl of Findlater, 20 Jan. 1775, AOLB.
15. Wedgwood to Bentley, 18 April 1772; Finer and Savage, op. cit., p. 121.
16. Boulton to Lord Cathcart, 30 Oct. 1771, Boulton and Fothergill Letter Book 1771–73, AOLB.
17. Wedgwood to Bentley, 10 April 1771, Finer and Savage, op. cit., p. 105.

18. Eliza Meteyard, *The Life of Josiah Wedgwood* (London, 1865), 2 vols., Vol. II, pp. 55–6 asserts that Boulton and Fothergill began in 1768 to export Wedgwood pottery to Cadiz and to the Baltic ports on their own account.
19. Ibid., p. 195.
20. Smiles, op. cit., p. 137.
21. Boulton to Watt, 7 Feb. 1768, AOLB.
22. Boulton to Wendler, July 1767, M.B. Letter Copy Book 1766–68, AOLB.
23. Boulton to M.R. Boulton, 26 Oct. 1789, AOLB (my italics).
24. Wedgwood to Bentley, 6 Nov. 1768; Savage and Finer, op. cit., p. 68 (Wedgwood's own italics).
25. Wedgwood to Bentley, 18 April 1772, Ibid., p. 121 (Wedgwood's capitals).
26. Wedgwood to Bentley, 6 Aug. 1775, WMSS. E. 18614-25, op. cit., McKendrick.
27. Wedgwood to Bentley, 30 July 1773, Finer and Savage, op. cit., p. 151 (Wedgwood's italics).
28. Nathalie Rothstein, 'Nine English Silks', *Bulletin of the Needle and Bobbin Club*, Vol. 48, Nos. 1 and 2, New York, 1964, p. 6 and 'Silks for the American Market', *Connoisseur*, Nov. 1967, p. 150. Also P.K. Thornton, *Baroque and Rococo Silks* (London, 1965), p. 18 *et seq*.
29. J. Evans, op. cit., pp. 192–3.
30. Ibid.
31. J. Fothergill to Boulton, 7 May 1762, AOLB.
32. For example, Boulton and Fothergill to Jno. Perchard, 27 March 1765, Boulton and Fothergill Letter Book 1764–66, AOLB.
33. Boulton and Fothergill to Jno. Perchard, 6 Aug. 1771, Boulton and Fothergill Letter Book 1771–73, AOLB.
34. J. Evans, op. cit., p. 181.
35. Finer and Savage, op. cit., p. 114.
36. W. Mankowitz, *Wedgwood* (London, 1953), p. 214. See also plates 1, 96, 97 and 98.
37. Eliza Meteyard, op. cit., Vol. II, p. 400.
38. Boulton and Fothergill to William Evill, 30 Dec. 1772, Boulton and Fothergill Letter Book 1771–73, AOLB. See also tortoiseshell box with Wedgwood cameo, Lady Lever Art Gallery.
39. Matthew Boulton Pattern Book, Birmingham Reference Library.
40. Wedgwood to Bentley, 14 July 1776; Finer and Savage, p. 195.
41. Wedgwood to Bentley, 18 May 1773; ibid., p. 149.
42. Wedgwood to Bentley, 7 June 1773; ibid., p. 150.
43. Wedgwood to Bentley, 23 June 1773; ibid., p. 151.
44. Wedgwood to Bentley, 14 June 1786, AOLB.
45. Ibid.
46. Ibid.
47. Wedgwood to Bentley, 3 Jan. 1768; Meteyard, op. cit., Vol. ii, p. 78.
48. Wedgwood to Bentley, 6 Nov. 1768; Finer and Savage, op. cit., p. 68.
49. Wedgwood to Bentley, 21 Nov. 1768; ibid., pp. 68–9.
50. Wedgwood to Bentley, ? July 1768, Wedgwood MSS, 1103, Ryland's Library, Manchester: also Wedgwood to Bentley, 27 Sept. 1769; Meteyard, op. cit., Vol. ii, pp. 212–16.
51. Wedgwood to Bentley, 24–26 Dec. 1770; Meteyard, op. cit., Vol. ii, p. 22.
52. J. Evans, op. cit., p. 163.
53. H. Perkin, *The Origins of Modern English Society 1780–1880* (London, 1969), p. 49.
54. *Williamson Letters 1748–65*, Bedford Historical Record Society (1954), pp. 2, 63–4; cf. Lady Verney (ed.), *Verney Letters of the Eighteenth Century* (London, 1930), 2 vols., Vol. ii, p. 127.
55. Fothergill to Boulton, 2 Nov. 1765, 3 Nov. 1765, and 23 Dec. 1765, AOLB, and Boulton to Fothergill 26 Dec. 1765, AOLB.
56. Boulton to Mrs Boulton, n.d. 9 Feb. 1772, AOLB.
57. N. Rothstein, 'Dutch Silks – An Important but Forgotten Industry . . .', *Oud Holland*, Vol. 79, (1964).

58. G. Rudé, *The Crowd in History* (New York, 1964), p.72.
59. The Grand Congress of Philadephia, 8–11 Oct. 1774, resolved: '... and on the death of any relation or friend, none of us, or any of our families, will go into any further mourning dress than a black crepe or ribbon on the arm or hat for gentlemen, and a black ribbon and necklace for ladies; and we will discontinue the giving of gloves and scarves at funerals'. *Lady's Magazine*, Dec. 1774.
60. Clare Williams (trans), *The Diary of Sophie von la Roche, 1786* (London, 1933), p.2.
61. For example, *Lady's Magazine*, June 1774, June 1776, and Dec. 1777.
62. R. Halsband (ed.), *The Complete Letters of Lady Mary Wortley Montagu* (New York, 1965), Vol. i, p.71.
63. *Lady's Magazine*, Sept. 1774, *The Retrospective Chronicle*, Aug. 1754.
64. *Lady's Magazine*, Feb. 1781: 'Fashion in High-Life. Embellished with an elegant Engraving of the PRINCESS ROYAL, in the Dress which she appeared in on the QUEEN'S Birth-day and at her Majesty's private Ball'.
65. G. Hill, *A History of English Dress* (London, 1893), 2 Vols., Vol. i, p.150.
66. Boulton to Fothergill to Col. Charles FitzRoy, 7 Nov. 1771, AOLB; Boulton to Moussin Pouschkin, 14 Dec. 1771, AOLB.
67. Op. cit., p.414.
68. Boulton to Mrs Boulton, 13 March 1772, AOLB.
69. Boulton to Lord Clermont, 8 Jan. 1772, AOLB.
70. J. Evans, op. cit., p.179.
71. Mankowitz, op. cit., p.228.
72. WMSS. L.H.P. JW to TB, 2 Sept. 1771; cited by McKendrick, op. cit., p.414.
73. McKendrick, op. cit., p.422.
74. Wedgwood to Bentley, 14 July 1776, Finer and Savage, op. cit., p.195.
75. J.T. Smith, *Nollekens and his Times* (London, 1828).
76. *Lady's Magazine*, Jan. 1780.
77. Ibid., July 1774.
78. Ibid.
79. *Morning Herald and Daily Advertiser*, 18 Sept. 1784. Of the fashions inspired by the Montgolfier brothers in France: suits à la Montgolfière, hats, parasols, canes, coiffures, all à la Montgolfière. S.T. McCloy, *French Inventions of the Eighteenth Century* (Kentucky, 1952), p.16.
80. *Gazetteer and New Daily Advertiser*, 19 Feb. 1784.
81. F.P. Hett (ed.), *Memoirs of Susan Sibbald, 1783–1812* (London, 1926), p.15.
82. J. Evans, op. cit., p.16.
83. *The Roxhurghe Ballads reprinted by The Ballad Society* (1869–80), 8 vols. Vol. III, p.776.
84. *British Magazine*, 1763, Vol. IV, p.417: cited by Perkin, op. cit., p.94.

FINANCING THE FRENCH NAVY IN THE SEVEN YEARS WAR: BEAUJON, GOOSSENS ET COMPAGNIE IN 1759

By J.F. BOSHER

Late in 1758, a year of distress in the French empire, the government of Louis XV took the unusual step of hiring merchant bankers to assist in financing the navy. Who they were, what they did, and how they failed to stave off bankruptcy in October and November 1759 makes an interesting short chapter in the history of the French navy, of the Seven Years War, and of the Bourbon monarchy.

In Bourbon France financing and banking were two related but different fields. Financiers dealt in government funds and the basis of finance was tax returns. From tax returns came the interest on financiers' venal offices, the reimbursement of funds they advanced to the government, the interest paid on these advances, the funds held by financiers and invested until required, and the credit permitting financiers to borrow and to speculate in business. The basis of banking, on the other hand, was trade in money as well as in merchandise. The banker was customarily a merchant who specialised in advancing money to other merchants in various ways and who expected interest on loans, commissions on services for distant correspondents, profits on discounted bills of exchange, premiums on marine insurance policies, and returns on investments in ships, goods, naval supplies, sugar refineries and other ventures. Financiers, too, might invest in all these ventures; merchant bankers (*marchands banquiers*), especially rich and ambitious ones, might buy financial offices; but banking and finance were nevertheless two quite different fields.[1]

The French navy was financed for the 20 years 1750 to 1770 by two financiers, the Treasurers-General for the Navy and their employees in Paris and the seaports. Before 1750 and after 1770, these financiers also financed the colonial services of the government, but in 1749 two new offices of Treasurer-General for the Colonies were created and sold to new men, so that during the Seven Years War the colonial administration was separately financed, even to the point of employing separate treasurers's agents at such major naval bases as Rochefort.[2] One of the motives for this separation was a desire to draw upon the services and the credit of four financiers rather than two, the War of Austrian Succession (1743–48) having imposed a severe strain on naval and colonial finances. As a result, the Secretary of State for the Navy and Colonies began to draw up separate tables of naval expenditure (*états de distribution*) to send to the Intendants of the naval bases, who spent the funds, and to the naval treasurers, who supplied them.

These new arrangements left the financing of the navy unencumbered by colonial financing and in experienced hands, for the two Treasurers-General who had both been in office since the early 1740s were not interfered with. During the odd-numbered years, 1755, 1757 and 1759, naval financing was managed by Marcellin-François-Zacharie de Selle (1704–59), a member of a large rich old clan of financiers which had been in naval financing for at least two generations before his. He had bought his office in 1740 from his father, Florent-Marcellin de Selle (1667–1743), and when he died in 1759 it was assumed by a first cousin, César-Luc-Marie de Selle de la Garéjade (1723–81). Garéjade spent his first three years, however, settling his late cousin's accounts and did not manage current naval financing until 1763. In other words, by a special arrangement the year 1761 was managed by the other Treasurer-General whose proper business was the naval financing for even-numbered years, 1756, 1758, 1760 and 1762. This was Louis-Barthélemy Moufle de Géorville, who had bought his office in 1743 from a relative, Barthélemy Moufle de la Tuilerie, and both had descended from notaries of Paris and Chartres of the early part of Louis XIV's reign, members of a large clan to be found in many parts of the royal service. In 1756, when Louis XV declared war on Great Britain, he can hardly have had two sounder financiers than these. Yet even with the colonial financing removed the naval service proved to be too much for the two Treasurers-General. Their failing credit was shored up by the banking firm of *Beaujon, Goossens et Compagnie* for eight months in 1759, but bankruptcy was imminent when one of them, de Selle, died suddenly on 15 October 1759, the day the government suspended the colonial bills of exchange; and de Géorville died a ruined man on 24 January 1764, a few months after the end of the war.[3]

The French navy's difficulties might perhaps be expressed accurately in figures by a professional accountant trained in eighteenth-century methods, for many reports and summaries survive in the archives, even though the principal accounts appear to have perished.[4] For my part, I have to confess a failure to see any relation between figures from different sources. I am not alone in this, however. Accounting for the sums raised and spent is a historical problem now because it was a practical problem then, as the Secretary of State for Foreign Affairs explained with reference to 1758:

> When the business of the navy, always unknown to the King's Council (the ministers entrusted with this department had long decided everything together with the King without even seeking the opinion of his council); when, I say, the inside of that administration was brought out into the open, the whole council trembled at an administration so vicious in its financial part; no accounting, no order, bills of exchange drawn on the Royal Treasury to pay expenditures of which the accounts were drawn up only several years after; the Intendants entitled to authorize payments as well as to review expenditures; in a word, a chaos, a chasm of abuses and of

> false administrative principles. It is not surprising that a machine so badly built almost perished.[5]

The confusion we find in the figures was inherent in the very system. We cannot be certain of naval accounts now any more than eighteenth-century ministers could then.

That said, we may again quote Cardinal de Bernis, who believed that in 1757 the navy spent some 60 million *livres* 'without paying a *sou* on its former debts, nor the greater part of current expenses'.[6] But according to another set of figures only 39 million *livres* of this were actually provided.[7] There was already a large deficit and it was seen as a serious problem. 'Where', asked de Bernis in January 1758, 'shall we find new financial resources?' In the course of 1758, some 42,370,149 *livres* were in fact found for the navy, but it spent no less than 55,306,482 *livres*.[8] In October, the Fontanieu Commission appointed to settle naval debts reckoned them at over 42 million of which 27 million had accrued since the beginning of the war.[9] In discussing the navy's financial difficulties it is usual to cite as an explanation a decision the royal *Conseil d'En haut* took in 1756 to give priority to the war on the European continent, but this seems unsound because the army was certainly no better off than the navy.[10]

The problems were deeper than mere priorities. By 1758 the war in all its theatres was being fought on credit, not only the organised credit of the Estates of Brittany, Languedoc and other provinces, but the short-term, haphazard, private credit of the government's financiers, including the Treasurers-General for the Navy.[11] As early as 1750, indeed, they had raised a loan of four million *livres* that was still outstanding in 1758 by which time the accumulated interest totalled nearly two million *livres*.[12] In 1758 the Treasurers-General and their agents in the ports were being pressed for more and more payments at a time when they could not recover their money by the usual method of negotiating *rescriptions* drawn by the Receivers-General of Finance on their own agents in provincial towns. The correspondence of Laurent Bourgeois, naval treasurer's agent at the small ports of Lorient and Port Louis, shows him advancing more and more of his own and his friends' money to settle naval debts with such merchants as Robert Dugard of Rouen, whose sailors, he reported, 'have been in the most frightful misery for a long time'.[13] By October 1758 he was desperately begging for funds and quoting his own advances in thousands of *livres*. His personal predicament reflected a general situation. On 11 July 1758 the Intendant of Finance charged with assigning tax revenues to the spending departments wrote, 'Our poor navy is already in enough disorder by its inability to cope with an infinity of essential payments, without the severe obstruction that the lack of 298,000 *livres* would cause us'.[14] The ministers were particularly alarmed at the enormous sums the colonial intendants were drawing in bills of exchange. If these bills were ever to be suspended, the Secretary of State for Marine and Colonies wrote to the Controller-

General of Finance in February 1758, the navy would be discredited and unable to carry on for lack of funds.[15]

It was in the difficult circumstances of 1758 that the firm of *Beaujon, Goossens et Cie* were called in to assist in financing the navy. In March, under the name *Michel, Beaujon et Goossens*, they signed a contract with the Secretary of State, Peyrenc de Moras, to lend the navy 1,500,000 *livres* and Moras reported this agreement to de Selle on 10 March.[16] On 25 March, de Selle gave the firm ten promissory notes for 150,000 *livres* each, notes that were to be cashed in repayment of the loan, one each month from January to October 1759. As it turned out, four of these notes had not been honoured by 15 October 1759, the day de Selle died, but even before the first of them was due the government made a much bigger contract with the firm. On 27 December 1758, *Beaujon, Goossens et Cie* undertook to advance the navy three million *livres* a month throughout the year 1759, and half a million a month to the fortification and engineering services which served the naval ports in various ways. Then, on 7 February 1759 they undertook to advance another two million directly to the Royal Treasury, making a total of 44 million of which 36 million were earmarked for the navy.[17] The firm was to advance these sums in the form of commercial bills of exchange drawn on their agents in the ports to order of one of the Treasurers-General, and it was to recover its funds by receiving and negotiating *rescriptions* of the Receivers-General of Finance and notes of the General Farm of Taxes. In January 1759 de Selle received 1,500,000 *livres* from the firm, de Géorville a million, and one of the Treasurers-General for the colonies 500,000 *livres*; but each of these three also received the same sum from other sources, so that the navy appears to have been counting on *Beaujon Goossens et Cie* to pay half of its anticipated costs.[18]

The government hoped for two main benefits from this unusual arrangement. The lesser of the two, but one explicitly stated in documents of the time, was to have funds sent out to the ports at lower cost. The first agreed to discount *rescriptions* and bills of the General Farm of Taxes at a commercial rate of 0.5 per cent a month or six per cent a year, which worked out at less than the financial charges the Treasurers-General were entitled to.[19] These charges consisted of a basic fixed allowance (*indemnité pour frais*) of 150,000 *livres* for paying the salaries of agents in the ports, a fixed percentage (*taxation*) of 0.4 per cent (that is, 40,000 *livres*) on the first 10,000 *livres* passing through the Treasurers-General's hands, 0.833 per cent of the next three million (that is, *deux sous pour livre*) and 0.416 per cent (that is, *un sou pour livre*) of everything over 13 million passing through their hands. 'It was to avoid expenses of that kind in 1759', an official memorandum declared in 1760, 'that *la finance* established the banking firm of *Beaujon, Goossens et Cie* with whom it made an agreement concerning the cost of discounting'.[20]

The other and more important benefit was the collective credit of the firm, especially of its merchant members, which the government hoped might extend the navy's credit from financial circles into the rich and cosmopolitan trading circles of the time. This was a plausible idea in the middle of the eighteenth century because maritime trade had been expanding and flourishing ever since the Peace of Utrecht (1713). The great ports of Bordeaux, Nantes, Le Havre and Marseilles had prospered in the West India trades, Saint Malo in the Newfoundland fishing trade, La Rochelle and Bordeaux in the northern wine and brandy trades and to some extent in the Canada trade, Lorient and Marseilles in the East India trades, Bayonne and Saint Malo in the Spanish trades, and many ports in the grain, timber and coastal trades. Everywhere rich families of merchants were building town and country houses, buying royal offices or shares in tax farms, and setting up as bankers. During the two mid-century wars, the Crown drew more and more heavily on this field of wealth to finance maritime and colonial fighting that seemed to be of direct benefit to the trading ports.

At the same time, the services of merchant bankers seemed indispensable in maritime and colonial warfare for importing naval supplies, timber and grain, for dispatching men and supplies to the colonies, and for making payments abroad. A vast cosmopolitan network of merchant bankers in Holland, Germany, Switzerland, Spain, Italy and England were accessible through the bigger French bankers, whereas French financiers, even the Farmers-General, were concentrated in Paris and somewhat limited in the scope of their business. The French government therefore drew more and more merchant bankers into royal finances. It did so much more obviously during the American War of Independence when it even appointed a Protestant Swiss banker, Jacques Necker, as Controller-General of Finance, but during the Seven Years War the hiring of *Beaujon, Goossens et Cie* expressed the same desire to tap commercial wealth and services for the navy's maritime and colonial warfare.

The same tendency led the government to engage a *marchand banquier* of Bayonne, Jean-Joseph de Laborde (1724–94) to furnish a million *livres* a month to the army by a contract of 3 December 1757; then, by another contract of 13 October 1758 to take charge of military financing in general up to 50 million or more a year; and finally, as Court Banker, to pay French diplomats abroad, subsidies to foreign allies and other such obligations, this beginning on 4 February 1759 with the retirement of the previous Court Banker, Jean Paris de Montmartel.[21] In June 1759 Laborde also accepted a post as a Farmer-General with a seat on the ruling *Comité des caisses*. Laborde's business connections were unusually wide and strong especially in Spain, his wealth was great, and he seemed pleased to put it at the disposal of the government in return for the personal friendship of various ministers, of Madame de Pompadour and especially of the Duc de Choiseul. When the financial crisis came late in 1759, Laborde held over 25 million *livres* worth of paper *rescriptions* for money advanced in the royal service. He had lent money to many official and semi-official agencies including *Beaujon, Goossens et Cie*, and he remained throughout a merchant banker proud of his position and scornful of the financiers who, he declared in his memoirs, were all against him.

Laborde was, it is clear, a friend and protégé of the Duc de Choiseul, but who were the friends and patrons of *Beaujon, Goossens et Cie*? Certainly not Laborde, who expressed a bitter enmity for them in his memoirs.[22] Certainly not Choiseul, who wrote to Louis XV after the war blaming the Secretary of State, Berryer, for the navy's decline 'because he was cheated by a rogue of a banker named Beaujon who, in spite of his knavery, has nevertheless maintained his influence at court'.[23] Choiseul, who had been ambassador to the Habsburg court in Vienna from March 1757, did not arrive in the French capital until November 1758 and was not appointed Secretary of State for Foreign Affairs until 3 December, too late to play any part in the arrangements for *Beaujon, Goossens et Cie*. It is possible that *Beaujon, Goossens et Cie*, a cosmopolitan group with Dutch, English and Huguenot links, were not suitable for the revolutionary new Bourbon–Habsburg alliance then being formed. It is possible, indeed, that *Beaujon, Goossens et Cie* were part of Paris de Montmartel's anti-Habsburg financial system built by Choiseul upon Laborde and a series of three celebrated marriages with the daughters of Mathias de Nettine, a great Belgian banker to the Habsburg government.[24] It is certain, at all events, that *Beaujon, Goossens et Cie* were engaged in 1758 by ministers with whom they already had business relations. Before Choiseul's time, the ruling faction at the court of Louis XV was a large group of financiers and their protégés, including Madame de Pompadour, and it was this faction that chose the Secretaries of State for the Navy and the Controllers-General of Finance who were in office during the early years of the Seven Years War. These ministers knew the five partners in *Beaujon, Goossens et Cie* well before the financial contracts of 1758. A study of these partners, each in turn, shows a tissue of relationships with the naval and financial services of the government.

Nicolas Beaujon (1718–86) was the son of a merchant of Huguenot origin, Jean Beaujon (*c.* 1680–1745), who was born to a village shopkeeper near Marmande (Lot-et-Garonne) but had made a fortune in the grain trade at Bordeaux and then gone into the colonial trades.[25] Jean and Nicolas Beaujon sent many ships to Canada and the West Indies during the 1730s and 1740s, and when Nicolas moved to Paris about 1751 he left relatives at Bordeaux, including Louis Beaujon of the well-known wine exporters, *Beaujon et Petit*. In 1753 when Beaujon married in Paris, he claimed to have no less than 122,000 *livres* invested in shipping ventures to the West Indies, the Guinea Coast of Africa, and Canada. He also claimed 42,000 *livres* from the navy, and this was not surprising as he and his father had shipped many a cargo for the government during the War of the Austrian Succession (1743–48). In 1756 Beaujon purchased the office of Receiver-General of Finance for even-numbered years in the *généralité* of La Rochelle, which gave him heavy responsibilities in the financing of the naval base at Rochefort.[26] His *rescriptions* drawn on his agent, Guitton, served as one of the main sources of funds for the Treasurers's agents at Rochefort in the years 1756, 1758 and 1760.

Meanwhile, in 1756 and probably as early as 1748, he had gone into the northern trades in timber and other naval supplies together with Goossens, his future partner in *Beaujon, Goossens et Cie*.[27]

Pierre-François Goossens (1701-?) was born into a Netherlands family settled at Bilbao, and after moving to Paris about 1741 and becoming a naturalised Frenchman in 1743, he kept in touch with his brother, Jean-Henry Goossens, who remained in trade at Bilbao until his death on 17 December 1777. Jean-Henry Goossens became the Bilbao agent for the big marine insurance company of Paris of which Pierre-François Goossens was one of the founding members in 1750. This company and a rival, *La Compagnie d'Assurance*, founded in 1755 by Paris bankers with shipping interests, in collaboration with others such as Jean-Pierre Kolly, a big naval supply merchant, preoccupied Goossens a good deal, especially during the pre-war years.[28] He found time, however, to form another company for six years with a Louisbourg merchant recently settled at La Rochelle, Michel Rodrigue (1710–77), for the purpose of fishing and trading cod and other fish products in French North America and selling them in France and the West Indies.[29] Meanwhile, between 1749 and 1757 Goossens alone and then with Beaujon endeavoured to develop trade with Saint Petersburg with a view to breaking the Anglo-Dutch monopoly in the Russia trade, and to importing Russian tobacco as an alternative to American tobacco from England and Scotland.[30] These grandiose plans, which seem to have come to nothing, grew out of a busy and profitable trade in northern timber and other naval supplies which Goossens had carried on since 1741 or earlier.

Supplying the navy was certainly the main part of Goossens' business, for in 1750 he described himself as 'intéressé dans les fournitures de la Marine'.[31] His name is mentioned in connection with the supply trades even in the early 1740s, and on 5 June 1750, before he had any formal association with Beaujon, he joined a company with two other naval supply merchants, a certain Pierre Babaud de la Chaussade who had been supplying anchors and other ironware since 1736 but does not play any further part in our story, and a Nantes merchant, Gabriel Michel, who does.[32] On the same day, this company signed a contract with the Secretary of State for the Navy, Antoine-Louis Rouillé, to supply masts, timber, pitch, lead, copper, hemp and other naval commodities to Brest, Rochefort, Le Havre and Toulon until 31 December 1754.[33] The scale of this business may be judged by a clause binding the navy to pay this company 100,000 *livres* each month on account. This contract was renewed in some form when it expired, but in 1757 and 1758 Goossens signed several other contracts with the navy to send supplies to the colonies.[34] He acted as a general manager of these shipping enterprises, employing his brother at Bilbao to send out Spanish ships, and local firms at French ports to send French ships. By this time, Goossens was associated with Nicolas Beaujon and on 26 December 1757 the Secretary of State, Peyrenc de Moras, wrote to ask Goossens whether he and Beaujon would undertake to buy 400 tons of wheat, 400 tons of rice, and

800 or 900 barrels of pork to ship with some passengers from Dunkirk to Canada.[35] Less than two weeks later, Goossens hired three vessels through the Dunkirk firm of *Pervilles, Salles et Cie* and signed a contract to ship the goods at a freight rate of 350 *livres* a ton. I have described this expedition elsewhere, and no more need be said here about Goossens' links with the navy before 1758, except to mention a memorandum of February 1757 which proposed to the ministry a scheme of Goossens for 'a loan of 20 millions for the navy by selling shares (*actions*) in the prizes taken by the King's vessels'.[36] Whether or not this scheme went any further, it shows Goossens' willingness to assist in financing the navy.

Goossens worked in association with Dutch merchant bankers whose capital and services appeared to lie behind his various enterprises. From 1 September 1756 he was in formal partnership with a Dutch banker in Paris, Jean-Baptiste Vandenyver, first as an equal partner and then, from 1 January 1760, as a silent partner with Vandenyver as the company's director.[27] They each held a three-sevenths share in the first company and the remaining seventh was held by Vandenyver's younger brother. It may be, as Laborde alleged, that Dutch loans to *Beaujon, Goossens et Cie* turned out to be small and brief, but during the Seven Years War, as before it, Goossens worked as the commission agent of a great many merchants of Amsterdam, Rotterdam and elsewhere in the Netherlands, managing their investments in French *rentes*, tax farms, and other government enterprises. For instance, in February 1756, while Goossens was on a business trip to Amsterdam, Vandenyver received 10,000 *livres* on his behalf from Micault d'Harvelay, Keeper of the Royal Treasury and future partner in *Beaujon, Goossens et Cie*, as a reimbursement from the French postal farm to a Rotterdam merchant, Hermann van Yzendoorn, whom Goossens had served since 1754 or earlier.[38] During the 1740s at least, Goossens was a busy and prosperous merchant banker specialising in the northern trades, and from 1749 his name was listed in the *Almanach royal* among the bankers.

The third partner in *Beaujon, Goossens et Cie*, Gabriel Michel (1702–65), came from another sector of French maritime trade, the slave trade, in which he and his family were leading merchants at the port of Nantes. According to a recent scholarly study, they dispatched 51 slaving ships, more than any other firm in France during the eighteenth century except two of their Nantes rivals.[39] When Michel moved to Paris sometime between the mid-century wars, he was already a director of the *Compagnie des Indies* and deeply enmeshed in government business, but he left a brother at home, François-Augustin Michel (1713–78), in a shipping firm, *Michel et Grou*, with whom he kept in touch.[40] Another brother, Jean-Jacques Michel, joined the marine insurance company of Paris in 1751, calling himself an *intéressé dans les affaires du Roi*.

By 1765 when Gabriel Michel died, he had most of his wealth in personal loans, *rentes*, and Paris property, but during the Seven Years War and earlier he invested heavily in the naval supply trades. He began to conceal his naval supply business during the war, perhaps because he had acquired an office of *Secrétaire du Roi* in 1756 and another of *Trésorier général de l'artillerie et du génie* in 1758. He had already acquired letters of nobility from the King in 1747. In any event, like many other rising merchant bankers, Michel used a front man (*prête-nom*) in his naval contracts. This was none other than the François Cohadon, *bourgeois de Paris*, so often named in lists of naval supply merchants during the Seven Years War. Perhaps Cohadon carried on some business of his own, but when he signed a contract on 2 July 1755 to supply the navy with masts, other timber and supplies for three years, he was recognised in Rochefort and Brest as Michel's agent, and in 1758 Berryer mentioned 'goods supplied by Sieurs Michel, Beaujon and Goossens under the name of Cohadon'.[41] Elsewhere Cohadon is described as Michel's cashier. Then, Michel had long been in touch with the Court Banker, Paris de Montmartel, for each had backed a large slaving company, Michel the *Société de Guinée* and Montmartel the *Société d'Angole*, which had been rivals until they had come to an understanding by negotiations signed on 25 September 1750.[42]

The fourth partner in *Beaujon, Goossens et Cie*, Jean Le Maitre de la Martinière (1715–?), had held the office of Treasurer-General of Fortifications (1749–56) until it was suppressed, and on 15 February 1760 was to take up the office of Treasurer-General of Artillery and Engineering (1760–74).[43] His sister was the wife of a senior Farmer General, a member of the ruling *Comité des caisses* from 1758 to 1761, Etienne Perrinet de Jars (1670–1762), whose son, David-Pierre Perrinet du Pezeau (1697–?), was Receiver-General of Finances for La Rochelle from 1729 to 30 June 1758, and therefore Beaujon's colleague from 1756 to 1758. These facts show Le Maitre de la Martinière as a financier with connections that might explain his appointment to *Beaujon, Goossens et Cie*, but there was also a commercial side to his family. He was the son of a Huguenot wine merchant of Paris, and his brother-in-law, Perrinet de Jars, was the son of a wine merchant of Sancerre (Berry). Furthermore, he had two brothers, Pierre and Caesar Le Maitre, Huguenot merchants who had settled in London as naturalised British subjects and had purchased British tobacco for the French Farmers-General during the 1730s and 1740s. They had both died before *Beaujon, Goossens et Cie* were in full stride as a banking firm, but one, Caesar Le Maitre, as recently as 1758. In any event, they had had some business relations with Etienne de Silhouette in their tobacco purchasing, and Silhouette was Controller-General of Finance from 4 March to 21 November 1759.[44]

Four of the partners, in *Beaujon, Goossens et Cie* had strong connections in the world of merchant banking, but the fifth, Joseph Micault d'Harvelay (1723–86), was entirely a financier unless we count his family's interest in the gunpowder and saltpetre farms as a form of trade.[45] The family had headed the royal gunpowder and saltpetre farms since early in the reign, and a younger brother, Jean-Vivault Micault de Courbeton, carried on in this field to become royal *Commissaire général des poudres et salpètres* when Turgot nationalised these farms on 1 July 1775. They were, however, the sons of a Farmer-General of Taxes from Beaune, Vivant Micault (1681–?), and the great-nephews of Jean Paris de Montmartel.[46] Montmartel had held the office of *Garde du trésor royal* since 1724 and given it over to Micault d'Harvelay in 1755, so that during the Seven Years War d'Harvelay was one of the two principal financiers whose business has always been described, somewhat confusingly to the twentieth-century mind, as 'the Royal Treasury'. In fact, he made such payments as fell to the *caisses* of the Royal Treasury in odd-numbered years, including 1759, in an age when that strange institution was neither at the centre of the royal finances nor in control of them. His position and his family connections were nevertheless qualifications enough for a place in *Beaujon, Goossens et Cie*, especially in view of Paris de Montmartel's strong hand in founding the company.

Such were the partners in this company, richer and more powerful than their obscurity might lead us to suspect, all involved in business for the Crown and yet most of them still merchant bankers (*marchands banquiers*) to some degree. The credit they could together bring to their enterprises was considerable, as they could attract investments in that world of naval business in Paris concentrated in the parish of Saint Eustache. There, in the Place des Victoires, lived Goossens near a Treasurer General for the Colonies, Tavernier de Boullongne, a former Secretary of State for the Navy, Claude-Louis Massiac, a big firm of bankers, *Tourton et Baur*, and a member of the naval victualling company, Jean-Laurent de la Porte. There, in the rue Vivienne, lived Gabriel Michel near several other directors of the Indies Company and near the central offices of the naval victualling company. Not all the partners in *Beaujon, Goossens et Cie* lived in the parish of Saint Eustache, but the centre of their activities was there where the three marine insurance companies had their offices, and where such big naval suppliers as Kolly and Babaud de la Chaussade, such bankers as *Dumas, Ricateau et Cie* and Jacob Dangirard, and such financiers as Perrinet du Pezeau and Antoine-François Hébert lived. No papers of *Beaujon, Goossens et Cie* survive, but the firm was certainly able to borrow in these circles. For example, one of the naval victuallers, Fossart de Rozeville, *écuyer*, invested 10,000 *livres* in two royal frigates, *Le Danac* and *L'Harmonie*, through a company (*société*) formed on 30 December 1758 by Michel, Beaujon and Goossens, a sum for which Goossens gave him a receipt which he still held at his death ten years later.[47]

The credit of *Beaujon, Goossens et Cie* was all the greater outside Paris by virtue of their network of agents (*correspondants*) in the seaports. These were substantial local businessmen, in some cases active merchant bankers in their own right. I have been able to identify a dozen of them:

Bayonne	Jacques Lasaga
Bordeaux	Blaise Jeandreau (1697–1780)
Brest	Yves-Augustin Bersolle (1702–74)
Cap François (St. Domingue)	Lorry
Dunkirk	Pierre Tugghe

La Rochelle	Jean-Baptiste-Pierre Guitton
London	Joshua Van Neck and Co.
Marseille	Isaac Rigaud et Cie
Port Louis	Jacques-Théodore Pesron (1701–64)
Quebec	Jean-Mathieu Mounier (1715–c. 74)
Rochefort	Joseph Ruffray (1716–71)
Rouen	Nicolas Baudoin
Saint Malo	Jean-Baptiste Magon de la Balue (1713–94)

Some of these, such as Bersolle, Tugghe and Ruffray, were Goossens' agents in the naval supply trades years earlier, all of them connected with other naval businessmen as well.[48] Ruffray, for instance, was the son of Charles-Pierre Ruffray, a Receiver-General of the *aides* in the region of the river Loire, who moved to Rochefort about 1738 as Treasurer of naval victualling (*Trésorier des vivres de la marine*) and made a second marriage in 1747 with the widow of the local controller of naval victualling. The son was already Goossens's agent at that time, and on 21 January 1747 he signed a contract with the local naval Intendant to supply English coal and lead. The name of Ruffray recurs in the records of every branch of the naval support business at Rochefort. The Ruffrays, Tugghes and Bersolles were much smaller fry, however, than the agents at the bigger ports, such as Magon de la Balue, from one of the oldest and richest of Saint Malo merchant families and destined to become a Farmer-General in 1763 and Court Banker, no less, in 1769. He, like Van Neck, was hardly inferior to any of the partners in *Beaujon, Goossens et Cie*. Jeandreau and Baudouin are more difficult to assess, being not among the successful merchants of their cities and yet related to successful merchants. Jeandreau, for instance, was related to the well-known Pourcin family at Bordeaux and his own brother, Jean Jeandreau, was a merchant. He himself managed the coffee entrepot for the *Consuls de la Bourse* during the 1750s and was at the same time a director of the royal mint at Bordeaux until late in 1758 when his nephew, Antoine Gallant, took the post. He had a royal title, 'Gentleman of the Great Falconry of France', and a modest fortune in *rentes*, tax farms and other investments, not to mention a town house, and a country estate at Gradignan, then about ten miles south of Bordeaux on the Bayonne road. At La Rochelle, the agent Guitton was employed as a clerk by Beaujon in his capacity as Receiver General of Finance: all the Receivers-General of Finance lived in Paris and employed clerks in the provincial capitals of their *généralités*. In general, the agents of *Beaujon, Goossens et Cie* were at the financial fringe of the maritime trading community; that is, they were in some cases men with financial origins and connections who had gone into naval business, but in most cases men with commercial origins and connections who were anxious to seize such contracts, offices and associations as the government might offer them.

By issuing bills of exchange drawn on these agents to the order of one of the Treasurers-General for the Navy, *Beaujon, Goossens et Cie* paid out 26,600,000 *livres* of which we have a record in the monthly tables of payment (*états de distribution*) for the first eight months of 1759.[49] This seems to be something approaching a half of the funds found in that period; and it may be a larger fraction than that. The principal destinations of these payments were, in order of total sums paid, Paris (11,099,796 *livres*), Brest (5,320,593), Rochefort (3,614,099), and Toulon (2,657,989), as might be expected. There were 15 other destinations, mainly Atlantic and Channel ports, but Auxonne-en-Bourgogne was also on the list. A great many of the payments to various Atlantic ports were in connection with the plan to invade Ireland with an army in rented ships and England with armies carried in specially-built invasion barges (*batteaux plats* and *prames*), a project for which the government allotted some 27 million *livres*.[50]

The Court Banker, Laborde, tends to disparage *Beaujon, Goossens et Cie* in his memoirs, pointing out that the funds they borrowed in Holland and London were a great deal less than they had expected.[51] But they were certainly a pillar of strength in financing the navy during the first nine months of 1759. Again and again the Secretary of State turned to them, to pay such debts as a million *livres* owing to Abraham Gradis of Bordeaux, or to honour such bills as those for 50,000 *livres* falling due at Le Havre on 18 October. 'I see no other expedient for meeting this indispensible payment', Berryer wrote, 'than to entrust it to Monsieur Beaujon'.[52]

By then, the financial system was beginning to collapse. In September, the Controller-General had reported to Louis XV:

> The many loans and the high interest to which money has been brought have warned the public of the State's distress. Any credit operations today will only have the fatal effect of revealing to the enemy that we are powerless and of making the peace more difficult. It is therefore only in increases of revenue that it is possible to seek further resources.[53]

But the rebellious sovereign courts stood in the way of increased taxes, as Silhouette discovered to his cost. On 15 October, payments on the bills of exchange drawn annually at Quebec and the other colonies on the Treasurers-General had been suspended and the funds earmarked for the colonies were turned over to the navy. The ministers had talked of this dreaded suspension for many months, as the sums needed in the colonies had been rising steeply with inflation due to wartime shortages and losses, and to corruption. The credit of the Treasurers-General was all but destroyed by this suspension, and it evaporated on 26 October suspending the *rescriptions* of the Receivers-General of Finance and the notes of the General Farm. *Beaujon, Goossens et Cie* were still solvent, however, and on 18 October Berryer's office had sent them the official tables of naval funding, confident that they could carry on.[54] It is true that the ministry was already beginning to defend the firm against prosecution in the courts for debt; on 29 October, the First President of the Parlement of Rouen complained to Berryer about this protection on behalf of the commercial court (*juges consuls*) of Rouen. 'I must thank you', Berryer wrote to Boullongne, Intendant of Finance, on 26 October, 'especially for what you are doing at this moment for a company which has been so useful to the navy this year and which, it is to be hoped, may be maintained for the service next year'.[55]

In spite of the Minister's hopes, the firm's days were numbered. They went bankrupt on 14 November in what was rapidly becoming one of the worst financial and business crises of the century. As early as 5 November, Magon de la Balue at Saint Malo wrote to *Magon Lefer frères* at Cadiz:

> You will have learned the sinister news from Paris, the suspension of payments of the bills from the colonies of which there are from 25 to 30 millions in the kingdom, that of many public bills (*effets publiques*), even of those reputed to be the most sound, the decision to free the endorsers of these (from any liability for them), the fear we have of new measures. All this came like a clap of thunder; a general distrust ensued. Everything is forbidden, credit stifled, Paris in a general consternation, the provinces too. Everyone is in a state of the most intense anxiety.[56]

In this 'violent crisis in French finances', as Berryer afterwards called it, he refused to buy for the navy even one copy of the Abbé d'Expilly's latest book, *Description, histoire et géographie des royaumes d'Angleterre, d'Ecosse et d'Irlande*, and refused the Abbé Reignière's new invention of 'An inflammable and inextinguishable firework suitable for being thrown by arrows, cannon or mortars onto the enemy's vessels'.[57] On 15 November the Bordeaux firm of *Beaujon et Petit* reported that Blaise Jeandreau had ceased paying there and closed his doors, that his employers, *Beaujon, Goossens et Cie* in Paris, had still been solvent on 10 November when the latest messenger had departed for Bordeaux, but there was much anxiety that they too might fail. They had, in fact, failed on the previous day, 14 November, as *Beaujon et Petit* were able to report by 22 November.[58]

French shipping merchants were in despair. Abraham Gradis declared that in all his years in business he had never seen things looking so black.[59] Such merchants as Desclaux, Latuillière and Petit (of *Beaujon et Petit*) journeyed hastily to Paris where Moise Gradis, Le Moyne of Rouen, and many others had for some time been trying to induce the government to pay its debts to them. Jeandreau also journeyed to Paris.[60] The failure of *Beaujon, Goossens et Cie* was, of course, only a part of the crisis, but it was a big part, especially in maritime trading circles. Their failure reverberated through Europe, affecting even such big bankers as André Pels and Sons and Thomas Hope and Company of Amsterdam, Pieter His and Sons of Hamburg, and George Fitzgerald and Joshua Van Neck of London.[61] When Fitzgerald, a Jacobite banker, went bankrupt early in December 1759 this was largely because of a letter he had received on 7

December from *Beaujon, Goossens et Cie* announcing that they would neither accept nor honour his bills of exchange, and his creditors later claimed at least 78,000 *livres* from the firm.[62]

The French government was now as bankrupt as an authoritarian government could be, short of a revolution. That is, all public confidence in its paper had crumbled, but it could fall back on royal decrees to defend itself against the otherwise inevitable and devastating legal prosecutions of its creditors, of its creditors's creditors, and so on *ad infinitum*. Under the umbrella of its own authority it could then receive and study all claims for payment, take stock of its debts, decide which to honour and which to repudiate, marshal the funds which accumulated meanwhile from tax revenues, resume payments through *Beaujon, Goossens et Cie*, the Treasurers-General of the Navy and others in their predicament, and so gradually restore its normal financial procedures and the public confidence that depended on normalcy.

All these things the government did as quickly as it could. On 30 November it published a general *arrêt de surséance* forbidding all prosecutions for debt against its financiers and bankers. Under this protection, *Beaujon, Goossens et Cie* carried on at their own pace, drawing bills of exchange for the navy's use in order to fulfil their commitments for the year. On 6 December Berryer declared that the Treasurers-General had received no funds for two months and he reckoned the sums owing to them at about ten million *livres*.[63] Payments to be made through *Beaujon, Goossens et Cie* totalled about seven million of this. They had been issuing IOUs (*reconnaissances*) to acknowledge bills and notes they could not honour, and many months were to pass before they could redeem them all. A ministerial table of October 1760 shows that the firm then owed more than 1,500,000 *livres* on its IOUs. Their debts accumulated in no less than 15 French ports, including Rochefort (for 540,803 *livres*), Le Havre (279,982), Toulon (99,613) and Saint Malo (77,444) to cite only the biggest claims.[64]

There was another side to such a bankruptcy, however, that could not be so easily put right. Accumulated debt might be deferred by decree and gradually repaid; current payments from tax revenues might be resumed; but fresh credit for the navy's needs could not be found by decree. For a time, at least, the French navy could expect few services or supplies on credit and could fit out few ships indeed. Whether the invasion forces were fully manned, equipped and ready on 20–21 November when Admiral Hawke defeated and dispersed the Brest convoy fleet in Quiberon Bay is not clear. The invasion project, *l'expédition particulière*, as it had been euphemistically called, was not the only project, however, that had to be abandoned. Early in December, Berryer composed a letter proposing to that old friend of the ministry, Abraham Gradis at Bordeaux, that he send a military expedition to Canada disguised as a trading expedition because 'at the moment the navy has not enough vessels to detach a force sufficient for that expedition'.[65] He soon thought better of this idea and decided on 10 December not to send the letter. But in January 1760, Berryer hatched another scheme for a privateering expedition to Canada to consist of three ships of the line, a frigate and two fly-boats to be financed by selling 400 shares worth 4,000 *livres* each and so producing 1,600,000 *livres*.[66] The Crown was to take 150 shares, Gradis 50, and the remaining 200 shares were to be sold in Paris by the banking firm of *Banquet et Mallet*. This scheme, too, was dropped. The tiny merchant fleet that sailed for Canada from Bordeaux in April 1760 accompanied by *Le Machault*, a royal naval vessel, was a subject of hard bargaining between the Minister and some Bordeaux merchants to make them pay for as much as possible.[67] Was this due to a lack of funds or only to Berryer's notorious parsimony?

Despite the government's authoritarian protection of *Beaujon, Goossens et Cie* and the apparent atmosphere of normalcy, the navy could scarcely carry on for lack of funds. A plausible set of figures, rounded off to the nearest million, shows how severely naval expenditure had to be curtailed:[68]

Year	*Funds Found*	*Spending*
1759	57	77
1760	24	34

Ministerial policy began to concentrate on repaying debts, such as the three million *livres* still due to the builders of the invasion barges in various Atlantic ports, and the large sums still due to several merchants on their contracts to transport troops to Ireland. These payments were slow indeed, and months later some merchants were content to settle for nine-year annuities bearing five per cent interest and negotiable on the market at 30 per cent loss.[69] In November 1761, two years after the crisis, Choiseul wrote to the Intendant of the naval base at Rochefort with a plan to pay off naval suppliers with the intention 'of reviving the credit of the navy in a manner that will be appropriate and safe for this service'.[70] Reforms were already under way and Choiseul was already looking forward to the next imperial war at sea.

York University, Toronto

NOTES

1. On French banking and bankers see Herbert Lüthy, *La Banque protestante en France de la Révocation de l'édit de Nantes à la Révolution* (Paris, 2 vols., 1959 and 1961); on French finance and financiers, J. F. Bosher, *French Finances 1770–1795: From Business to Bureaucracy* (Cambridge, 1970).
2. Henri Legohérel, *Les Trésoriers généraux de la Marine (1517–1788)* (Paris, 1965); and J. F. Bosher, 'Les Trésoriers de la Marine et des Colonies sous Louis XV: Rochefort et La Rochelle', *Revue de la Saintonge et de l'Aunis*, tome V (1979), pp. 95–108. There were three men in succession in each of the two offices of *Trésorier général des colonies*, then worth 800,000 *livres*: Jean-Baptiste-Jacques Boucher who died on 1 Aug. 1752 and was replaced by Georges-Nicolas Baudard de Vaudesir (1712–71) who was in turn replaced by his son, Claude Baudard de Saint James (1738–87) with effect from 31 Jan.

1758. The office for odd-numbered years (*Le Trésorier général alternatif*) was held in turn by Guillaume-Pierre Tavernier de Boulongne (1710–?), from 31 Jan. 1758 by Noel-Mathurin-Etienne Périchon (1698–1764) and from 11 April 1764 by Joseph de Saint Laurent (1707–73). An edict of Nov. 1749 set up the two new offices for the colonies; another of Feb. 1771 suppressed them; and another of Dec. 1759 temporarily reduced the two offices for the navy to a single one for Moufle de Géorville with effect from 1 Jan. 1760.

3. Archives nationales, Minutier central des notaires, Paris (hereafter abbreviated as AN, MC), étude LX, 24 Oct. 1759, post-mortem inventory for de Selle; étude LX, 3 Sept. 1743, post-mortem inventory for Florent-Marcellin de Selle; étude XV 417, 7 Feb. 1764, post-mortem inventory for Moufle de Géorville. Several hundred pages long, these inventories are closely-written manuscript lists of all property and papers with references to hundreds of other notarial contracts and other useful facts.
4. For instance, figures in the AN, Paris F^4 1008, 1077, and 1245; V^7 111, 112, 113 and 360; Marine B^2 361, 362, Marine B^1 66 and 67, Marine G^7 1830; figures at the Bibliothèque nationale (BN), ms. fr. 5399; figures in the voluminous ministerial correspondence with the naval ports in the Archives de la Marine (hereafter Arch. Mar.) in Paris, and at Rochefort, Brest, Cherbourg, and Toulon; and figures in the sources cited in Lee Kennet, *The French Armies in the Seven Years War* (Durham, NC, 1967), Ch. 8.
5. François Joachim de Pierre, cardinal de Bernis, *Mémoires et lettres, 1715–1758* (Paris, 2 vols., 1878), Vol. II, p. 86. These difficulties I have explained elsewhere, for example, in *The New Cambridge Modern History*, Vol. VIII, Ch. 20, 'French Administration and Public Finance'; and in my 'Government and Private Interests in New France', *Canadian Public Administration* (June 1967), pp. 244–57.
6. De Bernie, op. cit., p. 173 (25 Jan. 1758).
7. Cited by Henri Legohérel, op. cit., pp. 180 and 186, and taken from AN, G^7 1830.
8. Legohérel, op. cit., p. 186.
9. BN, ms. fr. 11340.
10. De Bernis, op. cit., Vol. I, pp. 303–8, often cited. On the army's finances, Kennett, op. cit., Ch. 8.
11. Armand Rébillon, *Les Etats de Bretagne de 1661 à 1789* (Paris, 1932), p. 730 showing six million *livres* lent to the Crown in 1758 and another six million in 1760, all at five per cent interest.
12. AN, F^4 1008, *Mémoire: situation du Sieur de Géorville*, 3 Feb. 1762.
13. Arch. Mar., Lorient, 1 E^5 1, the Bourgeois papers, Bourgeois to Moufle de Géorville, 23 Jan. 1758, etc.
14. AN, Colonies B 108, Le Normand de Mézy to Boullongne, Intendant of Finance. Jean-Nicolas de Boullongne (1726–87) took his father's office of Intendant of Finances on 25 Aug. 1757 when his father, Jean de Boullongne (1690–1769), was named Controller General of Finance. Until 1769, Boullongne supervised the treasury matters for the Controller General's department. See J.F. Bosher, 'The French Crisis of 1770', *History*, Vol. LVII (1972), p. 28.
15. AN, Colonies B 108, fol. 64–7. By April 1758, the Treasurers-General for the Colonies were unable to find a million *livres* to pay Simon Darragory, a French merchant in Spain, for shiploads of food sent to Canada on Spanish vessels with false neutral passports.
16. This contract is mentioned in AN, MC, étude LX, 24 Oct. 1759, de Selle's post-mortem inventory.
17. These contracts are explained in part in a printed *Arrêt du Conseil d'Etat du Roi concernant les lettres de change et billets des sieurs Beaujon, Goossens et Compagnie*, dated 14 Nov. 1759, which I read at La Rochelle in the archives of the chamber of commerce, bound volume 4. See also Moufle d'Angerville, *Vie Privée de Louis XV ou principaux évèvements, particularités et anecdotes de son règne* (London, 1781), Vol. III, p. 184.
18. AN, Marine B^1 66, fol. 123. If, as it appears in the figures in Legohérel, op. cit., p. 186, the navy spent 77 millions in 1759, the firm may well have managed about half of this sum.

19. Legohérel, op. cit., p. 313; and AN, Marine B^2 362 fol. 466, a letter of 28 July 1759 on the firm's rates.
20. AN, Marine B^1 67, *Mémoire sur les remboursements à faire par la finance à la marine rélativement à des dépenses* (15 May 1760).
21. Laborde's career and personal life are explained in his memoirs, edited and introduced by Yves-René Durand, in *Annuaire-Bulletin de la Société de l'Histoire de France, années 1968–1969* (Paris, 1971), pp. 75–162, and also in Yves Durand, *Les Fermiers généraux au XVIIIe siècle* (Paris, 1971). The Duc de Choiseul served as Secretary of State for Foreign Affairs from 3 December 1758 (following de Bernis), Secretary of State for War from 27 Jan. 1761 and Secretary of State for the Navy and Colonies from 13 Oct. 1761 (following Berryer). But Choiseul became a kind of chief minister from early in 1759 and had great influence at Court, forming almost a political party of his friends and protégés in those years and until his fall in 1770.
22. Laborde, *Mémoires*, pp. 157–159.
23. Choiseul, *Mémoire justificatif présenté au Roi en 1765* cited in *Mémoires du duc de Choiseul (1719–1785)* (Paris, 1904), pp. 405–6, and in André Masson, *Un Mécène bordelais, Nicolas Beaujon, 1718–1786* (Paris, 1937).
24. Laborde married Rosalie-Claire de Nettine on 12 April 1760; Micault d'Harvelay married Anne-Josèphe de Nettine in Jan. 1762 and Lalive de Jully, *introducteur des ambassadeurs* and protégé of Mme. de Pompadour married Marie-Louise de Nettine on 1 Aug. 1761. This system of Choiseul's and Laborde's is explained in Yves Durand, *Les Fermiers généraux*, pp. 80–81; and in Herbert Lüthy, *La Banque protestante*, Vol. II, pp. 657–9.
25. AN, T 306, marriage contract drawn up by the notaries Patu and Dutartre on 21 and 22 Oct. 1753 showing Beaujon's total assets at 490,000 *livres* when he married Louise-Elisabeth Bontemps, daughter of a courtier, *premier valet de chambre, etc.* The remark that Beaujon's family was of Huguenot origin is based on extensive documentary research in south-western France and explained in my forthcoming book, *The Canada Merchants, 1713–1763* (Oxford University Press, 1986).
26. AN, V^1 391 (1756) *provision d'office* dated 5 March 1754 as successor to Gracien Drouilhet who died on 30 Jan. 1756.
27. Arch. départementales de la Seine, Paris, D.C. 11 fol. 21, showing Goossens, aged 42, Catholic (he was in fact a 'New Convert') as required by the law, born at Bilbao, Spain, received *lettres de la grande chancellerie* at Versailles in Feb. 1743, naturalization, registered (*insinué*) in Paris on 7 March 1743. AN, MC, étude XLVIII 248, 22 May 1778 showing that Jean-Henry Goossens died at Bilbao on 17 Dec. 1777 aged 64, widower of Catherine Moriarty, leaving several children.
28. P.W. Bamford, *Forests and French Seapower, 1660–1789*, Toronto, 1956, p. 144; and J.F. Bosher, 'The Paris Business World and the Seaports under Louis XV: Speculators in Marine Insurance, Naval Finances and Trade', *Histoire sociale* (Ottawa), Vol. XII (1979), especially pp. 281–92.
29. For a summary of this fishing company, see J.F. Bosher, 'A Fishing Company of Louisbourg, Les Sables d'Olonne, and Paris: la Société du Baron d'Huart, 1750–1775', *French Historical Studies*, Vol. IX (1975), pp. 263–4.
30. Jacob M. Price, *France and the Chesapeake* (Ann Arbor, 1973), pp. 393–7.
31. AN, MC, étude LXXXIII 415 (22 July 1750), *Société Rodrigue et Goossens*.
32. AN, MC, étude XLVIII 114 (18 Aug. 1761), *transaction*.
33. AN, MC, étude CXV 585 (5 June 1750); and the full text is printed in Arch. Mar., Rochefort, 5 E^2 18–20.
34. Some of these are listed in AN, F^1 A vol. 42, with dates of 18 April 1758, 23 March 1758, 27 March, 1 and 11 April 1758, 8 Jan. 1758 and 27 Dec. 1757. AN, Colonies B 108, fol. 94, Peyrenc de Moras to Goossens 17 March 1758. Among the Spanish ships the Goossens brothers fitted out for Canada were *Le Saint Thomas, Le Grande Saint Louise* (180 tons), *La Ville de Bilbao* and *Le Jésus-Marie-Joseph* (150 tons).
35. AN, Marine C^7 123, dossier Goossens. I am grateful to Monsieur Etienne Taillemite, then director of the *section moderne*, for drawing my attention to these documents and allowing me to publish them in *Histoire sociale* (Ottawa), Vol. V (1972), pp. 79–85.

36. AN, Marine G 132.
37. AN, MC, étude XLVIII 108, Declaration of 6 March 1760; and Lüthy, op. cit., pp. 321–3.
38. Laborde, *Mémoires* (cited in note 21 above), pp. 149–50; AN, MC, étude LXXXIV 455, procuration 4 Dec. 1755 listing Vandenyver as Goossens's bookkeeper. For Goossens's clients in Holland, see AN, MC, étude LXXXIV 456, 6 Feb. 1756; CXV 714, 30 April 1758 and 721, 23 Jan. 1759; L, 14 Oct. 1743, 11 April 1752, 13 April 1752, 9 April 1758, and 15 Jan. 1750, and the *répertoire* of maître Patu's minutes. Patu's minutes are missing for the years 1752–60.
39. Robert Stein, *The French Slave Trade in the Eighteenth Century: An Old Régime Business* (Madison, WI, 1979), pp. 27 and 153. The firm of François-Augustin Michel (1713–78) and Jean-Baptiste Grou (1708–56) was prominent at Nantes.
40. AN, MC, étude LXXXIII 514, 17 Oct. 1765, post-mortem inventory for Gabriel Michel, who died on 27 Sept. 1765. During the Seven Years War, his notarial acts appear in two études: LXXXIII and XCV. AN, V^1 399 (1758) for Michel's purchase of the office of *Trésorier général alternatif de l'artillerie et du génie* for 600,000 *livres* with letters of provision dated 14 April 1758.
41. References to Michel's naval supplies under Cohadon's name are in AN, MC, étude XCV 253, 27 June 1757; BN, ms. fr. 11336, fol. 109, fol. 209 ff. and fol. 231; Arch. Mar., Brest, 1 E 149, Berryer to Hocquart, 11 Dec. 1758, 1 E 507, a three-year *marché* for northern masts which Cohadon signed on 2 July 1755, and Arch. Mar., Rochefort, 5 E^2 18–20 on the same contract; AN, MC, étude CXV 585, 5 June 1750, *marché pour le service de la marine*, 10 pp; and étude LXXXIII 506, 18 Sept. 1764, *procuration*.
42. Stein, op. cit., p. 28.
43. AN, V^1 361 (1749) and V^1 407 (1760) filed under name; *Almanach royal*, 1753, p. 315; the baptismal date is given, as usual, in the *lettres de provision* in the V^1 series.
44. AN, MC, étude XCI 861, 5 Feb. 1750, marriage contract for Perrinet de Jars and Martinière's sister; Yves Durand, *Les Fermiers généraux*, p. 82; J. M. Price, *France and the Chesapeake*, pp. 575, 1033 notes 67 and 68, and 1035, note 97.
45. On Micault d'Harvelay, Yves Durand, op. cit., pp. 84–5, H. Lüthy, op. cit., Bosher, *French Finances*, pp. 90, 96–7 and 334.
46. BN, Joly de Fleury Papers 1438 fol. 48–79; AN, P. 2519, *lettres d'honneur* of 16 Aug. 1780; V^2 41 and 44; T 200^7 d'Harvelay's succession. Micault de Courbeton married Marie-Françoise Trudaine.
47. AN, MC, étude LXXIII 901, 9 April 1768, post-mortem inventory for Alexis-Thomas-Edouard Fossart de Rozeville, *écuyer*. Hébert was a prominent partner in the naval victualling company during the Seven Years War. The addresses of Paris businessmen and officials appear in many of the documents already cited, notably documents concerning the marine insurance companies in AN, MC, étude CXVIII 459 and 460, étude XLV, 27 Sept. 1753 and LXXXIV, 7 July 1755, which are the founding acts and minutes of the three companies. The identities of these agents as working for *Beaujon, Goossens et Cie*, appear in scattered references, mostly manuscript, too numerous to cite, but let us acknowledge three printed references in H. F. Buffet, *Vie et société au Port Louis* (Rennes, 1972); Pierre Dardel, *Navires et marchandises dans les ports de Rouen et du Havre* (Paris, 1963), p. 367; and J. M. Price, *France and the Chesapeake*, p. 394.
48. Bersolle, born at Crozon near Brest on 13 July 1702, died at Brest on 15 June 1774 leaving ten children (see Arch. Munic. de Brest, dossier Bersolle); Jeandreau's will is in the Arch. dép. de la Gironde, Bordeaux, minutes of maître Faugas, 16 Aug. 1780, 15 Nov. 1759, etc.; Mounier is the subject of a biography in the *Dictionary of Canadian Biography*, Toronto, Vol. IV, etc.
49. The *états de distribution* are scattered through the correspondence in AN, Marine B^2 361 and 362. They give sums and destinations month by month, but only a few clues to the reasons for the payments.
50. Among the builders of invasion barges were Tugghe (50 *batteaux plats* at 2,800 *livres* each), Eustache *frères* at Rouen (24 *batteaux plats* for a total of 300,000 *livres*), de Launay at Caen, Raimbault at Nantes, and a great many more who might be identified.

51. Laborde, *Mémoires*, pp. 149–50.
52. AN, Marine B^2 362 fol. 485, Berryer to Boullongne, 17 Oct. 1759.
53. Charles-Joseph Mathon de la Cour, *Collection de Comptes-rendus* (Paris, 1788), pp. 31 ff.
54. The crisis of 1759 I have described from a different point of view in my paper, 'The French Government's Motives in the *affaire du Canada*, 1761–1763', *The English Historical Review*, Vol. XCVI (1981), pp. 59–78. Evidence for the chronology of events is in AN, Marine B^2 362.
55. AN, Marine B^2 362.
56. Arch. départ. d'Ile-et-Vilaine (Rennes), 1 F 1897, no. 42.
57. AN, Colonies B 111 fol. 8, Berryer to Vaudreuil, 22 Feb. 1760; Marine B^2 362, Berryer to Expilly, 10 Nov. 1759 and to Regnière, 23 Nov. 1759.
58. Arch. départ, de la Gironde (Bordeaux), 7 B 1025. *Beaujon et Petit* to Bory on 22 Nov. 1759 and 15 Nov. 1759. I mistakenly dated the failure of *Beaujon, Goossens et Cie* as 21 Oct. (over three weeks too soon) in my article cited above in note 54.
59. Arch. départ. de la Gironde (Bordeaux), 1 Mi. 112 (B1), Gradis to Marin, 22 Nov. 1759.
60. Arch. départ. de la Gironde (Bordeaux), 7 B 1025, Louis Beaujon to St. Fretté, 1 Nov. 1759; and *passim* in the letters Moise Gradis wrote from Paris in 1759, in 1 Mi. 112 (microfilm of the Gradis correspondence).
61. Arch. départ. de la Gironde (Bordeaux), 7 B 2126, da Silva to his son, Solomon da Silva in London, 20 and 30 Nov. 1759 and 2 Jan. 1760.
62. AN, MC, étude XLVIII 115 *indemnité* dated 23 Dec. 1761 listing Fitzgerald's Paris creditors; J. M. Price, *France and the Chesapeake*, p. 583.
63. AN, Marine B^2 362, Berryer to Boullongne, 6 Dec. 1759.
64. AN, Marine B^1 67 no. 19, *Etat des paiements* ....
65. AN, Colonies B 110, Berryer to Gradis, a letter dated only 'December 1759' with a note added, 'Le 10 Déc. 1759, Monseigneur a suspendu l'expédition de cette lettre et de l'état dont il y est question'.
66. Jean de Maupassant, 'Abraham Gradis et l'approvisionnement des colonies (1756–63)', *Revue historique de Bordeaux*, 2e année (1909), pp. 250 ff.
67. AN, Colonies B 112, Jan. to April *passim*.
68. Legohérel, op. cit., p. 186.
69. Paul Butel, *La Croissance commerciale bordelaise dans la seconde moitié de XVIIIe siècle*, thesis, Lille (Service de reproduction des thèses), 1973, Vol. II, p. 890.
70. Arch. Mar. (Rochefort), 1 E 168, Choiseul to Ruis Embito, 25 Nov. 1761.

DIRECTIONS FOR THE CONDUCT OF A MERCHANT'S COUNTING HOUSE, 1766

Edited by JACOB M. PRICE

Despite our increased understanding of the expansion and direction of British overseas trade in the seventeenth and eighteenth centuries, the inner life and procedures of merchant firms participating in that expansion remain largely unexplored. To be sure, the work of historians of accounting has established that from the late middle ages English merchants were becoming increasingly interested in adopting the more sophisticated double-entry bookkeeping procedures developed in Italy. This interest was sufficiently widespread by the mid-sixteenth century to make it worthwhile to publish English adaptations of continental textbooks of Italian-style accountancy. Publication of such adaptations and more original indigenous manuals became more frequent in the late seventeenth and eighteenth centuries in both England and Scotland.[1] We do not know, however, how carefully the average – or even the larger-than-average – firm followed the prescriptions of the textbooks or manuals. Only rarely does a complete set of a firm's books survive (wastebook, journal, ledger, etc.) and isolated volumes that do survive are often far from textbook perfect. If we know too little about accounting procedures, we know even less about the organisational and social character of the counting house in which this bookkeeping took place. How was work and responsiblity divided there? How was discipline maintained? Given our ignorance in these areas, it is of no little interest that a perhaps unique document has recently come to light spelling out in some detail the internal organisation and procedures established in 1766 for the counting house of Herries & Company of Jeffreys Square, London, a merchant firm trading primarily to the western Mediterranean.

The Herries firm of 1766 was the continuation of an older firm, Coutts Brothers & Company, which had originated in Scotland. John Coutts, originally from Montrose, had established a mercantile and banking business in Edinburgh *c.* 1730.[2] He prospered and became provost of Edinburgh, 1742–44, and a director of the Royal Bank of Scotland. Upon his death in 1750, Provost Coutts's firm was continued by his four sons, Patrick, John, James and Thomas. In 1752 Patrick (the eldest) and Thomas (the youngest) established a branch house in London, first in Philpot Lane, Fenchurch Street, but by 1754 in Jeffreys Square, St. Mary Axe. Brothers John and James were left to manage the older Edinburgh end. However, in 1755, James Coutts of Edinburgh married the niece and heiress of George Campbell, proprietor of the long-established Campbell or Middleton bank in the Strand, London. At the time of his marriage, James Coutts left his family's Edinburgh house and became a partner in

George Campbell's 'West End' bank. When Campbell died in 1760, James Coutts took his brother Thomas out of their family's Jeffreys Square house and made him a partner in the Strand bank which has survived to this day as Coutts & Company. These departures left brother John Coutts alone in charge of the family's old Edinburgh firm and brother Patrick in charge of the City branch. A crisis ensued in 1761 when John Coutts died and Patrick went insane. James and Thomas Coutts were unwilling to leave the prosperous Strand bank but wanted to continue the family's houses in Edinburgh and London (Jeffreys Square) as provision for some needy relatives.

New partners were therefore required for the old Coutts firm. These were found for the Edinburgh end in two of the firm's own clerks: Sir William Forbes, a landless baronet, son of an Edinburgh barrister, and James Hunter (later Sir James Hunter Blair, bart.), son of a merchant of Ayr. At the same time – 1762 – a senior managing partner at London was added in the person of Robert Herries of Barcelona. This Robert Herries was the son of an extravagant and improvident Dumfriesshire laird who was forced to sell his landed inheritance to a younger brother, a merchant of Rotterdam. Deprived of any expectation of inheritance in Scotland, young Robert Herries was sent for training to his uncle Robert's counting house in Rotterdam. After that uncle's retirement, young Robert went into business for himself in Barcelona in 1754 with the help of the great Amsterdam Scottish-Quaker firm, Hope & Company. He prospered at Barcelona and acquired interests in other firms in Valencia and Montpellier and was even for a time contractor farming the papal forests. A significant part of Herries' Barcelona business consisted of shipping brandy to the Channel Islands and Isle of Man for resale to the smuggling trade. When wheat harvests were poor in the western Mediterranean, his Barcelona house also handled grain shipments from North America which brought them into touch with major firms there such as Willing, Morris & Company of Philadelphia. Robert Herries had known John Coutts in his Rotterdam days and in Barcelona may have had dealings with the Coutts's London concern.

The reorganised Coutts house in London was from 1762 entrusted primarily to Robert Herries and a Coutts uncle, William Cochrane, who was pensioned off in 1766. The Edinburgh end was entrusted to the two new partners, Forbes and Hunter, and another Coutts uncle, John Stephen, who was also to be pensioned off in 1771. Although all six were initially partners in both firms, the London house (Jeffreys Square) was styled Herries, Cochrane & Company during 1762–66 and Herries & Company thereafter while the Edinburgh house continued to be known as John Coutts & Company until 1773 when its style was changed to Sir William Forbes, James Hunter & Company. Separate books were kept at each end. While the Edinburgh house gave up its corn trade and became essentially a bank, the Jeffreys Square business remained a merchant firm. (Herries later established a quite separate bank in St. James's Street.)

In 1766, when uncle Cochrane withdrew from active participation in the Jeffreys Square house, Herries or a partner very likely thought that its management needed some tightening up. On moving to London, Herries had retained an interest in his Barcelona house and visited it from time to time. Perhaps because he was away from the counting house for several months running, it was thought necessary to write out his instructions for the new, tighter scheme of management. He or a partner therefore prepared a 'Plan of the Business of Herries & Co. with Rules & Directions for conducting it'.[3] Although no trace has been discovered of records of Herries & Company of London, a copy of this memorandum has survived in the National Library of Scotland among the papers of the Edinburgh partner, Sir William Forbes.

The memorandum describes the procedures of a merchant firm with correspondents in Britain, Ireland, America, Holland, and the western Mediterranean. The clerks in its counting house were divided into two groups: one, under a senior clerk, George Keith, handled business originating in Britain, Ireland and America, while a second group, supervised by Herries himself, handled European business. Each group of clerks received two different afternoons off each week, governed by the different schedules for domestic and foreign posts. The opening pages of the memorandum give a rare view of the daily life of the counting house staff, most of whom appear to have been bachelors living in rooming houses, dining and whiling away their evenings in nearby taverns.

The clerks were trusted and were expected to merit that trust. They were sternly admonished not to convey to outsiders any details of the firm's business. Inside the firm, to avoid jealousy, their own salaries were also to be treated as strictly private and confidential and not specified in the firm's regular records. Little else, however, was kept from them. In fact, they were encouraged to use their spare time to read the firm's letter and memorandum books to familiarise themselves more fully with the details of the business. For, in the company's view, 'A Right Master, in order to be well served, ought to make no part of the Business a mistery to his Clerks, who on their part ought to be faithful to their trust, deserving of his Confidence'.

The last two-thirds of the memorandum is devoted to the accounting and record-keeping procedures of the firm.[4] In general, accounting followed the models presented in contemporary textbooks, with some interesting variations. For a substantial London merchant house, such as Herries & Company, bill of exchange services were particularly important. Its correspondents in Britain and overseas must have sent it hundreds of such bills yearly for collection and almost simultaneously drew on it for equivalent sums. Bills drawn on it by its Edinburgh alter ego, John Coutts & Company, and by its major Rotterdam correspondent, James Craufurd, were apparently automatically accepted. All other bills would have required normal checking before acceptance. So that such acceptance and other credit operations could be handled intelligently, the 'principals' of the firm would have required up-to-date information on active accounts. The provision of such information was facilitated by the unusual *check ledger* on which the memorandum is particularly informative.

Carrying entries from the wastebook to the journal to the ledger had to be done carefully and could be time-consuming, and not unusually in arrears. At Herries & Company the ledger was supposed to be checked against the journal and cash book once a week but was balanced only quarterly. However, for readier access to balances, entries were also carried immediately from the wastebook to a *check ledger* which was to be 'kept constantly up to the day, ... [so] that we may always know the state of our Correspondents Accounts by looking into it'. At the quarterly and annual balances, the check ledger was also compared with the regular ledger for an immediate indication of where errors might have occurred. The check ledger was therefore an important and useful variation from textbook practice. Was this something that Herries had learned in Holland?

On numerous points, the memorandum goes into more detail than contemporary textbooks, although some of the detail may represent procedures not generally followed. The firm did not keep a separate account for every firm with which it dealt but lumped the less important ones together in accounts for 'Sundry Debtors', 'Sundry Creditors' and 'Sundry Tradesmen'. Also noteworthy and perhaps exceptional was the practice (under 'Trade Necessaries') of deducting ten per cent per annum from the original cost of furniture and equipment 'for wear and tear'. Such systematic depreciation of the book value of capital equipment would appear to be unusual at this time.

Nevertheless, the greatest interest of the accounting sections of the Herries memorandum probably lies not in its exceptional features but in the picture it gives us of the way in which textbook models and procedures were utilised and adapted in a busy mercantile counting house.

The text of the Herries & Company memorandum is published here substantially as it appears in the original. Spelling and capitalisation have been left unchanged but abbreviations have been expanded and a few minor alterations made in punctuation. To improve clarity, a few section headings have been added in square brackets and some minor changes made in layout.

University of Michigan

NOTES

1. On the introduction of Italian accounting into England, see B. S. Yamey, H. C. Edey and Hugh W. Thomson, *Accounting in England and Scotland: 1543–1800: Double Entry in Exposition and Practice* (London, 1963); cf. also James O. Winjum, *The Role of Accounting in the Economic Development of England: 1500–1750* (University of Illinois, Center for International Education and Research in Accounting, monograph No. 6), (Urbana, IL, 1972).

2. The following section on the Coutts and Herries firms is based on Jacob M. Price, *France and the Chesapeake: A History of the French Tobacco Monopoly, 1674–1791* ... 2 vols. (Ann Arbor, MI, 1973), Vol. I, pp. 620–23 *et passim*; Sir William Forbes of Pitsligo, bart., *Memoirs of a Banking-House* (London and Edinburgh, 2nd edition, 1860), pp. 1–27. There are also many references to the Herries in Herbert Lüthy, *La Banque Protestante en France de la Révocation de l'Edit de Nantes à la Révolution (Affaires et Gens d'Affaires*, XIX), 2 vols. (Paris, 1959, 1961), Vol. II, pp. 657–63 *et passim*. For James Coutts, see also Sir Lewis Namier and John Brooke (eds.), *The History of Parliament: The House of Commons 1754–1790*, 3 vols. (London and New York, 1964), Vol. II, pp. 263–264.
3. National Library of Scotland, Fettercairn Papers (acc. 4796) box 201, bdle 11. It is possible that James Hunter of Edinburgh was the author or co-author of the memorandum. He was in London in early 1766 when the reorganisation of the firm took place. Forbes, *Memoirs*, 22.
4. I am indebted to Professor B. S. Yamey for valuable comments on the memorandum.

MEMORANDUM

(National Library of Scotland: Fettercairn Papers (acc. 4796), box 201, bdle. 11)

Plan of the Business of Herries & Co. of London with Rules & Directions for conducting it in the two following Departments:

Foreign – Comprehending all the Countries beyond Sea, excepting Ireland, the British Isles, and our Colonies in America

The Business of this Department will be directed by Mr. Herries, assisted by WEC. PG. & BR.

ihInland – Comprehending Great Britain, Ireland, and British America

The Business of this Department to be under the Care of Mr. Keith, assisted by WF. GM.

Hours of Attendance: The Clerks in each Department must be in the Counting house at Nine o'clock in the morning and remain till Two, coming back at Four & continuing till Eight at Night, or later, should the Business of the House on particular occasions require it, excepting, on two Afternoons in the Week, allowed them for their private Affairs or Amusement: Viz. for those in the

Days of Absence	Foreign Department Wednesday & Saturday Inland – Monday & Thursday	... P.M. only

Thus all of them will be in the way of Business every Morning of the week excepting Sundays, and on tuesday & friday they will likewise be all imploy'd in the Afternoon

[Daily Schedule of Assignments]

Monday Morning To bring up all the Books, and make any Entrys of what has pass'd in the preceding Week & not then attended to, for which purpose it will be proper to revise the Occurrences of that week. To mark on the Memorandum Book all Letters left unanswer'd, or to be immediately answered, noting any thing else that may appear necessary to be done, or any Appointments to attend on Business in the Course of the Week, and making the same Memorandums from time to time as Occasions offer – This must be done by Mr. Herries or

Mr. Keith, or in case of their being indisposed or not in the way, by the next in rank.

Afternoon Being the arrival of foreign Posts, all Entrys must be made from the Letters received, and the Answers advanced, so as to abridge the work of the General Post next day, Avoid hurry & Confusion, and have done by times.

Tuesday Morning. To see how our Accounts stand with our different Correspondents, both Inland & Foreign, What Sums to be drawn or remitted, what Bills to negotiate, and calculate whether by Arbitration [arbitrage] any thing can be made on our half Exchange Accounts with different places, Attend to the Sale of Foreign Commodities, To advance the Letters, Invoices &c. till Change time, and in the

Afternoon – The Bookkeepers & every body must lend a hand till the Business of the Post both foreign & Inland be dispatched, after which each to resume their Tasks till the hour of retirement.

Wednesday Morning To examine the Finances, sending all the Short Bills, due for week to come, to the Bankers. To check our Bills receivable with the quantity Columns in the Ledger. To give in Notes to Tradesmen of Orders for Goods, Dispatch what Business is to be done at the Custom house, and take measures for shipping such Goods, either orderd from us, or sent us to forward.

Afternoon – The Clerks of the Inland Department who will only be in the way [i.e., on duty] must bring up the Books committed to their Charge, and prepare every thing for the dispatch of the Inland post the next day.

Thursday Morning To examine the State of our Insurances & see that they be properly executed. To form States of Losses & Averages, and take the necessary steps towards their recovery. To prepare any Letters or Accounts, not only those to be forwarded this Evening, but such as belong to the Fridays post, so as to render it less heavy, and at all rates the Inland Letters must be ready before Change time – The

Afternoon – Being alloted for respite to the Clerks in that Department those in the foreign must take Care to bring up all their Books, make out a List of the Letters to be wrote, and forward as much as possible the Work of

Friday Morning When the same Measures must be observed in respect to Exchange Business &ca as has been mention'd in the Articles of Tuesday Morning, and in the

Afternoon – The Bookkeepers must equally assist in dispatching the post.

Saturday Morning. To look into the State of our Funds & see what Money will be wanted in the beginning of the Week. To prepare Letters &ca for Ireland as well as Great Britain & America, Make our bills of parcells, and attend to the delivery of any Goods that have been sold, to bring up the Occurrences of the Friday's post, and in the

Afternoon The Inland . . . Clerks after the post is dispatch'd must sort & arrange the different Books & Papers in their proper places & Order

General Rules

1. When any of the Clerks go out on the business of the House in the hours of attendance without being sent by a Principal [partner], he must put down in the Memorandum Book where gone to, about what, and

when he expect to be back, for government. The Principals will endavour to do the same.

2. If the Clerks fail to attend at the appointed hours, they must stay beyond them in proportion.

3. Should the Afternoons allotted in the respective Departments for their Recreation and pleasure happen at any time not to coincide with their own private Engagements they may in such a Case exchange with each other the day of respite, but they must not make a practice of doing so, since each is supposed to act best in his own province.

4. Should it be necessary for the dispatch of any pressing or unforeseen business to deny them absence on their appointed days of respite, the[y] will be told of it in the morning of such days.

5. It is expected that they will not of themselves pretend to judge of their presence being or not being necessary on the allotted days of attendance, since they cannot guess who may call, or what business may offer – They are therefore to wait the hour of retiring and if nothing appears to them to be done they may employ themselves in revising what has been done or in improving themselves by the printed Books on Trade bought for the use of the Counting house.

6. It is also expected before they go home at night that they will continue to ask the acting Principal, whether any thing further is to be done that night or any Message to be delivered before they return next morning –

7. That to prevent Jealousy among them as to their Merit in the Counting house, it is thought proper that their respective Salaries shall not appear in the Books (and they are for the same reason requested to conceal the same from each other) by placeing the Sums paid them from time to time to the debit of the acting Principal, which he must take their receipts for in a small private Book kept for that purpose, crediting their respective Accounts in that Book according to agreement with them, for the whole of their Salaries, which must go Quarterly, and in one Article to his Credit with the House.

8. The Partners in the joint Houses here & at Edinburgh, having no Concern in Mr. Herries's Settlements in Spain, he keeps a private Clerk to assist him in conducting such of their Affairs here, as from their Nature are not subject to a Commission, and gives him his Board & Lodging for these Services, which not being near sufficient to employ him, the Surplus of his Time must be dedicated to the House here, and recompensed as they may deserve, or the parties agree. The present private Clerk is D.M. who, not being ranked in any of the Departments, must occasionally assist in both, whenever his chief Object (Mr. Herries's private Affairs) does not require his attention or attendance, considering himself with respect to the days of respite *only*, in the *Foreign*.

Mr. Gentili having other Counting houses to attend, must be exempted from the Hours fix't upon for the others, but will be in the way [i.e., on duty] as hitherto four days in the Week.

9. The Writers of Letters must relate briefly what occurrs to be . . . [?] without omitting any material Circumstance, taking care to Mark at the bottom of the first Side, on reading them over, the number of pieces or papers to be inclosed, by as many strokes or short lines, thus (///). Each must fold up and address those he writes, but this must not be done till they be first copied & marked by the Copiers.

10. No Letters must be seald or shut till just before they be sent to the post office & this must not happen before Eleven O'clock on tuesday & friday and Eight O'Clock at Night on the other days of the week.

11. Any of the Clerks in want of any Letter or paper put up, must himself look for it and be sure to put it up again in the same place or order where he found it, taking care that no loose papers remain on the Desks lest they be mislaid or fall into Books which may very easily happen.

12. Those in waiting must be sure always to put down in the Address Book the Lodgings of persons recommended to the House, or others who call on business, when no Principal happens to be in the way [present]. They must not fail to inform such persons in such a Case of the days that he is to be found in Town, and of the hours of his Calls at the different Coffee houses about Change Viz. Tuesdays & fridays at Tom's about half past twelve, at the Jerusalem Garraway Loyds &c. about one, at John's about half past one, & after Change.

13. The Clerks in general are requested to remind each other in a friendly manner of any little Neglects, as well as the Principal when they perceive him wanting in any thing markd out to be done by himself, any engagements to attend on business &ca. making immediate Note thereof in the Memorandum Book, lest they afterwards should forget.

14. Each of them must constantly have on their Desks a few Sheets of waise [waste] paper sew'd together for immediate Notation of what may occurr to them in the Course of their work, as well as for cyphering and Calculations &ca., Each writing his name on the first page of these blotting Sheets and a list of the Books committed to his Charge.

15. They must not lock up in their Desks any papers relating to the Business of the House, lest such papers should be wanting when any of them happen to be out.

16. Each of them must take care to clear his own Desk when his Work is over, before he leaves the Counting house.

17. In order to have a right Notion of the thread of the Business, and be able to act their respective parts in it with propriety and judgement, they must at their spare moments read all the Letters received & wrote by the House.

18. They must take care that the Journal & Check Ledger be secured every night, along with the Bills & papers of most value in the Iron Chest, whereof the key is kept in the little private Book Case, & of the last Mr. Herries keeps one key & Mr. Keith another.

19. They must put down in the Address book where they lodge, and as often as they happen to change their Lodgings, likewise where they generally eat, or are to be found in the Evenings, lest in Case of Fire or any such Accident their presence at the Counting house be found necessary, altho' at untimely hours.

20. They must above all things observe & think themselves bound in honour not to divulge or reveal in the Course of Conversation or otherways, the Secrets of, or Occurrences in the Business of the House, for tho' a Principal ought never to plan or undertake anything that he need be

ashamed to avow boldly to the World if necessary, yet it may often be of great prejudice to him & his Co-interested, to have his Schemes blab'd out, and his measures exposed to be counteracted, or imitated by those who mind the Business of others more than their own, and without being themselves able to judge enter into projects purely by imitation, by which they only spoil Markets, without profiting by it. Many other Losses & Inconveniences, even of a more serious nature, may arise from tattling on the private affairs & operations of a House of Trade.

A Right Master, in order to be well served, ought to make no part of the Business a mistery to his Clerks, who in their part ought to be faithful to their trust, deserving of his Confidence.

Books in general used in the Business, how & by whom to be kept Viz.

Wastebook – by BR

Wrote on loose sheets of paper prepared & ruled for that purpose, narrating in the Journal style, all the Circumstances of every Transaction immediately as it passes, without care as to the manner of doing it, but particular attention must be paid to nothing being omitted from the Letters received or wrote by the House, marking on the backs of those Letters, and in the Margin of Copy Books of Letters, the folio of the Waste book and those that contain nothing recordable with a Zero thus (0).

This book is also partly formd from the Invoice, Sales, Account Current & postage Books marking in like manner in these Books the folio referred to in the Waste book which must be sew'd together every 3 Months and bound at the end of the Year.

It must never be a moment behind, & if thro' haste Errors should be committed they will be rectified in the

Journal kept by WF

and containing nothing more than a corrected Copy of the Wastebook, abridging what may appear superfluous, and adding when any Material Circumstance has been omitted, reverting to double Entrys, as well as to any that may have been overlook'd in the Waste book but care must be taken to mark such Alterations in this last, in order that the Check Ledger, which is posted from the Waste book in loose sheets, may also be alter'd, so as to agree with the principal

Ledger kept by WF

and posted from the Journal & Cash Book alternately as the dates happen to run. This chief Book must be kept constantly up, as of course those will from which it is formd, and the Accounts in it regularly closed in conformity to those we furnish to our Employers, or receive from those we employ.

It must be prick'd off with the Journal & Cash book every week, and compared with the Check Ledger every Quarter of a Year, when a Proof sheet of both must be made out, and from that at the end of the Year a regular Balance formd, closing all the Accounts which at the other three Terms need only be summed up.

Explanation of the General Accounts of the Ledger

Bills receivable: To this Account are placed all Remittances made us in London by John Coutts & Co. of Edinburgh & James Craufurd of Rotterdam, immediately on the receipt, and the same is balanced by Cash for the Bills discounted with or sent into the Bankers, by the Bank of England for those discounted there, and by their respective Accounts for such as are returned by J. Coutts & James Craufurd.

Discounted Bills to be alter'd to Remittances: This Account comprehends all Remittances made us by our other Correspondents, either on London or elsewhere, which are not placed to the Credit of their Remitters untill they fall due or are negotiated; this Account is balanced in the same manner as the preceding.

Bills payable: Is the Account to which we place all Drafts made on us by J. Coutts & Co. of Edinburgh or James Craufurd immediately on their being advised, and it is balanced by Cash when paid, or by the respective Accounts when their Bills on Ourselves are remitted us on account of our other Correspondents.

Merchandize Charges: To be closed the 1st July 1766 and the Balance divided proportionally between the Accounts of *Goods Consign'd, Goods Shipt & Exchange Account.*

Charges on Trade: To this Account is placed Clerks Wages & the Allowance for Housekeeping, Stationary Ware, and other Articles for the use of the Counting House, and any Charge of traveling &c on business concerning the House. It is balanced at the year's end and by Profit & Loss.

Merchandize General alter'd to Goods Shipt: We charge to this Account the amount of the Invoices or Bills of parcells of such Goods as are purchased on commission some time before the Invoice can be sent off, and it is credited by the proper account when that is dispatch'd.

Commission Account
Brokerage Account
Postage Account
Interest Account } Explain themselves

Insurance Account to be alter'd to Insurance Commission: To this Account we place our Commission on all Insurances made either on our own or other people's Accounts when any is charged. It is balanced at the end of the Year by Profit & Loss.

Sundry Debtors: Saves us the trouble of openeing accounts for such persons as we may probably have but one transaction with in a year, for Goods sold &ca. And

Sundry Creditors: Answers the same end for money lodged in our hands on accounts of people we are not in constant Correspondence with.

Sundry Tradesmen: To this Account we place all Bills of parcells of

Goods bought in Town and it is debited to Cash when they are paid.

Doubtful Creditors: We place to this Account such Debts as are not likely to be soon call'd for, and have lain long over.

Bills not appear'd: To this Account is placed such Bills drawn on us as are long overdue, and suspected to be lost.

Exchange Account: We place to this Account all Bills taken on speculation, or drawn in order to balance accounts, before they are negotiated, also the Charges of Commission, Postage &ca. on accounts Current received from our Correspondents, and the balances of the sterling Columns on those Accounts. It is also debited for all Notary's Charges, and credited by the respective Accounts that those Charges may regard when sent off, or the Concern'd advised of same. It is balanced at the end of the year by the General Balance for any Bills remaining on hand, and by Profit & Loss for the difference betwixt the debit & Credit.

To these it is proposed to add the following, viz.

Silks: To the debit of which is to be placed the Duty & Charges on all Silks we receive, either for our own Account or on Consignment. Also the Neat proceeds on sending off the Account of Sales of such as are on Consignment and the prime cost of those for our account. On the other hand it is to be credited by sundry Debtors, or the Buyer's proper account if he has any, for the amount of all Silks sold, and balanced by the quantity on hand, appearing by the quantity Column kept in Bales, and by Profit & Loss.

Wools: To be kept for all that concerns Wools in the same manner as that for Silks.

Raisins: To be kept in the same manner with the two preceeding for what concerns Raisins

N.B. The above three Articles being those in which we are principally concern'd, it is thought proper to open separate Accounts for them, and in order to enable us to form the Account Sales, Tarifs are to be made of the usual Charges which are always to be adhered to, except in extraordinary Cases. For other Consignments if not of great importance, it is proposed to raise a general Account under the title of

Goods Consignd: Which is to be debited for the Charges & neat proceeds of all Goods consign'd to us in general of what kind soever, and credited by Sundry Debtors or the Purchasers for amount of all Sales, balanced by the quantity on hand and Profit & Loss.

Trade Necessaries: To this Account we place the Cost of all Uttensils as Weights and Measures &c. for our Warehouses or Cellars as well as of all Desks, Book Cases, printed Books on Trade, Maps &ca. for the Use of our Counting houses, placing yearly Ten per Cent of their amount to Profit & Loss for Wear & Tear.

Cash Book or General Account of Cash, forming a part of the Ledger, and to be consider'd a folio thereof: kept by BR

This Book contains all Transactions, and is properly a corrected Copy of the Banker's Book; in it are placed to their proper accounts all Bills received payment of, or discounted, also all Bills paid as well as Accounts, which Articles are posted to their proper Accounts in the Ledger directly, without passing through the Journal. It is balanced Monthly.

Account Current Book

Is to be kept by the same person that keeps the Ledgers, who is at his Leisure to form from thence the Accounts Current of the different Correspondents, to be sent off half yearly, viz. at the end of the Months of June & December.

Check Ledger kept by BR

Is to be posted from the Wastebook & Cash Book and kept constantly up to the day, the intention of it being that we may always know the state of our Correspondents Accounts by looking into it. It is also of great use at the Quarterly & General Balances by frequently saving the trouble of pricking off the Books, by comparing it with the chief Ledger it is immediately seen where the Error (if any) lies.

Ledger of Bills kept by WEC

This Book contains in form of a Ledger Particulars of all the Bills remitted us by our Correspondents (except J. Coutts & Co. & James Craufurd) placed on receipt to the debit of every Remitter's Account, which is credited as each bill falls due, or is return'd. From this Book are to be taken daily the Bills that fall due that day, for which Discounted Bills or Remittances are to be made Debtor in the Journal to the Remitters Accounts if paid; if not, return'd Bills are to be made Debtor to and Creditor by the Remitter.

Sales Books kept by

On the Sinister Side of this Book are to be copied the Invoices of all Goods for sale, either for our own Account or on Consignment and the prime Cost in Sterling money extended in the outer Column, to which must be added the Charges, either form'd from the Tarif or Petty Cash Book, or both, thus we may see at one view what the Goods cost us and regulate the Sale accordingly. If no Invoice then the Marks & Numbers and quality of the Goods are sufficient to enter on the Sinister side, together with the limits fixt, if any, or any particular directions given concerning the Sale; on the Dexter Side, is to be enter'd from the Bills of parcells Book all the Sales made, when, to whom and at what price & terms of payment, extending the Amount in the outer Column.

Book of Accounts of Sales: Copied by W.E.C. [and] W.F.

In this Book are to be kept genuine Copies of Accounts of Sale transmitted to our Correspondents, which are to be form'd from the Sales Book, and enterd from this Book into the Journal.

Invoice Book: kept by

In this Book are to be first made out all Invoices of Goods shipt, from which Copies may be taken & transmitted to the Concern'd.

Bill Book: Kept by

In this Book are to be regularly entered, under their proper months, all Bills drawn on us, in the manner now practiced, and in a place set apart for that purpose, all Bills accepted by others made payable at our House, with the dates that they fall due. Any Bills drawn by J. Coutts & Co. or J. Craufurd accepted without advice the keeper of the Bill book is to give a Note of to the keeper of the Wastebook.

Book of Orders Received: Kept by

In this book are to be enter'd on receipt all Orders for Goods, or other directions from Correspondents relating to any other part of the Business, which cannot immediately be put in execution. A large Margin must be left for inserting any subsequent directions concerning same, and the manner of execution.

Book of Orders Given: Kept by

In this Book are to be copied all Orders given to our Correspondents abroad, and in the Margin, the manner in which they are executed, or the reason why not obey'd.

Book of Bills of Parcells Given: Kept by

In this Book are to be kept Copies of all Bills of parcells and other Accounts deliver'd in Town, and is from time to time to be look'd into by the keeper of the Wastebook, who is to make the necessary Entrys from same in the Books.

Credit Book: Kept by

In this Book are to be enter'd in form of a Ledger, all Credits lodged with us in favour of different people, mentioning on the Credit Side, by what letter received, and to what extent, & how long to subsist – On the Debit, the Sums paid in Consequence thereof, or when countermanded.

Bankers Book: Kept by G.K. [=Keith?]

Contains all Transactions with the Banker, is to be brought up daily, and balanced monthly.

Brokers Book: Kept by

... Accounts are to be opend in this Book for every Broker either in Exchanges or Goods, but particularly in Exchanges in which are to be enter'd to their Credit the amount of all the Bills of, or negotiated by them, which to be compared with their Accounts when delivered. In the Accounts of Brokers on Goods, they are to be credited for the amount of Goods sold by their intervention.

Remarks on Trade: Kept by

In it are to be copied all Remarks or Observations on Trade communicated to us by our Correspondents abroad, All pro forma Invoices & Accounts of Sale, also Calculations of Exchanges &c. And in general every thing worth observation that passes thro' our hands, relating to any particulars Branch of Trade.

Petty Cash Book: Kept by

Is in three Columns, one for the postages, another for Charges &ca. on Goods paid, and the last for Money received. It is enter'd into the Wastebook, and balanced monthly.

Correspondence Book: Kept by

Contains an Alphabetical List of the places of residence of our Correspondents, whose Names are inserted opposite thereto. Care must be taken to enter in it the Name &c. of every new Correspondent we write to, and any alteration in the Terms of our old. The Lines must be a sufficient distance from each other, to leave room to insert with a Circumflex the name of the partners that compose Trading Companies say Societies. The degrees of Credit are mark'd in the Margin by the five Letters in the Wood [?] Trade, as explaind in the first page, as well as the other initial marks.

Book of Occurences in Trade: Kept by

Contains a brief relation of any thing material say remarkable that happens in the Course of our Business, or in Trade in general. It must be inspected Weekly by the acting Partner and a Copy sent by the Thursday's post to those at Edinburgh. This Book has a large Margin for the dates and Additions or Alterations that may occur on the weekly revisal of it. The Copies to be wrote by the Inland Runner.

Copy Book of Bills to Negotiate

In this Book are to be inserted immediately on receipt Copies of all Bills remitted us to be negotiated, without Second & Thirds, in order that when they are negotiated there may be no occasion for taking Copies of them at that time, which being generally post days makes it inconvenient.

Address Book

Is to contain Alphabetically the Names of such of our Correspondents who have particular Addresses. Also the Lodging of the people in Town who call on business, or are recommended to the House, as well as those of our Clerks.

Warehouse Book

Contains on the left hand all the Marks Numbers & Weights of silks & other Goods, as received into the Warehouse; Also their Weights at the King's Beam And on the right hand the date of delivery & to whom, also the Weights & price.

Memorandum Book

Contains on the Sinister Side al[l] Memorandums Notes & Occurrences relating to the foreign Department, with a margin, where a mark must be made, according as things are complied with. The dexter side to be used for the same purpose in the Inland Department, to be wrote in & Look'd into by every body as they come in and go out.

Convention Book

Contains Extracts from the Letters we write & receive relating to any particular Agreement with our Correspondents, with regard to the mode of serving them, or being served by those we employ, particularly as to Credits & Advances, Interest & Commission &ca. to be charged by us or them, in the course of business, or in particular Cases. This Book must have an Alphabet kept in the same manner as that in a Copy-book of Letters, and there must be a large Margin for notation of any little Alterations made in these Agreements that do not deserve a fresh Entry. The use of it is obvious. It will prevent Errors in Accounts Current and recurring back to old Letters.

[Responsibilities and Procedures]

Customs House Business: To be managed by a person we have in view who serves several Houses in this business and does nothing else, having a certain Allowance in each Entry for his troubles and several Runners to assist him; but till we fix with him the:
Foreign by W.E.C. and the
Inland by G.K.
Drawing Bills of Exchange: Foreign: P.G. and W.E.C.
Inland: G.K.
Orders to Insurance Brokers: Foreign: W.E.C.
Inland: G.K.
Addressing Bills for Acceptance: W.E.C.
Copying Accounts Current: Foreign: W.E.C. & P.G.
Inland: G.K. & D.M.
Attending the Warehouse, Cellars &ca.: G.K., W.E.C.
According as the business of the respective Departments require their attendance, and they are in the like manner to regulate themselves with respect to:
Receiving & forwarding Goods
Examining Accounts-Received: Inland: W.F.
Foreign: B.R.

[Filing or Storage Procedures for Records]

Bills receivable & Remittances: To be kept in a Drawer of the private Book Case (where of Mr. Herries & Mr. Keith have, as has been already mention'd, each a key) in separate Division, examined daily and secured every night in the Iron Chest.

Explanation [examination?] of the Divisions & Drawers in Book Cases etc: to be sorted & Examined at the appointed times, under the inspection of the principals by DM

Foreign Letters Unanswered: On the Eves of the posts of this department & the Letters to be answer'd next day [to be] wrappd in the parchment for unanswerd foreign Letters, and left on the Desk

Foreign Letters Answerd: To be sorted & put under their proper letters of the alphabet twice a week, viz. Wednesdays & Saturdays, after being examined, and all the Entries found to be made.

Inland Letters Unanswer'd: To be examined on the evenings of Monday & Wednesday, and morning of Saturday, and any Letters requiring answers put up in the Inland parchment.

Inland Letters Answer'd: To be sorted in the same manner & at same time with the Foreign

Policys Depending: To be examined monthly, and those whose risques are determined put in their proper places, Viz. If arrive safe, in the place for Policys determined; if any Loss or Average in the Drawer for Losses to adjust.

Policies Determined: To be sorted & put by once a year.

Spanish Blank Bills Italian Ditto French Ditto Holland Ditto Inland Ditto	To be sorted monthly & first, seconds & thirds put in separate papers

Vouchers: To be wrapp'd up in paper & wrote on the back to whom belonging, and for what purpose.

Accounts not examined: To be examined & put in their proper places twice a week, Viz. on Wednesday & Saturdays

Bills to negotiate: to be examined on the Mornings of general posts and a List made out of such as are in course of Negotiation

Promiscuous papers Unsorted: Various Papers Sorted:	To be examined twice a week, any papers found belonging to any other places, they must be put in the proper ones, to be ready when wanted; at the end of the year to be put by.

Charter parties: to be put by once a year.

Papers belonging to others: to be kept in separate parcells wrapped up in clean paper mentioning to whom belonging. At the end of the year, such as are not likely to be calld for soon, to be put aside, & the others continued.

Alphabet: To be made up in separate parcells according to the Letters, and put by yearly.

Bills of parcells not enter'd: To be examined when any Invoice is sent off, and put, when enterd, on the file of Bills of parcells which are to be laid by yearly.

Losses adjusted: to be put by Yearly.

Losses to adjust: To be examined weekly, and if any Vouchers wanting, they must be wrote for; when adjusted they are to be put in the Drawer for Losses adjusted.

Powers of Attorney: To be sorted at the end of the year & such as there is no further occasion for put by.

2.^{ds} & 3.^{ds} of Remittances: to be sorted & put by yearly.

Receipts: Ditto

Retired Bills & drafts: To be sorted & put by monthly.

Bills for call of the 2.^{ds}: To be examined monthly, that none fall due without advising the person who sent it.

Protested Bills & Protests: To be examined monthly, and such as there seems no further occasion for put by at the end of the year.

Remittances on Ourselves: To be sorted monthly & put by amongst retired bills..

Acceptances retired: To be sorted & put by yearly.

Letters to forward: To be examined every post, & those to be sent off immediately to be taken out of the Drawer & put into the Desk-box intituled Copied Letters.

Letters requiring no immediate Answer: To be look'd into every post, and put in the proper parchments [files] as occasions offer to answer them and those remaining at the end of the Year put by Six months after the other papers.

INDEX

Printed in the United States
by Baker & Taylor Publisher Services

Printed in the United States
by Baker & Taylor Publisher Services